Fatema Mernissi for Our Times

Gender, Culture, and Politics in the Middle East
miriam cooke, Simona Sharoni, and Suad Joseph, *Series Editors*

Select Titles in Gender, Culture, and Politics in the Middle East

The Best of Hard Times: Palestinian Refugee Masculinities in Lebanon
Gustavo Barbosa

The Funambulists: Women Poets of the Arab Diaspora
Lisa Marchi

The Hammam through Time and Space
Julie Peteet

Iranian Women and Gender in the Iran-Iraq War
Mateo Mohammad Farzaneh

*Istanbul Appearances: Beauty and the Making
of Middle-Class Femininities in Urban Turkey*
Claudia Liebelt

*Quest for Love in Central Morocco: Young Women
and the Dynamics of Intimate Lives*
Laura Menin

*Sexuality in the Middle East and North Africa:
Contemporary Issues and Challenges*
J. Michael Ryan and Helen Rizzo, eds.

Sumud: Birth, Oral History, and Persisting in Palestine
Livia Wick

For a full list of titles in this series,
visit https://press.syr.edu/supressbook-series
/gender-culture-and-politics-in-the-middle-east/.

Fatema Mernissi
for Our Times

Edited by Minoo Moallem
and Paola Bacchetta

Syracuse University Press

This book will be made open access within three years of publication thanks to Path to Open, a program developed in partnership between JSTOR, the American Council of Learned Societies (ACLS), University of Michigan Press, and The University of North Carolina Press to bring about equitable access and impact for the entire scholarly community, including authors, researchers, libraries, and university presses around the world. Learn more at https://about.jstor.org/path-to-open/

Copyright © 2025 by Syracuse University Press
Syracuse, New York 13244-5290

All Rights Reserved

First Edition 2025
25 26 27 28 29 30   6 5 4 3 2 1

Chapter 4 credit: Fatema Mernissi contribution to LES LIONNES © 1974 by Fatema Mernissi. Used by permission of Edite Kroll Literary Agency Inc.

For a listing of books published and distributed by Syracuse University Press, visit https://press.syr.edu.

ISBN: 9780815638568 (hardcover)
9780815638575 (paperback)
9780815657354 (e-book)

Library of Congress Cataloging in Publication Control Number: 2024040395

Contents

List of Illustrations   *vii*
Acknowledgments   *ix*

Introduction:
Fatema Mernissi for Our Times
PAOLA BACCHETTA and MINOO MOALLEM   1

Section One. Epistemic Inventions

1. The Many Lives of Fatema Mernissi:
Dreaming and Trespassing
ZAKIA SALIME   23

2. The Mernissian Autobiography,
or the Limits of Self-Disclosure
AKILA KIZZI   41

3. *Jadal* and the War of Words
MINOO MOALLEM   60

4. *The Lionesses*:
A Film Project (1981)
HAMID BÉNANI, JALIL BENNANI, and FATEMA MERNISSI
Translated from French by Paola Bacchetta   78

5. Toward Decolonial Translating:
Reflections on "francophoning-anglophoning" "Les Lionnes"
PAOLA BACCHETTA   98

Section Two. Family and Kinship

6. Trespassing Queer Kinship with Mernissi's *Dreams of Trespass*
SIMA SHAKHSARI   127

7. Boundary Breaking and Boundary Making:
Fatema Mernissi's Paradoxical Narratives
SUAD JOSEPH   153

8. Fatema Mernissi's Situated Perspective:
The Mirror Effect
FATIMA AIT BEN LMAMDANI
Translated from French by Paola Bacchetta   167

Section Three. Feminism and Islam

9. Fatema Mernissi and the Question
of Women's Agency and Power in Islam
AZADEH KIAN   185

10. Fatema Mernissi's Heritage and the Pathway
for French Muslim Women's Autonomy
HANANE KARIMI
Translated from French by Paola Bacchetta   216

11. Fatema Mernissi and Animating *The Four Hijabs*
MANAL HAMZEH   234

12. Fatema Mernissi:
A Personal Memory
AMINA WADUD   243

Section Four. Mernissian Critiques of Coloniality, Orientalism, and Capitalism

13. Scheherazade and Sustainable Development
MOUNIRA HEJAIEJ   251

14. Fatema Mernissi, Intersectionality,
and the Decolonization of Knowledge:
Rural Women's Work versus the Harem Myth
NASIMA MOUJOUD
Translated from French by Paola Bacchetta   278

Editor and Contributor Biographies   295
Index   301

Illustrations

1. Jamal Mehssani, *Femmes en trance (Maroc)*   79
2. Three friends at the beginning of *The Four Hijabs*   235
3. The four hijabs on stage—the visual, the ethical, the spiritual, and the spatial   239

Acknowledgments

This volume is the culmination of papers presented at a conference we organized in honor of Fatema Mernissi on October 6 and 7, 2016. We thank the University of California Humanities Research Institute (UCHRI), Sultan, and Al Falah for providing funding that allowed us to bring together a group of national and international scholars to talk about Mernissi's contributions to feminist scholarship. We are also indebted to the following at the University of California, Berkeley, for their support and sponsorship: the Center for Middle Eastern Studies, the Gender and Women's Studies Department, the Center for the Study of Sexual Cultures, the Center for Race and Gender, and the Townsend Center. We are grateful to Gilliam Edglow, our fantastic research administrator, for her assistance; Pamela Matsuoko for her help with the conference poster; and Jeannie Imazumi for her financial assistance. We are deeply grateful to our editor, Laura Fish, who took over this project from Peggy Solic at Syracuse University Press and worked patiently with us on this volume. In addition, we are grateful to two anonymous reviewers of the manuscript for their helpful comments and suggestions.

Minoo Moallem: I first met Fatema Mernissi when I was a graduate student in Montreal in 1987 and met her again later at Harvard. These encounters, along with the subsequent close reading and teaching of Mernissi's work for many years in my course "Women in the Muslim and Arab Worlds," have influenced my understanding of Islamic feminism, colonialism, and the critique of local and global patriarchies in the context of West Asia and North Africa. I extend my special thanks to Emily Gottreich—who, at the time, was the director of the Center for Middle Eastern Studies at UCB—for supporting this project and acknowledge the contributions of Gayatri Spivak, Sunaina Maira, Thoraya Tlatli, and Huma Dar to the conference. Furthermore, I am grateful to my research assistant, Madeleine Calvi, for her hard work in assisting with the conference and to my amazing undergraduate students Midori Chen, Edie Sussman, and Alondra Martinez, who volunteered to help during the conference. I also wish to thank my graduate assistant, Akshaya Lakshmi, for her help with the edited manuscript. Thanks to my friends Inderpal Grewal, Caren Kaplan, Parama Roy, Deniz Gokturk, Ella Shohat, Robyn Weigman, Sima Shakhsari, Sherene Razack, Eric Smoodin, Renate Sadrozinski, and Christopher Flores as well as to my extended family—Shahin, Arash, Brita, Yara, and Kaveh Baytamakou; Abbas, Mahnaz, Mehraneh, and Ahmad Moallem; and Mahmoud Bodouhi. I dedicate this work to the memory of my mother, Mohtaram Shariatpanahi, who taught me the first lesson about being independent and not afraid of questioning patriarchal oppressive forces wherever I am.

Paola Bacchetta: I thank Jalil Bennani for suggesting I translate *The Lionesses* but also for generously following through with vital discussion at every stage. Thanks also to Stefania Pandolfo for the kind conference invitation that allowed Jalil and me to meet. I thank the Mellon Foundation for a grant to support my trip to Rabat, Morocco, while I was translating *The Lionesses*. I am grateful to Ahmed Moatissime and Nicole Khoury for first introducing me to Fatema Mernissi's work when I was a student at the Institut d'études du développement (Institute for the Study of Economic and Social Development) at the Sorbonne in Paris. I thank Ritu Menon in Delhi, who made sure Mernissi's work was published in India and invited her home to Delhi. My gratitude to my colleagues and friends at the Decolonizing Sexualities Network, with whom dialogue over more than the past decade has always nourished my thought. I thank Norma Alarcón and Norma Cantu for our conversations about translations. Thanks to my family, especially Gia Bacchetta, Chelsa

Dames, Nigel Dames, Urias Dames, Jennifer Jimerson, Tyla Newark, Amos Vogle, Autumn Vogle, Elijah Vogle, Lily Vogle, Steph Vogle, and Laila Zolner. Thanks to my favorite troublemaker, JazzCat. I am grateful to Angela Figueiredo for being there. I hope for a better world for all of us.

Fatema Mernissi for Our Times

Introduction

Fatema Mernissi for Our Times

PAOLA BACCHETTA and MINOO MOALLEM

This volume aims to honor and celebrate the life and work of the pathbreaking feminist sociologist and writer Fatema Mernissi (Fez, Morocco, 1940–Rabat, Morocco, November 30, 2015).[1] The chapters bring into relief and engage with her immense contributions for our times. Mernissi produced critical and creative work in many genres, mainly academic books and articles, literature, and (fictional) autobiography. She also coauthored a film, *Les Lionnes* (The Lionesses, 1981), whose script appears in this book for the first time anywhere in any language, here translated from French into English. She has inspired reems of analytical and creative writing, artwork, innovative films, and important forms of activisms.

Mernissi was born into an upper-middle-class family in Fez and lived in the extended family household of her maternal grandfather. She first attended a gender-mixed Qur'anic school, then a girls' school run by the colonial French protectorate. After graduation, Mernissi studied political science at Mohammed V University in Rabat. She then went to Paris to study sociology at the Sorbonne. From there

---

1. There are two correct spellings of Mernissi's first name: "Fatima" and "Fatema." She preferred "Fatema," the more intimate rendition, and thus we use that spelling here. But she also signed as "Fatima Mernissi"; for example, she signed *Les Lionnes* (The Lionesses), the cowritten film project, with "Fatima Mernissi."

1

she transferred to Brandeis University in the United States, where she earned her PhD in sociology in 1973. Her dissertation title was "Effects of Modernization on the Male–Female Dynamics in a Muslim Society." It soon became in somewhat revised form her first book, *Beyond the Veil: Male–Female Dynamics in a Modern Muslim Society* (1975), now a classic.

After earning her PhD, Mernissi returned to Morocco. At first, she taught at the University of Rabat. In 1980, she began teaching in sociology at her alma mater, Mohammed V University, in Rabat. She also did research with the university's affiliated research center. Very early on with other intellectuals in Rabat, Mernissi cocreated a moving pedagogical unit called la Caravan Civique (the Civic Caravan). Its goal was civic education specifically for rural girls and women. Later she created many different kinds of workshops, most notably ones oriented around situated, contextual knowledge production by rural working-class women through storytelling. Mernissi continued to be based in Rabat throughout her life. She was regularly invited to speak in various venues in Europe, the United States, Canada, India, and many other places. She published primarily in French and English but also in Arabic. Mernissi's work has influenced feminist scholars, activists, and artists in the Muslim, Arab, Amazigh, and North African worlds and their diasporas as well as far beyond them. Her writings have been translated into a plethora of languages, and that trend continues. She had strong relations with feminists across the Maghreb and sub-Saharan Africa as well as in India, Pakistan, Mexico, France, Spain, the United Kingdom, the United States, Australia, Latin America, and elsewhere. She is most known for critically challenging gender and sexual relations of power in Muslim contexts and for her anticolonial critiques of gender and sexual relations of power in the global North as well. Mernissi insisted on reaching out to a younger generation of scholars and activists. She touched many of them deeply. This volume reflects and continues her efforts to induce and nurture critical thought around women, gender, sexuality, and colonialism in earlier and current generations and in generations to come. It demonstrates how her work can help us all grapple with some of the most basic and acute social crises of our times.

Mernissi's works are increasingly being recognized by a widening transnational audience. Prior to her passing, she was the recipient in 2003 of Spain's prestigious Prince of Asturias Prize for the Spanish versions of her work. In 2004, she received the Erasmus Prize in the Netherlands. In 2011, *The Guardian* listed her as one of one hundred women who influenced the world. Posthumously in 2017, she was honored by the Middle East Studies Association as it established the Fatema Mernissi Book Award. Thus far, three chairs have been created in her name in universities transnationally in Brussels, Rabat, and Mexico City. Her work has recently been the subject of international conferences in Belgium, Morocco, France, and the United States. Her critical feminist thought is also the subject of a film by Saddie Choua aptly entitled with Mernissi's own words from a US television interview: *Je crois qu'il y a une confusion chez vous. Vous croyez que moi je veux vous imiter* (I Believe You Are Confused. You Actually Think I Want to Imitate You, 2017). It is also the topic of an animated short film by Manal Hamzeh entitled *The Four Hijabs* (2016). We include in this book Hamzeh's own commentary about Mernissi and the film.

Mernissi in Context(s): Morocco, North Africa, Middle East, the World

Primarily four areas of Mernissi's work are of particular importance to her immediate context but also have much broader implications for the world: history, contemporary sociology, rethinking Islam, and literature. Her historical and sociological studies focus mainly on critical readings of power structures and patriarchy, especially misogyny in Morocco and more widely in Muslim-majority societies. Mernissi was a pathbreaker in rethinking Islam in light of feminist epistemologies. She revealed complex and multifaceted genealogies of Islamic discourses and interpretive politics across different slices of time. She challenged earlier and contemporary authoritative Islamic sources and interpretations, pointing to colonial and local rewritings that have invariably worsened women's social positionings. She advocated for reform within the context of Muslim societies and Islamic "traditions" (which she understood not as eternal but rather as historically crystalized practices), including the hadith. And she is globally known for her continuous efforts to promote gender justice. Mernissi called women the builders of civil society and urged them to create both social and epistemic change. Her literary writing further explores these same thematics in a genre that allows for broad schemes of affect and identification with her heroines and her social critiques. She often tells her stories through the eyes of some of the most subaltern subjects in Muslim societies. And she sometimes turns her focus toward an analysis of Western presumptions about Muslim cultures and women.

Mernissi published with an array of publishers, from small women's presses such as Simorgh in Pakistan to commercial presses that are against the elitist academic approach to publication gatekeeping.[2] As a multilingual subject, she was very aware of her audiences, their linguistic groundings, epistemic realms, and modes of reception. When she wrote or gave speeches, she articulated her ideas in or translated them to a language that responded to the specific contexts within which she addressed audiences. Her ability to convey her thoughts and make them appealing to particular audiences was crucial in challenging geopolitical power relations. In contrast to many feminists who export Eurocentric ideas to other parts of the world and thereby continue to invest in hegemonic Western epistemologies, Mernissi challenged the coloniality of knowledge through decolonial insight. She also transcoded and resignified some of the

---

2. See the following examples: *Beyond the Veil: Male–Female Dynamics in Muslim Society* (Mernissi 1975), *Woman in the Muslim Unconscious* (1984, published under the pseudonym "Fatna Aït Sabbah"), *The Veil and the Male Elite: A Feminist Interpretation of Women's Rights in Islam* (1991b), *Islam and Democracy: Fear of the Modern World* (1992), *The Forgotten Queens of Islam* (1993), *Dreams of Trespass: Tales of a Harem Girlhood* (1994), and *Scheherazade Goes West: Different Cultures, Different Harems* (2001).

dominant tropes circulating in the West, including the Orientalist trope of the harem.

As a measure of self-protection and to ensure unbridled speech, Mernissi signed some of her most politically sensitive publications with a pseudonym—especially when she took on the task of rewriting the cultural Muslim heritage and especially in relation to legal sources of Islam, the Qur'an, and the hadiths. This strategic move enabled her to analytically engage with more controversial issues that may have offended those with an affective and foundational attachment to the sacred texts and thus closed to any alternative form of interpretation. An example of one such publication is the very provocative and controversial text *La femme dans l'inconscient musulman*, which she published under the pseudonym "Fatna Aït Sabbah" in 1982.[3] In this book, she writes about how the female body becomes a field of sacred writing and male power as she analyzes the erotic aspects of love, desire, and male pleasure in what she calls the orthodox discourse of Islam to challenge the conventional interpretation of Islam as heritage (Aït Sabbah 1982, 8).

In another of her critically challenging books, *Islam and Democracy* (1992), Mernissi refers to the twelfth-century Iranian Sufi poet Farid al-din Attar and his famous long poem *Mantiq ut-Tayr* (*Conference of the Birds*) in order to dream of a new world or "a global mirror in which all cultures can shine in their uniqueness" (174).[4] Mernissi's dream of a new global world is an optimistic imagining of a world guided by Sufi poets, going beyond the fear of uncertainty, the fear of freedom of thought, the fear of the past and the

---

3. This book was translated into English by Mary Jo Lakeland in 1984 under the title *Women in the Muslim Unconscious*. Mary Joe Lakeland was the excellent translator of many of Mernissi's books. One of us (Minoo) met with her many years ago in Berkeley and appreciated her commitment to making Mernissi's work available for English readers.

4. Farid ud-Din Attar Nishabouri was a prominent Iranian poet and Sufi thinker who had a significant impact on Sufism and Persian poetry. Attar was murdered by Mongol soldiers in AH 627 (1230 CE).

present, and any form of xenophobia or fear of the stranger (the *gharib*). At the center of this dream is Mernissi's optimistic reading of the opportunities for a better world that does not limit women's freedom. In this project, she sees as comrades Arab and Muslim men who refuse the ancestral violence of patriarchy. Mernissi consistently critiques the Moroccan modernist and male literary elite and their depiction of women's bodies. Yet she also challenges Western democracies for continuing to invest in modern forms of patriarchy and the stereotypical and Orientalist ideas of Arab men and women. To challenge both currents and Muslim patriarchal systems, she crosses the boundaries of the public and the private as well as the global and local to show how both individual and collective forms of violence are exercised against women. As a feminist, Mernissi did not limit herself to an analytical approach to patriarchy but tried to unearth how women could liberate themselves from the disciplinary forces of colonialism and of patriarchal orders and borders.

Mernissi's vast knowledge of Islamic and Arab literature and history made her work and her feminist framework trailblazing. Each writing or publication refers to a body of literature and historical figures in the Arabo-Islamic world whose voices and governance practices could potentially inspire the present. For example, in *Islam and Democracy* (1992) she invokes the eleventh-century ruler Fatimid Caliph al-Hakim as well as the centrality of light and time and the blossoming of astronomy under his rule. Expanding on this ecological vision of governance throughout the Qur'an, she argues that being Muslim "means being master of time and the stars, which Allah created to permit us to establish a 'Tarikh' 'calendar'" (132). In her view, both mathematics and astronomy as marvels created by Allah represent Muslims' historical awareness of the cosmos. Yet she criticizes the current rules of the Muslim world as detached from any relationship with a cosmic dimension and the West for monopolizing scientific knowledge and constructing modernity into a homogenous entity located within the linear narrative of Western progress. In one of her interviews, Mernissi noted that her interest in reading Ibn Arabi and studying Sufism had to do with movement without frontiers: "Your space is there, you are in your dimension, but you meet the stranger: this is globalization" (Leccese 2006, 347).

One of her most significant contributions is her revisiting of Islamic texts in light of history. She reveals how Islamic texts have been mediated by a patriarchal male elite, thus opening up space for Islamic feminism with the task of revisiting and revising this history and the texts subjected to such manipulations. Although some feminists reject the idea of feminist interpretation of Islam, Muslim feminists currently constitute a strong force challenging patriarchal interpretations of religious texts and have used multiple strategies to challenge sexist aspects of Islam. Some reinterpret earlier Islamic texts for today. Others drop parts of religious texts that convey sexist language by positing them against the same texts' egalitarian passages, statements, and stories. Mernissi uses *tafsir* (exegesis) to open possibilities for different interpretations of religious texts by feminist and queer theologians. She challenges the historical mediation by the male elite in their preservation and reinvention of patriarchal traditions. She mobilizes these devices to open up space for a new understanding of the sacred and historical texts.

Mernissi's work on sexuality contributed sometimes directly and sometimes indirectly to what later became the field of Islamic feminisms and—for some authors—what is emerging as forms of queer theorizing of the theological in Muslim contexts across the Maghreb and beyond. From the time of her first book, *Beyond the Veil: Male–Female Dynamics in Muslim Society* (1975), Mernissi wrote directly not only against the grain of colonial and Orientalist representations of Muslim women as eternal victims of Islam and Muslim men but also about sexuality. For her, women are subordinated in Muslim societies, but they are equally subordinated in the West, albeit differently and according to disparate logics. Contrasting the work of the Islamic theologian al-Ghazali and the Western psychoanalyst Sigmund Freud on sexuality, Mernissi points to how in Islamic texts women's sexuality is conceptualized as active, whereas in Western texts it is assumed to be passive. In other works, Mernissi highlights how the Islamic representation of Muslim women as sexually active led to some Muslim men in power imagining women as a threat to the social order and requiring control via external measures such as gender separation and covering. In contrast, in the West women's imagined passivity led to measures to make them internalize their oppression to become self-policing. Mernissi points out how women in Morocco are free in their bodies compared to Western women. In Morocco, women wear comfortable clothing and shoes and are free to eat what they want, while in the West they are constantly on display for men, wear tight clothes and high-heeled shoes that destroy their vertebra, and suffer from anorexia and bulimia. Besides Mernissi's contributions to feminist and queer interpretations of Islam, in retrospect we can also understand from a decolonial point of view how in the juridical systems that colonizers imposed in many places, when homosexuality was outlawed, only male homosexuality was banned as the colonizers imagined women to be too passive to have any sexuality together.

Mernissi not only critiques dominant sexist interpretations of Islam by Muslim male theologians and politicians in power and by global northern dominant feminisms but also provides precise alternative perspectives. In her book *The Forgotten Queens of Islam* (1993), she shows Muslim women as intellectuals and leaders. In her cowritten film script *The Lionesses* (chapter 4 in this volume), she opens up women's current Sufi practices of resistance. Her challenges to dominant interpretations of Islamic texts, her notion that the gender binary is a social construction without basis in Islam, her insistence that Muslim women are powerful subjects, her notion of women's active sexuality, her demonstration that sexuality is not demonized in Islam but rather can be understood as a force (that sexist men want to control), and her reminder that Islam is concerned primarily with social justice have opened a way for queer readings of the Qur'an and other Islamic texts.[5] Importantly at this time, a field

---

5. Indeed, Mernissi figures in the important text *Queer Maroc: Sexualités, genres et (trans)identités dans la littérature marocaine* by Jean Zaganiaris (2014),

of queer theological readings, theorizations, and practices of Islam is forming and expanding. It includes scholars such as Ghazala Anwar, amina wadud, and Samar Habib, among others.[6]

There are many additional striking examples of Mernissi's use of history and her own interpretations of texts for the present. Each brings us something radically important to consider. For instance, in her short book *Can We Women Head a Muslim State?* (1991a) Mernissi engages new questions about gender and political power. She gives the example of Umma Salma, the Prophet's wife, who raised many questions regarding women's equal treatment, including "Are we partners in Islam?" (42). She writes:

> Not only was the question of equality raised in the Prophet's (pbuh [peace be upon him]) Medina, but women received positive answers to their queries. Divine revelations assured them that the new religion was truly revolutionary. That the era of Jahiliya, of violence and the subordination of women was over. The new Islamic era meant a new status for women. The verse about the Queen of Sheba raised high the aspirations of women by providing them with the role model of woman as head of state. And many women in Muslim history did aim that high and were successful in their endeavor. (37)

In a similar vein, in *The Forgotten Queens of Islam* (1993), Mernissi revisits the history of Muslims through the case of Benazir Bhutto, the prime minister of Pakistan at the time Mernissi wrote this book, to demonstrate women's political leadership regardless of

---

alongside authors such as Abdellah Taia, Tahar Ben Jallooun, Mohamed Leftah, and others.

6. Transnationally, a range of Muslim queer activist groups are proposing and living queer interpretations of Islam, from Al Fatiha Foundation (founded in 1997) in the United States to the Safra Project (founded in 2001) in London. There are queer mosques in South Africa, Canada, Paris, Los Angeles, Berkeley, and many other sites across the globe. Mernissi's work, as a precursor in rethinking gender in Islam and in the West, opened up many possibilities for current queer Muslim thought and movements.

the patriarchal interpretation of Islam. She refers to the concept of "queen" in Islamic history to show that while women have not carried the title *caliph* or *imam* in the current masculinist applications of these titles, they have taken part in positions of power under the title *sultan*, *malik*, and *al-hurra* (free woman) (13–14). She points out that the word *caliph* exists only in masculine form and cannot be used in the feminine, yet both *sultan* and *malik* have referred to men and women. She returns to her argument that, "paradoxically, while Islam was born of a democratic design that limited the power of aristocrats, the word *ashraf* was never devalued; in fact, the contrary is true" (15). She explains that the word *al-ashrif* referred to "the privileged ones who can trace their ancestry to Fatima, his daughter, and to Ali, his son-in-law and cousin" (15–16). In *The Forgotten Queens of Islam*, she carefully illustrates cases of numerous Muslim women leaders from India to Spain to North Africa.

The concept of fundamentalism—which first arose in contexts of Christianity in the West—is currently strategically used to depict the other of modernity and increasingly to single out Muslims as fundamentalists (Moallem 2005).[7] Although Mernissi does not challenge the idea of fundamentalism, she engages with the reasons for which right-wing and fundamentalist movements have gained popularity in the Muslim and Arab world. In her small book *The Fundamentalist Obsession with Women: A Current Articulation of Class Conflict in Modern Muslim Societies* (1987), she criticizes Western notions of fundamentalism as "uneducated, uncultured, blood-thirsty, woman-hating, politically frustrated, terrorist and loaded with guns and bombs" (17–18). Countering this image with reality while acknowledging that religion-based right-wing political formations are a growing tendency in Muslim and Arab societies and around the world, Mernissi argues that this tendency is related to an identity crisis provoked by colonialism and capitalism. She writes, "Identity

---

7. See also "Whose Fundamentalism?" (Moallem 2002), a statement on the current events.

is a sense that one's life is meaningful, that, as fragile as one may be, one can still have an impact on one's limited surroundings" (6). She writes that fundamentalism "is a political statement about men undergoing bewildering, compelling changes affecting their economic and sexual identity—changes so profound and numerous that they trigger deep-seated, irrational fear" (5). Mernissi emphasizes that mass access to universities has significantly affected the relationship among knowledge, power and information (19).

Mernissi's critique of Western democracies and Arabo-Islamic patriarchies provides a framework for thinking about feminist politics that brings the geopolitical into conversation with feminist theory and practice in everyday life. As several scholars working in decolonial studies have demonstrated, since the sixteenth century and with the epistemological hegemony of colonial modernity, diverse ways of producing knowledge have been replaced with the hierarchal and evolutionary methods of knowledge production according to colonial binary categories in colonial modernity—from traditional to modern, from barbaric to civilized, and from underdeveloped to developed.[8] Mernissi is a feminist who offers a different way of thinking about gender and women's issues by revisiting lost or forgotten knowledge that colonialism and nationalism have suppressed.

The circulation of Eurocentric knowledge as "the knowledge" and the marginalization of a plurality of epistemes from the global South have been challenged in postcolonial and decolonial feminist and queer scholarship.[9] Yet Eurocentric hegemonic feminisms continue to circulate across much of the world. Mernissi's work has been more legible to Western feminist circles because of her ability to engage either liberal or socialist feminist traditions critical of patriarchy and gender inequality, yet teaching her work takes

---

8. For a critique of the notion of tradition and traditional, see the book *Between Warrior Brother and Veiled Sister* (Moallem 2006).

9. See, for example, Bacchetta 2020; Shohat and Stam 1994; and texts, discussions, and podcasts on the Decolonizing Sexualities Network website at https://decolonizingsexualities.org.

place primarily in courses specifically on the Middle East or Arabo-Islamic work. Even though gender studies and women's studies have resisted canonization for many years, US-centric knowledge frames have unfortunately gained hegemony and established a canon that is reflected in many courses offered by gender and women's studies departments in the United States and sometimes elsewhere. As a result, feminist knowledge produced by scholars outside US or European circles has been marginalized and taught in new and old "area studies" venues.[10] This volume attempts to offer a broad reading of Mernissi work from multiple positions to make it more legible to academic circles and activist organizations. Lack of horizontal feminist conversation and the influence of vertical and hierarchical modes of knowledge circulation, especially from the global North to the global South, have been significant components of such a condition.

Mernissi recognizes that because of globalization and the division between the global North and global South, we all are now tied together in "fortune and misfortune," as she puts it in *Islam and Democracy* (1992, 168). She strategically redeploys and expands some of the colonial and Orientalist concepts, tropes, and symbols that Westerners often use to depict the oppression of Muslim women and to talk about local, regional, and transnational divisions. For example, she uses the concept of veiling and the hijab to talk about the Berlin Wall as the "Berlin Hijab" and reflects upon the perception that "behind every boundary something terrifying is hiding" (1992, 6). Invoking the Arabic concept of *hudud* (borders, limits), she engages the boundaries that "separate and create order and stand for all the others" (8).

The term *public intellectual* is rarely used to describe feminist thinkers. Yet Mernissi, in our view, was one of the most influential feminist public intellectuals across the Arab world, North Africa,

---

10. For a feminist critique of Middle Eastern studies as area studies, see Moallem 2001.

and the Middle East and had an even broader transnational reach far beyond these regions. Her work was also published and circulated in Europe, North America, South Asia, and sub-Saharan Africa, and in translation it traveled to Japan and Indonesia. In Morocco, Mernissi was part of feminist and people's activist collectives. However, her impact on activism reaches far beyond those borders. For instance, in this volume Hanane Karimi tells us about the centrality of Mernissi's work to Muslim feminist organizing in France. Mernissi was also read by Muslim activists in India and Pakistan, instigating struggles there. In her later years, her talks and interviews appeared on YouTube, thereby opening access to her by a broader popular audience, whether literate or not. As mentioned earlier, her work has inspired artists, filmmakers, and other cultural workers across generations.

Structure, Organization, Contributions

This book is divided into four sections. Although many chapters make contributions to the themes of two or more sections, we organize them in this way to highlight specific aspects of Mernissi's work and life for the readers' convenience.

Section one, "Epistemic Inventions," includes chapters that speak to Mernissi's creative insistence on knowledge production, both her own and that of the rural, working-class Muslim women in Morocco with whom she worked closely. The five chapters in this section present and analyze Mernissi's contributions in this area. Some propose concepts with which to understand Mernissi's life and works.

The opening chapter, "The Many Lives of Fatema Mernissi: Dreaming and Trespassing" by Zakia Salime, offers an insightful overview of Mernissi's life and importance for feminist studies and practices over time. Salime engages Mernissi's writerly and academic evolution, her activism on behalf of rural, subaltern women, and her creation of counterspaces inside and outside institutional settings and established political realms. Mernissi, writes Salime, created new spaces where she was able to reinvent herself, always dreaming and always trespassing. Mernissi intervened in or in relation to ever-changing gendered, political, and economic struggles in Morocco.

Here we get an unparalleled sense of Mernissi's intellectual and political trajectory inside the political conditions of her times.

In chapter 2, "The Mernissian Autobiography, or the Limits of Self-Disclosure," Akila Kizzi analyzes Mernissi's *Dreams of Trespass: Tales of a Harem Girlhood* (1994), translated into French as *Rêves de femmes: Une enfance au harem* (1996). Kizzi shows how Mernissi disrupts global northern autobiographical conventions and defies dominant referentiality as her "I" becomes an "I-we" or collective subject. Her narration is not fully intelligible to epistemically privileged readers. She displaces autobiography as a genre when in note 2 of chapter 3 of the French edition—a language that Moroccans read more often because of colonialism—she reveals that the text is fictional, a point lost on English-only readers. In the French edition, Mernissi respects *hurma* (modesty, avoidance of public exposure) in narration and visuality. For example, in contrast to Eugène Delacroix's classic Orientalist-exhibitionist painting *Women of Algiers* (1834, 1847–49), she uses for the book's cover the image of three Moroccan women who turn their backs to viewers, refusing the public gaze.

Chapter 3 is Minoo Moallem's "*Jadal* and the War of Words," a text that elaborates on the power and pleasure of Mernissi's work by bringing to light her inquiries into the burden of cultural and social inheritance in a postcolonial or neocolonial context. One of many Arabic concepts she uses is *jadal*, the art of dialogue and debate. *Jadal* consists of well-informed, rigorous, witty, courageous, bold, and skilled debate at the intersection of knowledge and power. Moallem argues that Mernissi's reference to the art of dialogue in Muslim cultures provides an epistemological and pedagogic tool to open up both Orientalist and anti-Muslim discourses as well as foundationalist, masculinist, and absolutist readings of Islam.

Chapter 4 provides Mernissi's film script *The Lionesses* (1981), cowritten with Jalil Bennani and Hamid Bénani, translated from French to English by Paola Bacchetta. *The Lionesses* creatively suggests how spiritual spaces and practices enable subalternized women. It presents contextual epistemic categories and definitions—that is, for illness, healing, emancipation, sainthood, and temporality. It centers four women: Fatima, who after failed Western psychiatric treatments tries a sanctuary; Zhor, who leaves a boring life for a sanctuary; Halima, who after a long unhappy marriage becomes a *chouaffa* (clairvoyant); and the Amazigh historical figure Lalla Aziza Tagurrami, a saint who reconciled warring tribes at some unknown historical time. Each puts into relief some of what sanctuaries offer women: therapy, entertainment, charismatic power, and political power, respectively.

In chapter 5, "Toward Decolonial Translating: Reflections on 'francophoning-anglophoning' *Les Lionnes*," Paola Bacchetta discusses translating Mernissi's cowritten polyvocal film project from one dominant language (French) to another (English) as a postcolonial-decolonial text. She offers the notion of "pretranslation" to put into relief the (silenced) presence of prior subalternized languages in the text, here Darija and Amazigh in particular. For Bacchetta, pretranslation elements may surface in the various dimensions of the text: rhythm, lexicon, grammar, imagery, orality, sensuality, temporal-spatialities, or symbolic. She addresses "translation-pauses," or different kinds of narrational haltings that pretranslation components may induce. She also reflects upon the post-translation dimensions of the translated text's condition(s) of reception. The chapter is a contribution to reflections upon theorizations and practices of decolonial translations to come.

Section two, "Family and Kinship," consists of chapters that address Mernissi's critiques of global northern feminist presuppositions about the family and her thinking on family and kinship. It includes reflections on the queer potentiality of Mernissi's writing on this topic. Together the chapters pose questions about what constitutes a family and kinship for dominant transnational feminist and queer theory.

In chapter 6, "Trespassing Queer Kinship with Mernissi's *Dreams of Trespass*," Sima Shakhsari focuses on Mernissi's book *Dreams of Trespass* (1994) to consider the limits of epistemic assumptions, categories, and thematics in dominant US queer theory and how they render non-US writing in this field unintelligible. For Shakhsari, this text is queer even beyond its presentation of nonheteronormative identities, the figure Badur's transgressive drag, and relations outside procreative kinship. Drawing on Elizabeth Freeman's (2007) notion of kinship as renewal and regeneration, "being long and belonging," Shakhsari discusses how Mernissi figures women cocreating kinship by both repeating established codes of conduct and violating them. This chapter offers much about kinship for queer refugees, refugee studies, and a deeply context-sensitive transnational queer studies.

Suad Joseph's chapter, "Boundary Breaking and Boundary Making: Fatema Mernissi's Paradoxical Narratives," also addresses Mernissi's *Dreams of Trespass*, in this case to consider Mernissi's childhood in the 1940s. Joseph highlights Mernissi's observations about her family's urban and rural homes and relations with her many different relatives. Mernissi's concept of "patriarchal connectivity" usefully signals the intersection of affect (love) and power as the glue within a sexist kinship system but also the ways that lived relationality defies this intersection. For Joseph, Mernissi's writing mobilizes a childlike voice to bring us through boundaries, to trespass with her. Joseph's chapter opens with a reflection on how childhoods that are different but have similar relational possibilities can be sites of trespass.

In chapter 8, "Fatema Mernissi's Situated Perspective: The Mirror Effect" (translated from French by Paola Bacchetta), Fatima Ait ben Lmamdani engages Mernissi's critiques of multiple relations of power and the positionality of the speaking subject, which in the United States and France are theorized as, respectively, "intersectionality" and the "situated viewpoint." She highlights how Mernissi always analyzed colonialism, class, capitalism, gender and sexuality, and rural–urban relations of power, language, and religion inseparably. She reflects on how Mernissi not only resisted colonial and Orientalist discourse but also turned the terms of that discourse back upon the West. For instance, in 1996 Mernissi called the French Senate, which at the time was only 4 percent women, a "harem." Here, Lmamdani's work is intertextual with Karimi's chapter, which remarks that Mernissi called the Berlin Wall the "Berlin Hijab."

Section three, "Feminism and Islam," comprises chapters that engage with Mernissi's complex reflections on this topic. Some analyze shifts in Mernissi's thought on feminism and Islam in relation to colonial-Orientalist and racialized discourse in the United States, France, and Morocco.

Azadeh Kian wrote chapter 9, "Fatema Mernissi and the Question of Women's Agency and Power in Islam," in France during ferocious attacks against postcolonial and decolonial studies, intersectionality, and studies of Islam. Kian clarifies Mernissi's pertinence to this context. Mernissi opens up the (otherwise homogenized) category "women" as she engages class, religion, ethnicity, languages, rural and urban space, and access or inaccess to formal and other kinds of education. She not only frontally challenges French colonial Orientalist-essentialist-culturalist notions of Islam and of "Muslim women" as timeless victims, devoid of agency and in need of rescue, but also enables critique of the essentialist-culturalist views of Muslim women held by some Muslims in France today.

In chapter 10, "Fatema Mernissi's Heritage and the Pathway for French Muslim Women's Autonomy" (translated from French by Paola Bacchetta), Hanane Karimi shows how Muslim feminists of Maghrebian origin in France collectively use Mernissi's work to contest hegemonic, sexist Muslim religious knowledge of Islam and to critique the French state's Islamophobia. For Karimi, Mernissi's "democratic writing"—or writing by and for the author, not for the reader—helpfully centers Muslim feminist concerns. In France, some women are mobilizing Mernissi's subversive definitions of theological concepts such as *hudud* (borders, limits) and "hijab" (as a space and as a symbolic territory) and her critiques of colonial-Orientalist unveiling for resistant and emancipatory purposes. Karimi hints at francophone Muslim feminist scholarly intertextualities as she cites Nasima Moujoud and Fatima Ait ben Lmamdani's concept *le voile de la rupture* (the veil of rupture), or the break with both the Western model for women and the one that threatens the Western model.

In chapter 11, "Fatema Mernissi and Animating *The Four Hijabs*," Manal Hamzeh discusses the centrality of Mernissi's *ijtihad* (intellectual struggle and rigorous theorizing committed to gender justice) to Hamzeh's book *Pedagogies of Deveiling: Muslim Girls and the Hijab Discourse* (2011) and her coproduced film *The Four Hijabs* (2016). Hamzeh's book and film take up Mernissi's critical rereading of Qur'anic verses on the hijab to open up a different kind of conversation. For Hamzeh, the hijab is often reductively discussed as "to veil or not to veil," yet "the real question is about four distinct hijabs that appear in sixteen Qur'anic verses." Hamzeh offers a detailed account of these hijabs and a rich analysis of bridging the theoretical, narrational, and visual for a popular audience.

This section concludes with amina wadud's chapter "Fatema Mernissi: A Personal Memory," which reflects on the links between Mernissi's work and wadud's own work on women, feminism, and Islam as well as on a missed encounter in Morocco toward the end of Mernissi's life.

Section four, "Mernissian Critiques of Coloniality, Orientalism, and Capitalism," includes two chapters that engage with Mernissi's critiques of how multiple relations of power—especially colonialism, coloniality, Orientalism, and capitalism—work together inseparably with gender and sexuality. This section also puts into relief how Mernissi's work has been ignored in much dominant global northern feminist scholarship and discusses what that work can bring to both expand and profoundly transform this scholarship.

In chapter 13, "Scheherazade and Sustainable Development," Mounira Hejaiej mobilizes the figure of Scheherazade in Mernissi's writing to illuminate Mernissi's ideas about what rural subaltern women's narratives bring to critical social and economic development. The empirical sites for Hejaiej's reflections are the water-related Women's Empowerment Projects in rural Tunisia. Mernissi argued that projects based on local social capital—networks of trust, caring, and shared responsibility—succeeded where World Bank and International Monetary Fund structural-adjustment programs failed miserably, thereby frontally challenging the dominant Western vision of development. Mernissi emphasized Moroccan notions of *hanan* (tenderness), *tiqa* (trust), and *ta'awun* (cooperation) as well as subaltern women's voices "from below" as vital for social and economic development and the creation of other ways of life.

In chapter 14, "Fatema Mernissi, Intersectionality, and the Decolonization of Knowledge: Rural Women's Work versus the Harem Myth" (translated from French by Paolo Bacchetta), Nasima Moujoud addresses Mernissi's texts in French from the 1970s and 1980s on two thematics: the exploitation of women's labor and the colonial construction of the harem. Whereas in dominant scholarship on labor, including labor and gender, these themes are generally understood as separate concerns, for Moujoud they are integral, and Mernissi was committed to deconstructing colonial categories, including the harem, by making women's work visible. Moujoud highlights that Mernissi emphasized how colonialism is "a principal tool for the expansion of capitalism" and worked to decolonize knowledge, analyze power, and reveal women's labor exploitation. Though ignored in official, dominant French feminisms, Mernissi contributed centrally to women's liberation in both France and Morocco.

༄༅

We offer this collection of texts with the hope that readers will find it as immanently useful as we have for critical feminist, gender, decolonial, and anticapitalist scholarship and activism for our times and for the future.

References

Aït Sabbah, Fatna [Fatema Mernissi]. 1982. *La femme dans l'inconscient musulman.* Paris: Albin Michel.

———. 1984. *Women in the Muslim Unconscious.* Translated by Mary Jo Lakeland. Oxford: Pergamon Press.

Bacchetta, Paola. 2020. "Decolonial Sexualities." *Interventions: International Journal of Postcolonial Studies* 22, no. 4: 574–85.

Freeman, Elizabeth. 2007. "Queer Belongings: Kinship Theory and Queer Theory." In *A Companion to Lesbian, Gay, Bisexual, Transgender, and Queer Studies*, edited by George E. Haggerty and Molly McGarry, 293–314. Oxford: Wiley Blackwell.

Leccese, Francesco Alfonso. 2006. "The New Arab Mass-Media Vehicles of Democracy? Interview with Fatima Mernissi." *Oriente Moderno*, New Series, Year 25, 86, no. 2: 345–56.

Mernissi, Fatema. 1975. *Beyond the Veil: Male–Female Dynamics in Muslim Society*. Cambridge, MA: Schenckman.

———. 1987. *The Fundamentalist Obsession with Women: A Current Articulation of Class Conflict in Modern Muslim Societies*. Lahore, Pakistan: Simorgh.

———. 1991a. *Can We Women Head a Muslim State?* Lahore, Pakistan: Simorgh.

———. 1991b. *The Veil and the Male Elite: A Feminist Interpretation of Women's Rights in Islam*. Translated by Mary Jo Lakeland. Cambridge, MA: Perseus.

———. 1992. *Islam and Democracy: Fear of the Modern World*. Translated by Mary Jo Lakeland. New York: Basic.

———. 1993. *The Forgotten Queens of Islam*. Translated by Mary Jo Lakeland. Minneapolis: Univ. of Minnesota Press.

———. 1994. *Dreams of Trespass: Tales of a Harem Girlhood*. Cambridge, MA: Perseus.

———. 1996. *Rêves de femmes: Une enfance au harem*. Translated by Claudine Richetin. Paris: Albin Michel.

———. 2001. *Scheherazade Goes West: Different Cultures, Different Harems*. New York: Washington Square Press.

Moallem, Minoo. 2001. "Middle Eastern Studies, Feminism, and Globalization." In "Globalization and Gender," edited by Amrita Basu, Inderpal Grewal, Caren Kaplan, and Liisa Malkki. Special issue, *Signs: Journal of Women in Culture and Society* 26, no. 4 (Summer): 1265–68.

———. 2002. "Whose Fundamentalism? A Statement on the Current Events." *Meridians: feminism, race, transnationalism* 2, no. 2: 298–301.

———. 2005. *Between Warrior Brother and Veiled Sister: Islamic Fundamentalism and the Cultural Politics of Patriarchy*. Berkeley: Univ. of California Press.

Shohat, Ella, and Robert Stam. 1994. *Unthinking Eurocentrism: Multiculturalism and the Media*. New York: Routledge.

Zaganiaris, Jean. 2014. *Queer Maroc: Sexualités, genres et (trans)identités dans la littérature marocaine*. Paris: Ailes sur un tracteur.

Section One
Epistemic Inventions

1

The Many Lives of Fatema Mernissi
Dreaming and Trespassing

ZAKIA SALIME

To me, the act of writing about Fatema Mernissi is emotionally driven. The overwhelming memories of gatherings, food sharing, field trips, and walks on the beach infiltrate and corrupt the act of writing like an academic, who usually speaks to the intellectual impact of an author. How to condense the many lives of Fatema Mernissi in one single narrative about her intellectual legacy? How to do justice to her incredibly inspiring and rich theoretical and methodological contribution without recalling the moments, the spaces, and the lives she profoundly shaped and touched? By "many lives" in my title, I point to the plural ways in which Fatema Mernissi affected not only feminist knowledge but also its modes of production, its publics, its meaning and places of construction. To highlight the "synergies"—to use Mernissi's own term—she created, I would need to situate her legacy in a broader politics of knowledge production and feminist practice. I would need to recall the counterspaces she created at the fringes of public academia and informal politics. I would need to rethink her work and commitment to feminist epistemology at the interstice of scholarly work and activist involvement. The many lives of Fatema Mernissi are also about long-lasting friendships, numerous communities of work, research collectivities, food, humor, happiness, and hope.

Multiple Legacies

Fatema Mernissi earned her PhD in sociology in 1973 from Brandeis University, where she set feminist inquiry into the heart of Islamic theology. She was a professor of sociology at the University Mohamed V in Rabat before joining the Institut de recherche scientifique (Institute of Scientific Research), established by the same university. She found the institute's insular character, its purely academic (elitist) mission, and its lack of resources very annoying yet not limiting. She responded to its lack of funds by fundraising, to its elitism by combining scholarly work and activism, and to the rigidity of its institutional spaces by opening her own home.

Her first book, *Beyond the Veil* (1975), put her work on the syllabi of most women's studies departments in the United States and around the world. When feminism was embracing Marxism and liberalism and denouncing patriarchy, Mernissi embraced religion as a central field for the construction of a feminist critique of the cultural and institutionalized spheres of the subjection of women. She pioneered definitions of the Islamic textual tradition of prophetic rhetoric—hadith—as interpretive, contingent, and subject to human scrutiny. In her books, including *Beyond the Veil* (1975) and *La femme dans l'inconscient musulman* ([1982] 1986, written under the pseudonym "Fatna Aït Sabbah"), Mernissi shed doubts on a whole tradition of interpretation of sharia by prominent Muslim scholars and theologians, including al-Ghazali. The centrality of Islam as a tradition of knowledge seeking, knowledge production, border crossing, and trespassing by both men and women is best represented by Mernissi's use of Sinbad and Scheherazade. They were emblematic figures in her writing and understanding of voice, travel, and imaginative futures.

To her readership in the West, Mernissi was one of the most inspiring figures of contemporary Arab feminism. She dared to excavate the theological grounds on which the relationship among gender, sexuality, and Islamic patriarchal ideologies rest by uncovering the traces of sexism in the Islamic textual tradition. *Beyond the*

Veil (1975) opened a new field of feminist inquiry into Islamic theology, setting the grounds for the emergence of what is now known as Islamic feminism. The latter brings Islam and gender in constant conversation. She continued to question this relation in many of her writings—first by revealing the political regimes that oppress women and second by foregrounding women's agency and their power of disturbing and trespassing.

To my generation of women, Mernissi was an entire school in her own right. Her impact extended beyond her immediate circle of Moroccan intellectuals to foster feminist activism in the North African region of the Maghreb. In her writing, we could feel the life-power of words, find the pride of belonging, and discover the noninterrupted line of women's rebellion, which started before the advent of Islam and is not showing signs of waning. For those of us who knew her as a person, she was a force of nature. She crossed and trespassed all physical and symbolic boundaries to propose a situated feminist theory that cuts across multiple disciplines, methodologies, and epistemologies, affecting several generations of women and providing them with the tools of argumentation, knowledge production, collective power, and decolonial sensibilities. Her work reads as a powerful account of women's fields of power and agency rather than of their victimhood or oppression. In her work, despite her own incisive voice, it is indeed all other women that we hear—the peasant, the factory worker, the homemaker, the carpet weaver, the activist, the artist, and the writer. This is why I speak about the many lives of Mernissi but also about her plural audiences. Mernissi did not write or speak only to a scholarly community. She instead engaged with students, street vendors, and factory workers, among others. She let them speak through her work. This is why her influence extended beyond academia to penetrate and infuse people's fond memories, including that of a fifty-year-old female artist who claimed to have "become an orphan after Fatema's death."[1]

---

1. Artist in Salé, Morocco, interviewed by the author, May 2017.

Up to the late twentieth century, programs of gender studies were missing in Moroccan universities. Academia in Morocco also lacked (and is still lacking) any significant government funding for research projects, which laid the ground for the rise of consultancy among researchers as a substitute for publicly funded research. A first generation of women academics stepped in to fill the gap by forming instead the first independent research groups, seeking external funding, and working outside proper institutional settings. Championed by Mernissi, these groups started to inject a feminist discourse back into academia through the production of collective books and their writing in leftist academic journals, notably *al-Assas* and *Lamalif* (see Daoud 2007). Mernissi's own writings formed the backbone for this emergent feminist knowledge production.

The Academic

Throughout her exemplary career, Mernissi documented specific turning points in the history of political and intellectual debates that Muslim societies generated in their relationship to Western modernities, colonial interventions, and neocolonial aggressions. The Gulf War (1990–91) was one of these turning points. In Morocco, the US-led war on Iraq generated a massive protest that drew an estimated one million to the streets of the capital city, Rabat, alone. Mernissi's book *Islam and Democracy: Fear of the Modern World* (1992), published a year after the war, reads as a powerful reaction to the US war on Iraq and to the Arab leadership's complicity and fear of democracy by revisiting the Islamic intellectual tradition of political debate, *jadal*, and rational thinking.

She pioneered a feminist reading of the Islamic textual tradition of prophetic rhetoric—hadith—as interpretive, contingent, and subject to human scrutiny. Her loving incursion into the life of Prophet Muhammad, exemplified in her book *The Veil and the Male Elite: A Feminist Interpretation of Women's Rights in Islam* (1991), generated one of the most powerful paradigms in feminist epistemology by widely opening the realm of hadith and Islamic studies to feminist scrutiny. The French version of the book, *Le harem politique: Le*

Prophète et les femmes (Mernissi 1987a), was banned in Morocco and other Arab countries because of its challenge to the authenticity of certain hadiths and their reciters—most notably Abu Huraria.

In *Le harem politique*, she centered women's voices by showing their daily questioning and challenges to the way the Qur'an addresses humankind or mankind rather than women explicitly. She dared to make the Qur'an respond to women's questioning by highlighting new revelations where the Holy Book addresses women specifically in specific verses or whole chapters devoted to women. She challenged Islamic jurisprudence by showing the contingency of some widely known misogynistic hadiths, shedding doubts on their authenticity, and questioning the legitimacy of hegemonic reciters. She engaged in a counterdiscourse that located those misogynistic hadiths at the juncture of political unrest following the Prophet's death and that identified the leading roles women took in the wars between his successors. The book also challenged the perception of the mosque as an exclusive male space for prayer by claiming that the mosque had initially been an open platform for political debates and feminist contestation of Qur'anic revelations, Islamic jurisprudence, and established patriarchal practices.

Mernissi's understanding of the importance of debate grew first from her embrace of Islamic philosophy and its articulation of the Qur'anic principle of argumentation, *jadal*—as she stated in one of her interviews with Al Jazeera (Al Jazeera 2014)—and second from her later encounters with Sufism. Though Sufism is the least well-known aspect of her intellectual and spiritual trajectory, her last publications bear its traces, including *L'amour dans les pays musulmans* (Love in Muslim Countries, 2012a), and *Les 50 noms de l'amour:* Le jardin des amoureux (2011). In a public space saturated by talks of war, acts of violence, xenophobia, and Islamophobia, love has a pacifying power. And, as usual, Mernissi digs into Islamic philosophy, reading eleventh-century writings by Muslim theologians to expose an Islamic (yet profane) tradition of love unraveling its Arabic expressions and showing this tradition's engagement with spirituality, emotionality, physicality, connection, and passion.

Her reference point in *L'amour dans les pays musulmans* is the eleventh-century Andalusian theologian and poet Abu Mohammad Ibn Hazm. His treatise of love, *Ṭawq al-hamāmah* (1022; *The Ring of the Dove* [1953]), gained universal appeal through numerous translations into many European and non-European languages, as Nazan Yıldız shows. Written as a collection of poetry, explains Yıldız, the treatise "becomes the representative of profane and courtly love in the Eastern literature," forming "a bridge between the studies on love in the medieval Eastern and Western literature" (2013, 497). This bridging most likely inspired Mernissi's choice to focus on this particular classic.

For *L'amour dans les pays musulmans*, Fatema Mernissi traveled across time and geographies, navigating the virtual pathways of the internet to see how young Moroccans express their longing for love and how they speak about it as a personal search, a longing, and a conquest. Mernissi's dream in the book is to allow a young generation of Muslims to reconnect with a culture of love as a practice of listening and of surpassing oneself. *Les 50 noms de l'amour:* Le jardin des amoureux (Mernissi 2011), the Moroccan version of *L'amour dans les pays musulmans* (Mernissi 2012b), takes the same theme of love by exploring another classic, the fourteenth-century book *Raoudatul muhibbin wa nuzhatul-nushtaaqeen* (*The Garden of Lovers*) by the Muslim theologian and imam Ibn Qayyim al-Jawziyya (see Ibn Qayyim al-Jawziyya 1431 AH/2010 CE). This time Mernissi opted for an art book by having three contemporary Moroccan artists—Mohamed Bannour, Fatema al-Ourdighi, and the calligrapher Mohamed Idali—contribute illustrations in paint and calligraphy of every one of the fifty different words expressing love in the Arabic language.

Her focus on love in this stage of her life was not only spiritual but also political. Her aim was to uncover another facet of Islamic theology and Arabic literary production in which love is a constituting part. What best to illustrate this facet than the writing of Imam Ibn Qayyim al-Jawziyya, a prominent Muslim cleric. Sufism, the notoriously declared enemy of political Islam, is where Fatema

Mernissi took most of her lessons about love as a path to knowledge and reconciliation. Revisiting Jawziyya's book was her way of pacifying a social space that had become too infused and confused with violence. Indeed, her very last edited volume, *Réflexions sur la violence des jeunes* (2015), published a few months after her death, dealt directly with the question of urban youth violence in the Moroccan public space.

Paradigm Shift

Mernissi's most powerful intellectual contribution to Moroccan gender studies stems from her interrogation of the structures of capitalist patriarchy and her definition of modern state institutions through women's positionalities, subjectivity, and spoken words. Many articles and books represent this phase (see, e.g., Mernissi 1987a, 1987b, 1988a). In her work and despite her incisive voice, we clearly hear other women. This is most exemplified by her book *Le Maroc raconté par ses femmes* (1986), translated into English under the title *Doing Daily Battle: Interviews with Moroccan Women* (1988a), as well as by numerous articles about women's place in the modern state. For instance, *Doing Daily Battle* offers an inside perspective into working-class women's conditions and struggles in the city of Rabat by foregrounding their voice and individual stories. Through a series of interviews with women living in the city and with migrants into it, the book presents a powerful illustration of women's agency as they struggle against marginalization, gender oppression, and economic precarity. As Mernissi puts it in the book's introduction, the goal is to illustrate the discrepancies between the legal definition of women as dependent housewives and their lived reality as economic agents and breadwinners.

This focus on labor and women's economic activity injected ordinary women's standpoint and a feminist materialist perspective into the women's movement's demands for reform to family law in the 1980s and 1990s. The feminist notions of experience, voice, and standpoint are central to this book's methodology. Though the interviews for *Doing Daily Battle* took place in the 1970s, the publication of the book in the 1980s came in support of women's groups' mobilization against family law. *Doing Daily Battle* invites almost a visual representation of these women's everyday struggle against economic necessity and their agency as they fight the structures of vertical (state-based) and horizontal (community-based) patriarchies and sexism. We are speaking about an important moment in the history of the feminist movement in Morocco—a moment in which this movement was facing not only the postcolonial legal apparatus but also most importantly the mounting Islamist forces and their patriarchal understanding of gender roles.

Mernissi's impact on feminist theory and gender studies stems from a major paradigm shift. She never claimed space or rights for women. Rather, in all her writing she showed that women have always been taking that space without asking permission. This was also her understanding of the rise of the most conservative forces in political Islam. Political Islam is not to be viewed solely as an utterly patriarchal interpretation of the sharia but as a fear of women's massive presence in public spaces and of their irreversible engagement with the structures of knowledge acquisition and with the institutions of the modern state (see Mernissi 1987a 1987b, 1988a, 2001).

In *Le harem politique* (1987a), she traced the emergence of these conservative forces back to the early time of the revelation, putting them in dialogue with Muslim women's early reflections and contestation of the Holy Book, the Qur'an, always in dialogue with Prophet Mohammed. It is no wonder why the book was banned in most Arab countries after its publication in France. In her books, she engaged what the prominent Moroccan sociologist and philosopher Abdelkbir Khatibi (1985) called "a double critique." In her case, this means speaking back to patriarchal Islamic institutions as well as to Western truncated views of Muslim women's lives and assumption of their powerlessness and utter oppression (Mernissi 1994, 2001).

By engaging this double critique, Mernissi became an inspirational figure for generations of women whose lives were marked by a convergence of colonialism, nationalism, modernization, Islamism, and revolution. Her navigation of these legacies and political currents were prominent themes in her scholarly research, public sociology, books, and novels. As she consistently reinvented herself, she was by the same token reinventing new communities of researchers and activists and new scholarly, literary, and artistic production. As she traveled across ideological currents, she always wrote against the grain, broadening the scope of creativity and debate, leading from center stage as well as from behind the scenes. *Bridging, inventing,* and *subverting* are terms that condense Mernissi's great intellectual legacy and human fingerprint, best expressed in her world-renowned novels *Dreams of Trespass: Tales of a Harem Girlhood* (1994) and *Scheherazade Goes West: Different Harems, Different Cultures* (2001).

The Scholar/Activist

I first met Mernissi in 1991 while attending the yearly international Multaqa al Ibda'e al-Nisa'i (Forum of Women's Creativity), organized by a group of women academics from the University of Fez. The symposium came at a politically charged moment. It was meant to showcase women's contributions to art, literature, and science across the Arab-speaking region. Organized with funding from the socialist City Assembly and hosted in the city hall, the forum was another venue for generating public support for feminist demands for the amendment of family law, or *mudawana*. As scholars and artists from the Arab world were discussing their works, the organizers were circulating a petition, the "One Million Signature Campaign against the *Mudawana*." Mernissi's presence at this forum and many others gave this mobilization a great impulse.

As a newly appointed assistant professor at the École normale supérieure in Fez and a fresh graduate from a sociology program in France, I was still trying to grapple with the cultural shifts that had taken place in less than a decade at the level of public debate and university setting. How did we shift from leftist ideologies of Third Worldism and socialism to an Islamist-inspired student population? How did that population manage to infuse academic debates with reinvented Islamic paradigms? Obviously, we had skipped the *feminist revolution* in both phases.

The presence of Mernissi at the Forum of Women's Creativity was a strong selling point. Like others, I attended the forum not only to sign the petition but also to hear Mernissi address the issues of the day: the mounting power of conservatism and the need for gender equality before the law. To my surprise, she addressed neither the petition nor the rising power of Islamism nor the reform of the *mudawana*. She did not speak about her own work, either. She instead highlighted all the freshly published books by the forum's women participants and organizers. She commented on the originality of the books, highlighted their major contributions, and proposed new collaborative platforms in which women and men participants could continue to work together. Later, when I became a regular member of meetings organized by Mernissi, I realized that her charismatic presence and incisive voice never overshadowed other people's presence.

Mernissi was not only a powerful federating force but also a visionary. She unsettled the newly segregated gender spaces by convening men and women to work together on generating new ideas and publications. Layla Chaouni, her Moroccan editor and director of Éditions Le Fennec, was central in this process. Chaouni opened her own publishing house to many of these meetings, enabling the young scholars to develop an insider perspective on the market of ideas and books. Mernissi created this synergy by putting a potential author close to a publisher, an activist close to a funding-program officer, and an artist close to a curator. Sometimes she had all of them around the same table, and many times she brought them around a special visitor and the dinner table at her own home. All were carefully chosen for the originality of their ideas and for their involvement with communities across Morocco. Mernissi was a firm believer in the power of writing, the power of reinventing communities, the transformative power of mixed spaces and groups, and the importance of creating alliances around these groups.

Unlike most other prominent sociologists at the Institut de recherche scientifique, Mernissi decided to weave together the academic and the activist worlds. Whether in her apartment in Rabat or in her four-story home on the Harhoura beach on the Atlantic coast,

Mernissi brought scholars, writers, journalists, and activists together to think about new projects and engage in collaborative ones. For decades, Mernissi's homes were a vibrant place for *reorganizing gender* by mobilizing groups around writing projects. To challenge the insular and elitist character of her own workplace, the Institut de recherche scientifique, Mernissi created laboratories in her homes for generating new ideas and new communities, transforming her personal spaces into regular destinations for groups of activists, artists, and first-time writers. At the same time, her apartment and house walls served as a permanent exhibit for artwork by marginalized women artists, including the late Benhila Regraguia, a painter from Essaouira.

Though Mernissi never associated her name with a specific woman's organization or political party, she accompanied the creation of most women's rights groups, notably those with a leftist or a liberal inspiration, including the transnational North African Collectif 95 Maghreb égalité and Maghreb 2000. She also backed the creation of the first leftist feminist magazine, *Thamania Mars (March 8)*. But she was never a member of any of these organizations. Despite her commitment to feminist spaces, Mernissi never claimed to own any of them and never attempted to influence their political or ideological stand. Having said that, I must also add that Mernissi was at the same time very generous with her time and connections but incredibly protective of her own personal space and timetable.

When I met her in the early 1990s, she resisted the label *feminism*. She did not want to "create another harem," she repeatedly said. She did not want to be viewed as a woman who works on women with other women. At that point, she was compiling a list of names that she would propose to universities around the world when they invited her to speak about gender. She told these universities that there were many women in Morocco who could do the job. Despite her reluctance to be defined exclusively as a gender scholar, Mernissi was the first Moroccan intellectual to engage in a systematic production of feminist knowledge by forming research groups across disciplinary divides. With the sociologist Aisha Belarbi, she formed the first feminist research group, Approches (Muqarabat). The two sociologists alternated in editing ten anthologies on women. Between 1987 and 2001, Approches published *Portraits de femmes* (Mernissi 1987b), *Femmes et pouvoir* (Mernissi 1988b), *Femmes partagées: Famille/travail* (Mernissi 1989), *Corps au féminin* (Belarbi 1991), *Couples en question* (Belarbi 1992), *Etre jeunes filles* (Belarbi 1994), *Femmes rurales* (Belarbi 1995), *Femmes et Islam* (Belarbi 1998), *Initiatives féminines* (1999), and *Femmes et democracie* (Belarbi 2001). The Approches series contributed to the dynamics triggered by the debate about reforming family law and the proliferation of activist/scholarly platforms on women's rights. These books also challenged the fragmentation of disciplinary fields as well as the bifurcation of these fields into either Arabic or French publications by instead being inclusive of both Arabic- and French-writing authors.

After her *gender phase*, the 1990s bear the trace of Mernissi's infatuation with the idea of *civil society* and with the satellite dish, especially with the advent of MBC (formerly Middle East Broadcasting) and Al Jazeera. She saw their potential as democratizing, modernizing, and liberating forces against both political Islam and social conservatism. I could not disagree more, but I chose not to open that conversation with her.

Mernissi hailed the rise of civil society but adopted a very pragmatic take on it as a space of creativity and imaginative future. Though she never took a formal stand on domestic politics, her involvement with civil society players was always a response to political conjunctures, including the creation of the Union du Maghreb Arabe (Union of the Maghreb Arab) in 1987 by the heads of states of Mauritania, Algeria, Tunisia, Libya, and Morocco.

As the devastating Algerian Civil War (1991–99) was ravaging that country, Zine al-Abidin Ben Ali was rising to power in Tunisia and undermining the possibilities of an actively independent civil society. In contrast, the Moroccan monarchy was slowly engaging in a process of political liberalization (see Brand 2004; Salime 2011), which made Morocco the only viable option for meeting among women's groups from the three countries. Mernissi played a central role in these meetings as a charismatic figure. She aligned herself with the feminist movement in these countries where demands for reforming family law were reaching a tipping point. She accompanied the creation of the Collectif 95 Maghreb égalité and Maghreb 2000 and responded with new book series, including Femmes citoyennes du Maghreb and Femmes citoyennes de demain. These publications brought new authors to the public's attention and raised hotly debated issues about women's legal status and their place as agents in the modern states of the Maghreb. They also carried the mark of Mernissi's endeavor to connect local players with international donors, which materialized in more publications, including in the two series Profiles de femmes and Visibilité féminine, which cover all fields of women's work from art and media to social security, law, and politics.

Working in activist forums compelled Mernissi to engage in fundraising for her numerous workshops and publications. She responded to an international conjuncture in which all funding programs were hunting for alternatives to Islamism among women's groups and "civil society" players. Some of these programs were notorious for supporting "democracy building" across the region, notably the German foundations Frederick Ebert Stiftung and Konrad Adenaur, which worked closely with the feminist networks Collectif 95 Maghreb égalité and Maghreb 2000 to sponsor their publications in French and translations into Arabic. The National Endowment for Democracy and the United Nations University for Women were also involved in funding Mernissi-led publications on Islam, civil society, and women. Other funds were also secured through the Canadian Agency for Development, ACDI (formerly Agricultural Cooperative Development International), Oxfam, and many other organizations. Two series of books, Women: Future Citizens of the Maghreb and Humanistic Islam, were the culmination of Mernissi's endeavor to bring together researchers and activists from the Maghreb with international funding programs.

Mernissi's thesis was simple: to defeat the fundamentalists (the term Mernissi's chose to use), civil society players must create a counterdiscourse and open counterspaces. The private sponsoring of an inexpensive Islamist literature played a crucial role in the diffusion of a conservative discourse among high school and university students and larger publics. This informal exchange of books and audiovisual material by women and men shaped the creation of what I have called an *embedded counterpublic* (Salime 2016) in homes, schools, and the workplace. From within existing institutions, the embedded counterpublic was challenging existing "un-Islamic" ways, so it then became imperative to invent new spaces and imagine a publication policy that could counter this proliferation of an Islamist genre and its influence in everyday lifeworlds.

At the discursive level, Mernissi believed, "civil society" (notably women's groups) must be able to dig into Islamic sources to show that the fundamentalists do not speak in the name of Islam. At the most material praxis, this public knowledge must be produced at an affordable price to compete with the inexpensive Islamic literature. Mernissi's politics of funded publications was meant to enable Le Fennec to continue producing books at an affordable price. Her strategic choice was to support the creation of alternative platforms to the Islamist market. To the previous book series that dealt with women, she added ones that uncover the human and even secular face of Islam. For instance, L'Islam humaniste is a collection of books written and directed by North African scholars to disclose the roots of human rights and secularism in Islamic thought.

In addition, Mernissi never shied away from joining activists in rallies and action across Morocco. She performed field visits to artists and to projects managed by activists in remote regions in southern Morocco. She labeled each one of these projects for marketing purposes, as we can see on her website, but also to emphasize her numerous interventions with multiple communities. Several books were born from these projects, including the collected volumes *Generation Dialogue: Journalistes marocaine* (Mernissi 2012b) and *Les Sindbads marocains: Voyage dans le Maroc civique* (Mernissi 2004). Notably *Les Aït-Débrouille: Un reportage sur des ONG rurales du Haut Atlas* (Mernissi 1997), a book based on Mernissi's field trip in the high Atlas Mountains of Morocco and published with funding from the World Bank, illustrates her understanding of civil society as a substitute for the missing state.

The Birth of a Feminist Press

Mernissi's book series produced also the main feminist publishing house in Morocco, Le Fennec. Its director, Layla Chaouni, recalls her first meeting with Mernissi. Chaouni was a young editor in a publishing house when Mernissi's *Sexe, idéologie, Islam* (1983, a translation of *Beyond the Veil* [1975]) was issued by a French publishing house. She met Mernissi at a book exhibit and approached her with a very attractive offer: the production of an Arabic translation of the book in a pocket format that would bring the price close to the buying power of students and teachers. Further discussions between the two women led to the creation of the first feminist press in North Africa, Le Fennec, in 1987, notably after Chaouni secured the production of the Approches series as well as the Moroccan editions of all Mernissi's books produced abroad. The collaboration between the two women lasted until Mernissi's passing in 2015. During the 1990s, when I contributed to the Approches series (Salime 1999, 2001), Le Fennec was not simply a feminist press but also the destination for many women's groups and a focal point for Mernissi's workshops outside of her own home.

Visiting Chaouni in Casablanca in May 2017 felt like undertaking a journey back into fond memories of a space that enabled dreams to come true, friends to meet, and solidarities to take shape. In that space as well as in others, Mernissi had the reputation of getting people out of their comfort zone, sometimes in uncomfortable ways. Her guests, not necessarily all Western-trained intellectuals, enjoyed hearing her stories embedded in popular wisdom and common sense and seeing her tap into the repertoire of ordinary women's words, daily practices, and stories. Layla Chaouni and I remembered how Mernissi would be speaking about a project of writing but then suddenly start to weave her thought into a story from her childhood in Fez or an anecdote about the street vendor from whom she learned something or a handcraft woman who made her a garment or a piece of jewelry. Mernissi, we restated, was connecting different worlds, bridging past and present while dreaming about the future.

In 2015, Chaouni, Fatema Mernissi's editor, was expecting to receive from Mernissi the new preface to an old book and could not understand the delay. Most of us, including Mernissi's close friends and family members, did not know about the state of her terminal illness—only her Moroccan doctor, personal driver, and housekeeper did, friends told me. Mernissi died on December 9, 2015, but continues to live in the communities she created, the chances she gave, the opportunities she opened, and the ideas she formed. As a final closing thought, no one put it better than Leila Chaouni when she ended our conversation with this statement: "Fatema lived free and died dignified." Though Mernissi did not live to see the *better world* she worked for, she firmly believed it was possible.

References

Aït Sabbah, Fatma [Fatema Mernissi]. [1982] 1986. *La femme dans l'inconscient musulman*. Reprint. Paris: Albin Michel.

Belarbi, Aisha, ed. 1991. *Corps au féminin*. Casablanca, Morocco: Le Fennec.

———, ed. 1992. *Couples en question*. Casablanca, Morocco: Le Fennec.

———, ed. 1994. *Etre jeunes filles*. Casablanca, Morocco: Le Fennec.

———, ed. 1995. *Femmes rurales*. Casablanca, Morocco: Le Fennec.

———, ed. 1998. *Femmes et Islam*. Casablanca, Morocco: Le Fennec.

———, ed. 1999. *Initiatives féminines*. Casablanca, Morocco: Le Fennec.

———, ed. 2001. *Femmes et democracie*. Casablanca, Morocco: Le Fennec.

Brand, Laurie. 1998. *Women, the State and Political Liberalization: Middle Eastern and North African Experiences*. New York: Columbia Univ. Press.

Daoud, Zakya. 2007. *Les années* Lamalif: *1958–1988, trente ans de journalisme au Maroc*. Casablanca, Morocco: Tarik.

Ibn Hazm, Abu Mohammad. 1953. *The Ring of the Dove: A Treatise on the Art and Practice of Arab Love*. A translation of *Ṭawq al-Ḥamāmah* (1022 CE) by Anthony Arberry. London: Luzac Oriental.

Ibn Qayyim al-Jawziyya. 1431 AH/2010 CE. *The Garden of Lovers and The Excursion of Those Who Yearn*. Mecca: Muʾassasah Sulaymān ibn ʿAbd al-ʿAzīz al-Rājiḥī al-Khayriyyah and Dār ʿĀlam al-Fawāʾid.

Al Jazeera. 2014. "Fatema al-Mernissi." YouTube video, posted by Dr. Adil, July 11. At https://www.youtube.com/watch?v=nlaUJP_Vk0w&feature=share.

Khatibi, Abdelkbir. 1985. "Double Criticism: The Decolonization of Arab Sociology." In *Contemporary North Africa: Issues of Development and Integration*, edited by Halim Barakat, 9–19. London: Croon Helm.

Mernissi, Fatema. 1975. *Beyond the Veil: Male–Female Dynamics in Muslim Society*. Cambridge, MA: Schenckman.

———. 1983. *Sexe, idéologie, Islam*. Paris: Tierce.

———. 1986. *Le Maroc raconté par ses femmes*. Rabat, Morocco: Société marocaine des éditeurs réunis.

———. 1987a. *Le harem politique: Le Prophète et les femmes*. Paris: Albin Michel.

———, ed. 1987b. *Portraits de femmes: Changements et résistance*. Casablanca, Morocco: Le Fennec.

———. 1988a. *Doing Daily Battle: Interviews with Moroccan Women*. Translated by Mary Jo Lakeland. London: Women's Press.

———, ed. 1988b. *Femmes et pouvoir*. Casablanca, Morocco: Le Fennec.

———, ed. 1989. *Femmes partagées: Famille/travail*. Casablanca, Morocco: Le Fennec.

———. 1991. *The Veil and the Male Elite: A Feminist Interpretation of Women's Rights in Islam*. Translated by Mary Jo Lakeland. Cambridge, MA: Perseus.

———. 1992. *Islam and Democracy: Fear of the Modern World*. Translated by Mary Jo Lakeland. New York: Basic.

———. 1994. *Dreams of Trespass: Tales of a Harem Girlhood*. Cambridge, MA: Perseus.

———. 1997. *Les Aït-Débrouille: Un reportage sur des ONG rurales du Haut Atlas*. Casablanca, Morocco: Le Fennec.

———. 2001. *Scheherazade Goes West: Different Harems, Different Cultures*. New York: Washington Square Press.

———. 2004. *Les Sindbads marocains: Voyage dans le Maroc civique*. Casablanca, Morocco: Marsam.

———. 2011. *Les 50 noms de l'amour:* Le jardin des amoureux. Casablanca, Morocco: Marsam.

———. 2012a. *L'amour dans les pays musulmans: A travers les texts anciens*. Casablanca, Morocco: Le Fennec.

———, ed. 2012b. *Generation dialogue: Journalistes marocaines*. Casablanca, Morocco: Marsam.

———, ed. 2015. *Reflexions sur la violence des jeunes*. Casablanca, Morocco: Le Fennec.

Salime, Zakia. 1999. "L'entreprise féminine à Fès, une tradition." In *Initiatives féminines*, edited by Aicha Belarbi, 31–46. Casablanca, Morocco: Le Fennec.

———. 2001. "Femmes-politique: Alliance difficile: Paroles de jeunes." In *Femmes et democratie: La grande question*, edited by Aicha Belarbi, 37–66. Casablanca, Morocco: Le Fennec.

———. 2011. *Between Feminism and Islam: Human Rights and Sharia Law in Morocco*. Minneapolis: Univ. of Minnesota Press.

———. 2016. "Embedded Counterpublics: Women and Islamic Revival in Morocco." *Frontiers: A Journal of Women's Studies* 37, no. 3: 47–73.

Yıldız, Nazan. 2013. "A Bird after Love: Ibn' Hazm's *The Ring of the Dove* (*Tawq al-Hamamah*), and the Roots of Courtly Love." *Academic Journal of Interdisciplinary Studies* 2, no. 8: 491–98.

2

The Mernissian Autobiography, or the Limits of Self-Disclosure

AKILA KIZZI

This chapter considers the issue of writing the self in Fatema Mernissi (1940, Fez, Morocco–2015, Rabat, Morocco). To understand the importance of self-writing among North African women, I analyze Mernissi's writing along with that of the Algerian writer Assia Djebar (1936, Cherchel, Algeria–2015, Paris, France). I choose this comparative method to shed light on the personal trajectory and historical context of colonization that influenced the way these two women approached their writing. I look at their social status and commitments, feminist or otherwise, in North African society. My analysis points to similarities in their life and career paths and underscore the historical importance of their emergence on the literary scene. I use an intersectional approach to (re)think gender, race, and class-based dominations as well as to reflect on plural identities and shed light on both the mechanisms of oppression and the strategies women writers have used to resist them.

Fatema Mernissi and Assia Djebar knew each other and worked together on postcolonial feminist writing projects, including, for instance, the Tunisian writing workshops of the 1980s and 1990s. In their works in French, both contributed to the future of such projects, elaborating their ideas on it from within a culturally situated feminist knowledge. Through these feminist writing projects, Djebar and Mernissi wanted to reinvigorate the feminist movement in the South, particularly in Africa and the Arab world. The aim was to bring women's aspirations to the forefront of political agendas in their cultural context and specificity. It was not a question of countering the Western feminism of the time, but a way of distinguishing the struggles of women in the South and giving them a place in a homogenizing world.

The trajectories of the two women differ, but what brought them together was this ardent desire to develop feminist thinking in North Africa.

This chapter is based mainly on previous research on self-writing in French among North African women of the twentieth and twenty-first centuries. This research has allowed me to discover many women writers who are less well known or not known at all. It also shows the two women's way of approaching the French language as the language of the other, the colonizer. But the most striking thing revealed was their way of writing about themselves, knowing that the autobiographical register requires a certain revelation about oneself and about the people around women writers, thereby bringing the intimate out into the public space. This gesture can be understood as a transgression, which is why women who undertake to write in the autobiographical register must use strategies to avoid being publicly vilified.

To understand the issue of the emergence of North African women writers in the contemporary francophone literary landscape, it is important to know how their writing was first received. The works of the first generation of women writers under colonization passed almost unnoticed in France, where they were published. The themes they addressed did not meet the expectations of French readers. The latter, fed on Orientalist imaginaries and attentive to cultural details under a voyeuristic gaze, were disappointed by a content that did not give importance to these kinds of fantasies.

Fatema Mernissi is one of the few North African women to write in several languages, including English, French, and Arabic. If we must analyze this point, we could think that she was looking for a language that fulfilled her in every aspect—a language that allowed her to say that she is a North African woman and a feminist at the same time, a language capable of translating her thoughts without distorting them. She was looking for a language that would welcome her aspirations as a free woman aware of the power of writing in advancing the cause of women of color.

One can even concede to her not only the genius of breathing into her several written languages all the African and Amazigh imaginaries that attached her to her native Morocco but also a desire to universalize those imaginaries denigrated by colonization.

As its title suggests, this chapter aims to show how Fatema Mernissi foils the rules of autobiographical writing to avoid the disclosure of the self that is inherent to the genre. I do not analyze all of her works but focus instead on *Dreams of Trespass: Tales of a Harem Girlhood* (1994), translated into French under Mernissi's supervision as *Rêves de femmes: Une enfance au harem* (1996).

This book is significant to the analysis of the contributions made by North African women writers, especially Mernissi, to the transformation of the genre of autobiography and the proposal of a new autobiography. In my analysis, I engage with stories as well as with the narrative strategies and aesthetic choices necessary for their construction because I don't think narrative strategies can "underlie" the stories. Form and content are always inseparable and crave for simultaneous or hybrid rather than hierarchical analysis. I will, of course, consider the sociocultural context of Mernissi's work and her situated knowledge.

Fatema Mernissi was born into a Muslim family attached to tradition. She spent her childhood in what she called the "domestic harem," which brought together an extended family consisting of her parents, her paternal grandmother, her uncles, her paternal aunts, and her cousins. Mernissi was part of a generation of girls who benefited from education thanks to an intercessor and a progressive father. Her personal trajectory is similar to that of Assia Djebar, who was the first Indigenous woman accepted in the École normale supérieure under French colonization, also thanks to her father. It is also significant that both Mernissi and Djebar came to a feminist awareness early on thanks to this educational opportunity.

Fatema Mernissi published her first book, *Beyond the Veil: Male–Female Dynamics in Modern Muslim Society*, in 1975 in the United States and then her first book in French, *Sexe, idéologie, Islam*, a translation of *Beyond the Veil*, in 1983. In 1987, *Le harem politique: Le Prophète et les femmes* (The Political Harem: The Prophet and Women) was issued. These books make Mernissi one of the most influential writers of her generation in Morocco and North Africa. However, she didn't just write but was also committed to feminist activism. She created a network of international relations called "Civic Caravans" and "Women, Families, Children" that work on the social, cultural, and economic level everywhere in Morocco, especially in isolated and disadvantaged regions.

Mernissi's activist and intellectual work is highly esteemed, and she was honored with the Erasmus Prize in the Netherlands in 2004. In 2003, she received the Prince of Asturias literary prize in Spain, the equivalent of a literary Nobel. She disappeared from public life on November 30, 2015, a few months after the death of her friend and fellow writer, the feminist Assia Djebar.

All about *Dreams of Trespass:*
Tales of a Girlhood in a Harem

Dreams of Trespass (1994) is presented as a memoir: an autobiographical narrative in which Mernissi speaks of her life in retrospect. She was fifty-four years old when she began the story of her childhood. The text begins with a date, a place of birth, and a first-person narrator: "I was born in 1940 in a harem in Fez" (Mernissi 1996, 5).[1] This begins the story that evokes Mernissi's childhood in Medina. Through the gaze of a curious little girl, the author invites us to dive into the closed world of women. She draws a beautiful fresco of figures of traditional women, feminists, former slaves of or fighters

---

1. Instead of citing and quoting Mernissi's English book *Dreams of Trespass*, I cite and translate the French version, *Rêves de femmes*. This is my personal translation, which I have conceived as a performative exercise of translating Claudine Richetin's translation and thus of translating and rethinking Mernissi's work.

against the French or Spanish, and storytellers of Arabian nights. She writes of their dreams of a world where there are no more borders (*hudud*).[2]

Mernissi creates narrative in the form of a tale where the real and the imaginary, the marvelous, the humorous, and the tragic all find their meaning in the reality of the harem. Like Assia Djebar, Mernissi positions herself as a historian to report facts about the political struggle for progressive ideas and considers the future position of girls and women as fundamental to the new, independent North African countries. Her thought allows a deconstruction of the Orientalist and colonial idea of the harem in North Africa.

In her story about borders, Mernissi mixes autobiographical facts and sociological reflection. The protagonist is a girl who questions her place in the world and on the borders (*hudud*) fixed by a patriarchal society.

Mernissi locates what she calls "the borders of my harem," where women of the extended family live in seclusion in a big house built around a walled courtyard. Through the stories and discourses that construct this place, young Fatema learns the notion of borders, of limits, which is the foundation of the harem and which she compares to the border invented by the French and the Spanish to delimit the conquered territories. In this closed space, one of the most important images that the stories convey is that of solidarity among the women of the harem.

The Analytical Relevance of This Book

Rêves de femmes: Une enfance au harem (1996) was previously published in English in 1994 under the title *Dreams of Trespass: Tales of a Harem Girlhood* and translated into French in 1996 by Claudine Richetin, a translation reviewed and adapted by the author. By studying the two versions together, one can elucidate some aspects of Mernissian autobiographical writing. In its English version, the book

---

2. *Hudud* is an Arabic word that means "frontiers," "borders," "limits." Mernissi draws on the notion of *hudud* to develop her idea of transgression.

is classified in the genre of memoir, and the narrator seems to be addressing primarily a Western audience (Bourget 2013). In the French version, the footnotes of chapter 3 added by Mernissi are an interesting read. Note 2 explains some of author's narrative choices. It takes only one sentence to kill the hopes of readers and critics who had been reading the English version as a purely autobiographical book. "This book is not an autobiography, but a fiction that takes the form of tales told by a child seven years old" (Mernissi 1996, 234–35n2).

After this statement on the book's literary genre, the remainder of the note refers to the relationship with her readers that the writer has chosen to highlight. Mernissi further explains her artistic choice: "To complicate things, we must also remember that the version I presented coincided with a literary packaging that I needed to seduce my reader" (1996, 235 n. 2). These additions in the French version are reflections of a desire for freedom in the Mernissian writing to stand out from the Eurocentric autobiographical genre. We can also read Mernissi's explanations in light of postcolonial thought, considering the stakes of autobiographical writing by North African women within French language and literature. Why did the author not feel the need to justify her story's presentation as a memoir in the English version and yet decide to do so in the French translation? Did her relationship to the French language differ from her relationship to the English language? Were the weight of colonial history and geopolitical hegemony not valid reasons to settle her accounts with the French language and the choice of refusing the French autobiographical genre? These power relationships create identity tensions and a desire to legitimize the expression of other local languages, such as Amazigh and Arabic.

By refusing the stereotypical categorizations that her writing would be put in because of who she was and what she represented, did not Mernissi also avoid the French autobiographical genre? All these questions find answers in the thought that she presents in her works and in her postcolonial feminist political positions.

Writing is at the crossroads of subject, text, and the world, and these three elements are subject to infinite reciprocal influences.

In the context of literary creation, these data are embedded in canonical systems, and to break through those systems these elements must meet or at least resort to certain rules and discursive modalities. Every writing assumes a reference space in which sometimes the writer's subjectivity is felt voluntarily or involuntarily in the manner of approaching their text. In Mernissi's case, this reference space is crossed by several influences in style and approach. These influences tend to make *Dreams of Trespass* a book that opens the way to the *nouveau roman*, the "new novel," because its author places it in the fiction genre.

Thus, this writing escapes the problematic posed by the description of the referential space in the literary field to make it the object of situational writing. For Mernissi, it was essential to situate her story in the Moroccan cultural private space that she knew so well, to confer to this space not only a reference value but also to impose it as a major reference of her text. Mernissi was fifty-four years old when she wrote this book; she had traveled a great deal and had become familiar with several cultures around the world. In her novel, we can find historical and cultural sources from different contexts integrated into the text to locate her own reference space on the chessboard of the world.

Thus, she valued this private feminine space that geopolitical power relations have devalued and placed as secondary. North African women in their private space were the center of interest for Mernissi, who aimed to change the ethnocentric and colonial prejudices of the West. It is important to remember her pioneering PhD dissertation on women's sexuality. Sexuality was also the subject of her first book published in the United States under the title *Beyond the Veil* in 1975, then published in French under the title *Sexe, idéologie, Islam* in 1983.

This book is one of the first to deal with the question of racialized women—North Africans and Muslims—and their double alienation. From a feminist point of view, Mernissi and Djebar made this double alienation their struggle on two fronts: first in their own society to show the contributions by women in Islam, then in Western society by questioning Western clichés that put racialized women in a submissive position, ignoring the specific contexts of their struggles for emancipation.

What Does It Mean for North African Women to Write in French?

To explain what it means for North African women to write in French, I must first give a sociohistorical overview of the relationship of North African women writers to the French language. My aim is not to define this relation but to better understand it. The French language is linked to personal trajectories, historical subjectivities, and the domination that characterizes this relationship. It cannot be treated outside politics because it is essentially nourished by the vivid memories of colonization. This language is the *butin de guerre* (spoils of war) for those who keep it alive today outside the metropolitan center. These people's real involvement in its present and its future development is to question their relationship to it because their voices on the periphery remain inaudible to the center.

Under colonization, at least in Algeria, we cannot really speak about a choice of a language to write in because French was imposed, and there was no place for other languages such as Amazigh and Arabic. Assia Djebar analyzed this "choice" in her later work, and this analysis opens the way to a reflection on the place reserved for francophone writers after independence. Thanks to French schooling, North African women acceded to writing and made it a means of resistance in the North African sociocultural context. These women, who were mostly of modest social classes, felt the need to speak up to signify their role as citizens in a society strongly dominated by patriarchy. They were aware of the weight of their words in defending their rights and abandoning the silence imposed by tradition and reinforced by religious prohibitions. In *Rêves de femmes*, Mernissi describes this alienation in her concept of the harem through the voice of the little girl she was: "The word *harem*, she said, was a slight variation of the word *haram*, the forbidden, the proscribed. It was the opposite of *halal*, the permissible. . . . The *harem* was about private space and the rules regulating it. In addition, Yasmina said, it did not need walls. Once you knew what was forbidden, you carried the harem within. You had it in your head, 'inscribed under your forehead and under your skin.' That idea of an invisible harem, a law tattooed in the mind, was frightfully unsettling to me" (Mernissi 1996, 61–62).

Mernissi's work in the 1980s on the freedom of women to speak out had a resonance in feminist circles, particularly with the Approches collection and its first publication, *Portraits de femmes: Changements et résistance* (Mernissi 1987b).[3] This collected volume edited by Mernissi has the merit of being cited because it highlights the social progress of the struggles of North African women and their strategies of resistance.

In *Rêves de femmes*, the freedom of North African and Arab women to express their desire finds its place in the portrait of Chama, who puts on plays that challenge the rules of the harem and its traditional tapestries. When Chama wants to speak about women's freedom, the example of the famous Arab singer Asmahan comes to reinforce her feminist determination: "Asmahan wanted to go to chic restaurants, dance like the French, and hold her Prince in her arms," she would say. "She wanted to waltz away with him all night, instead of standing on the sidelines behind curtains, watching him deliberate in endless, exclusively male tribal counsels. She hated the whole clan and its senseless, cruel law. All she wanted was to drift away into bubblelike moments of happiness and sensual bliss. The lady was no criminal; she meant no harm" (Mernissi 1996, 110).

Writing gives power and brings women's words out of confinement into the traditional inner space to develop their own dreams, first by appropriating the language and the words to speak out. Mernissi's narrator uses words to deconstruct borders: "The magic of words will carry her dream. 'I will make myself a magician, I

---

3. This publication lists the social and political achievements of women in North Africa by drawing portraits of several women who resisted and struggled for change.

will cheat the words, to share dreams with other women and make borders useless.'" She analyzes this female space with remarkable lucidity: "The concept of harem is intrinsically spatial [as] an architecture where the public space, in the Western sense of the term, is inconceivable because there is only an interior space where women have the right to exist and an outer male space from where women are excluded" (Mernissi 1996, 109–10).

For Mernissi, writing has power, and words are tools that help break free of boundaries and realize her dreams as a woman. She describes this impact: "When you happen to be trapped powerless behind walls, stuck in a dead-end harem," she would say, "you dream of escape. And magic flourishes when you spell out that dream and make the frontiers vanish. Dreams can change your life, and eventually the world. Liberation starts with images dancing in your little head, and you can translate those images in words. And words cost nothing!" (Mernissi 1996, 114).

"Writing Is Speaking Out, Writing Is Exposing Oneself"

How to write without the risk of falling into exhibition, especially in the case of women from former colonies?[4] This question is to be analyzed from the angle of an intersectional approach that considers the postcolonial cultural and feminist identity of these women writers. It is necessary for them to reclaim the French language and perhaps reinvent it strategically according to the cultural and linguistic context from which they speak. This problem emerges in the French intellectual landscape. Researchers have examined the involvement of francophone writers in the future of the French language: "They are French-speaking writers outside France who have to invent their own writing language in a context where French is in competition, even in conflict, with other local languages. This leads both to invent

---

4. The quote in this section's subhead comes from Maïssa Bey in an interview by Lebdai Benaouda (Bey 2007).

various strategies to allow the languages of their community to be heard without falling into the exotic marking" (Gauvin 2016).[5]

According to Gayatri Chakravorty Spivak's (2006) thought about the subaltern, we can situate North African speaking through writing as a process of rehabilitating an expression confiscated during colonization but also after independence. North African women writers have managed to break into the literary space traditionally occupied by men. As a result, they legitimize this expression to advance their social struggles. During workshops in Tunis,[6] Fatema Mernissi managed to resituate the writing of North African women by giving it a political base. She worked for the creation of a North African feminist *entre-elles*, a womanist space, from situated knowledge, as demonstrated by the symposium "Des voies vers un féminisme maghrébin" (Pathways to Maghrebian Feminism) in 1985.

For Djebar, the *qalam*—the pen—became an invincible weapon in Mernissi's hands, especially during the Years of Lead, when women became the target of massive conservatism and orthodox ideologies.

To encourage women to write, Mernissi had recourse to all kinds of strategies. She set up her theory of writing as a *rejuvenation cure (l'ecriture = cure de rajeunissement)*, using a certain intelligence, humor, and relaxed attitude in getting this message through to North African women. Thus, she noted: "A true revitalizing treatment, writing is used daily. Upon waking from the first erasures on the blank sheet, the writing stimulates cell activity, eyelids swell, your skin wakes up! By late morning your skin is at its best. Thanks to its structuring assets, writing has reinforced the structure of the

---

5. All translations from text in French are mine unless otherwise noted.
6. Maghreb Feminist Days, held in Tunis on May 20 and 21, 2016, in tribute to the writer, sociologist, and feminist activist Fatema Mernissi. These workshops resulted in the publication of *Fatema Mernissi la pensée féministe au Maghreb*, edited by Fatiha Talahit and Rachida Ennaifer. It contains many contributions from North African feminist researchers, including one by Amel Ben Aba, "Fatima Mernissi, accoucheuse d'écrits de femmes tunisiennes." See Ben Aba 2016.

epidermis. In the late morning the features are smooth, wrinkles are less apparent" (quoted in Ben Aba 2016, 50).

Thus, she made writing a remedy against crises of all kinds, including that of real or symbolic wrinkles. To bring women to writing, Mernissi did not spare words. She urged North African women to write: "Write daily for an hour, anything, even a letter to the electricity compagny in your neighborhood. You have no idea of the effect of this daily exercise" (Mernissi 1991, 10).

A sociological field investigation conducted by Christine Détrez with sixty women writers in Algeria and Morocco shows the importance of writing for North African women and the power it gives them to be individuals in a society marked by gender inequalities. For Soumaya, writing is a "purge," and for Baha it is "psychotherapy" that helps them to cope with the daily difficulties related to their status as women. Labsira goes a long way in describing the comfort that the act of writing gives her, admitting: "Sometimes I feel bad if I do not write. Very badly, I sink like that, I find myself in the dark. While when I write . . . even by describing characters that have nothing to do with me . . . by rebuilding these things, I feel very good. This thing, these people have nothing to do with my personal life, have nothing to do with me. Seeing them live in a context like that in a page, I feel very well" (Détrez 2012, 81).

Labsira's comments about her own writing and the genre she has chosen show the North African's distrust of linking the events or characters described to their own lives. To avoid any rapprochement or parallel with their own lives, they prefer to say it upfront, "This is not my life, and the character is not me." This can be read as a precaution taken when North African women writers start putting into words what is "private" or simply write about "themselves."

Toward a Feminist and North African Postcolonial Autobiography

North African autobiographical writing escapes definitions of the genre imposed by researchers such as Philippe Lejeune, who describes autobiography as "a retrospective narrative in prose that a real person makes of his own existence, when she focuses on her individual life, especially on the story of her personality" (1998, 14). Mernissi signs a pact other than that of classic autobiography with her reader. Her writing does not follow the requirements of referentiality, subverting the rules through a new use of the personal "I," which is replaced by an "I-we," a collective subject. This new speaker represents Moroccan women collectively and in particular and North African women in general.

For *Dreams of Trespass*, Mernissi made a significant choice regarding its cover. She left no place for detail because she was conscious of the weight of history and the voyeuristic look of the *other* from abroad. The cover shows a group of three women dressed in traditional Moroccan outfits, their backs to the photographer's lens so that the reader looking at them cannot see their faces. We can make an intertextual link between this image chosen by Mernissi and the well-known painting *Femmes d'Alger dans leur appartement* (Women of Algiers in Their Apartment, 1833) by Eugène Delacroix, widely analyzed by Djebar in her book of the same title (Djebar 1980). On this cover, Mernissi had women avoid exposing themselves to the foreign gaze, an exposure exemplified in Delacroix's painting. By turning their backs on the public, the women are avenging their Algerian sisters, who under colonialism were imagined solely as objects of desire in French artists' and writers' Orientalist vision.

Through her approach, Mernissi deconstructed the canonical rules of writing and the genre in which she was expected to write as a North African woman exoticized in the gaze of her Western readers. The work is marked by an atypical writing charged by the author's desire to tell herself and to confide the anxieties that undermine the young Fatema. Mernissi has her hand on her system of enunciation as an original development that guides the text to describe the space of the harem and the women who occupy it without playing the game of gaining the approval of the other, the Western reader.

If we have to classify this writing according to the classical Western models of autobiography and self-writing, Mernissi's work cannot be placed in any category and/or can be placed in all categories at once. Her desire to always want to escape the binary categories continues even in her writing. She creates thus an *entre-deux* (between two) in which she classifies her writing. She opts for a new self-writing of North African women. This writing escapes Western classical rules and becomes unclassifiable, so it is stigmatized and marked by a lack of canonical recognition. Thus, Mernissi's work remains marginal in France.

For a Hybrid "I"

It is interesting to analyze the complexity and the hybridity of the autobiographical "I" used in particular by Mernissi but also globally by North African women writers. It can be read as a rejection of the classical form of autobiography known in the West and, more precisely, in France. North African women writers do not simply reject the classical autobiographical genre but also replace it with a new genre that escapes the constraints of self-writing with a clear and direct "I." A result of this new use of the "I" is a performative writing where the personal pronoun refers not only to the author but to all women in North Africa, as is the case with Mernissi and Djebar. It is an "I-we" that refers to the group, the community, and everything that forms the North African cultural universe in general and the Mernissian universe in particular. *Dreams of Trespass* abounds with references to a "we" that is expressed through the "I" of the narrator. This does not go unnoticed by readers who are attentive to Mernissi's thought and her desire to unburden her writing of the weight of Eurocentric autobiographical classicism, where the value of the "I" is superior and individualized when it is placed outside of the group. This thought should not be read as advocating the supremacy of the collective over the individual but rather as contributing to the collective's reinforcement. When one knows the North African societies well, one realizes that Mernissi's choice to emphasize the collective is not an obstacle to the freedom of the individual. On the contrary, it endows the individual with an additional power to gather the group of women around common struggles and thus to create solidarity among them. So Mernissi's "I" integrates the "we" of women into her feminist expression. This practice contributes to the emergence of new, complex, and hybrid identities in the writings of North African women. I have treated this hybridity in my research on the autobiographical work of Fadhma Aïth Mansour Amrouche, *Histoire de ma vie* (The Story of My Life, 1968), which shows the different aspects of identity and culture to be taken into account in a North African woman's autobiography (see Kizzi 2016, 2019, 2020).

As Samira Farhoud (2013) points out, this "I" testifies to the richness of the autobiographical genre practiced by the Maghrebi authors, which refers to a "we" of sorority. This use of the "I" shows a cultural specificity to be considered in the analyses of canonical knowledge.

Beyond the practice of a literary genre, it is a question of claiming and imposing a new francophone, deeply feminist writing that finds its essence in these women's permanent need to express themselves and use this discourse as a weapon against the injustices related to their condition. North African writers such as Mernissi and Djebar are aware of the impending horizon (*horizon d'attente*) and the theory of the reception of a work either in the West or in North Africa (Jauss 1990). Therefore, they are always looking for strategies to circumvent this expectation and the Western reference system in general. Mernissi gives writing an unorthodox dimension that presents as a (dis)ordered methodology. She deconstructs the process of writing: "One of the privileges of writing, for me in any case, is to write what goes through my head, as I do now. But when I say 'what goes through my head,' I do not mean that it's messy. The process of writing is very mysterious. But what is certain is that he is not disordered. He obeys an order that is not that of the reader, that's all. Often, in some kinds of writings, the most interesting in my opinion, this order escapes the author too" (Mernissi 2009, 7).

The French readership expects a North African and feminine "autobiographical" work to offer crisp details nourished (un)consciously by the Orientalist imagination. This expectation is doubled in the case of the autobiography of North African women compared to French women. In order to show the specificity of the receptive experience, to introduce the subjectivity of the author, the intersubjective and social dimension of the aesthetic experience, women's autobiography of North Africa comes close to the renewal offered by the works of Hans Robert Jauss on the question because it makes it possible to forego the analysis of the forms and the categorization of literary genres, the authors, and their works. Thus, Jauss makes the concept *horizon d'attente*, "waiting horizon," an informal one by introducing a multitude of variations of it. According to him,

> The analysis of the reader's literary experience will escape the psychologism of which it is threatened if, to describe the reception of the work and the effect produced by it, it reconstructs the waiting horizon of its first public—that is to say, the system of objectively formulated references that, for each work at the moment of the history in which it appears, results from three main factors: the prior experience that the public has of the genre to which it belongs, the form and the theme of previous works whose knowledge it presupposes, and the opposition between poetic language and practical language, imaginary world and everyday reality. (1990, 49)

If North African women writers try to reinvent autobiographical writing in the Western reference system from a personal and cultural point of view, they must also justify this reinvention in their own societies. As noted earlier, according to religious and social custom, the writing of women in North Africa must observe a certain modesty (*hurma*) because public unveiling is badly perceived, and the author of such work is sometimes sanctioned. Yet being denuded in the French language is also complicated because it might imply accepting the symbolic rape always implied in the gaze of the colonizer, as Frantz Fanon showed in his essay "L'Algérie se dévoile" ([1959] 2011). As a result, for North African women, the practice of writing means struggling simultaneously on two fronts, confronting a double alienation.

Even if at first sight this writing experience seems like a doomed mission, the fact remains that works such as Djebar's *Women of Algiers in Their Apartment* and Mernissi's *Dreams of Trespass* are almost unique in the use of an annoying "I" that disturbs and disrupts not only the borders of literary genres but also the boundaries of gender in North African cultures and in the Western referential system. This is what Mernissi calls *hudud*, the (in)visible borders. This thought, which runs counter to the dominant Western thought, is perceived as a challenge and a mistrust of canonical knowledge, which is one of the reasons why such work remains marginal and without recognition in the West.

Patricia Hill Collins (1986) discusses the creative use of the place of Black women's marginalization in society to develop theories and thought that reflect different perspectives. Thus, thinking about other places of discourse depends on the importance of bringing other perspectives that break with the unique history. Like Collins, Mernissi also developed her thinking around this idea of marginality, criticizing the hierarchy of knowledge as a product of classification and preferring to speak from the margin. That is to say, those who possess social privilege also have epistemological privilege because the model of universally appreciated science is white. As a result, this hierarchization positions the Eurocentric epistemological explanation as superior. It confers on Western modern thought the exclusivity of valid knowledge, structures it as dominant, and renders futile the experiences of knowing racialized women.

To conclude, I could say that in *Dreams of Trespass* Mernissi poses a major challenge to the autobiographical genre, opting for a writing that considers the political, feminist, and postcolonial positions of writing North African women. Assuming this choice, she puts her concept of symbolic and (in)visible *hudud* in perfect harmony with the novel genre she offers to the readership.

References

Aïth Mansour Amrouche, Fadhma. 1968. *Histoire de ma vie*. Paris: La Découverte.

Ben Aba, Amel. 2016. "Fatima Mernissi, accoucheuse d'écrits de femmes tunisiennes." In *Fatema Mernissi la pensée féministe au Maghreb*, edited by Fatiha Talahit and Rachida Ennaifer, 46–52. Paris: CNRS.

Bey, Maïssa. 2007. "L'être et les mots." Interview by Lebdai Benaouda. *El Watan*, Sept. 6.

Bourget, Carine. 2013. "Complicity with Orientalism in Third-World Women's Writing: Fatima Mernissi's Fictive Memoirs." *Research in African Literatures* 44, no. 3: 30–49. At https://doi.org/10.2979/reseafrilite.44.3.30.

Collins, Patricia Hill. 1986. "Learning from the Outsider Within: The Sociological Significance of Black Feminist Thought." *Social Problems* 33, no. 6: S14–S32. At https://doi.org/10.2307/800672.

Détrez, Christine. 2012. *Femmes du Maghreb, une écriture à soi*. Paris: La Dispute.

Djebar, Assia. 1980. *Femmes d'Alger dans leur appartement*. Paris: Femmes.

Fanon, Frantz. [1959] 2011. "L'Algérie se dévoile." In *L'An V de la révolution algérienne*, 17–50. Paris: La Découverte.

Farhoud, Samira. 2013. *Interventions autobiographiques des femmes du Maghreb: Ecriture de contestation*. New York: Peter Lang.

Gauvin, Lise. 2016. "Statut de la parole et traversée des langues chez Assia Djebar." *Carnets*, 2nd series, 7 (May 31). At https://doi.org/10.4000/carnets.908.

Jauss, Hans Robert. 1990. *Pour une esthétique de la réception*. Paris: Gallimard.

Kizzi, Akila. 2016. "L'accord im/possible: Écriture, prise de parole, engagement et identités multiples chez Taos Amrouche." PhD diss., Université Paris 8.

———. 2019. *Marie Louise Taos Amrouche: Passions et déchirements identitaires*. Paris: Fauves.

———. 2020. "Indigenous Algerian Women Artists in the French Landscape: Baya Mahieddine and Taos Amrouche." In *Under the Skin: Feminist Art from the Middle East and North Africa Today*, edited by Ceren Özpinar and Mary Kelly, 115–28. Oxford: Oxford Univ. Press.

Lejeune, Philippe. 1998. *Pour l'autobiographie*. Paris: Seuil.

Mernissi, Fatema. 1975. *Beyond the Veil: Male–Female Dynamics in Muslim Society*. Cambridge, MA: Schenckman.

———. 1983. *Sexe, idéologie, Islam*. Paris: Tierce.

———. 1987a. *Le harem politique: Le Prophète et les femmes*. Paris: Albin Michel.

———, ed. 1987b. *Portraits de femmes: Changements et résistance.* Casablanca, Morocco: Le Fennec.

———. 1991. *Le monde n'est pas un harem: Paroles de femmes au Maroc.* Paris: Albin Michel.

———. 1994. *Dreams of Trespass: Tales of a Harem Girlhood.* Cambridge, MA: Perseus.

———. 1996. *Rêves de femmes: Une enfance au harem.* Translated by Claudine Richetin. Paris: Albin Michel.

———. 2009. *L'amour dans les pays musulmans.* Paris: Albin Michel.

Spivak, Gayatri Chakravorty. 2006. *Les subalternes peuvent-elles parler?* Translated by Jérôme Vidal. Paris: Amsterdam.

3

Jadal and the War of Words

MINOO MOALLEM

In her remarkable contributions to feminist scholarship, Fatema Mernissi weaves together various threads—from a variety of genres to an awareness of her audience to a multiplicity of cultural and linguistic texts and contexts.[1] She invites the reader to share the pleasure of what Roland Barthes calls "the wake of what has always already been read, seen, done and lived" (quoted in Culler 2008, 33). For example, in describing paradise, Mernissi reconstructs it as an imaginary utopian feminist space in contradistinction to the

---

1. I first met Fatema when I was a graduate student at the University of Montreal. She was invited to give a talk at McGill University. I had just finished reading *La femme dans l'inconsciente musulman* (Aït Sabbah 1982) and was amazed by the author's brilliant writing, not knowing that "Fatna Aït Sabbah" was Mernissi's pseudonym. After the talk, she invited me to a workshop at Harvard and to an interview as part of her work on Muslim women academics who self-identified as feminists. She was interested in the moments when one revolts against patriarchal cultural and institutional practices. During the interview, we talked about our strong mothers, aunts, and grandmothers and their influence on our becoming feminist scholars. What was fascinating in her talk at McGill was the way she challenged the religious and secular nationalism and fundamentalism of antifeminists, both Muslims and non-Muslims. I was impressed not only with her historical knowledge but also with her style and aesthetic approach to Muslim societies, cultures, and histories. She was engaged both in deconstructing the past and in bringing to life the "forgotten queens of Islam" (the title of one of her books) by challenging masculinist narratives of Arab-Islamic history.

dominant patriarchal notions of it. She imagines paradise as the absence of fear and pain and a place for gentle and nonpossessive relations. She writes: "Paradise is a place where hugging is about soothing, a place where embrace is a soft opening of oneself, not possession, a place where soothing and opening up have no power connotations. They have nothing to do with weakness, fear, vulnerability, pain" (1986, 22).

Central to Mernissi's work are the relationship between reality and an affective sensibility as well as the need to open up Islamic discourses and practices that colonial modernity has isolated in a religious space. She has consistently argued that every text, religious or secular, is mediated by what she calls "la chaines de transmetterus" (a network of transmitters) (Mernissi 1987b, 19) restricted to privileged classes and ethnicities, especially the male elite. This mediation between Islamic knowledge and Western knowledge in our times has been entangled with relations of power, both local and global, and is established "a la fois lointaine et proche" (at the same time far and nearby). In Mernissi's terms, the hegemonic draws consensus from the past by concealing it: "D'abord ceux de nos contemporains . . . maquillent le passé pour nous voiler notre present" (Our contemporaries . . . conceal the past to veil our present) (1987b, 19). Thus, the power of her work lies in creating space to investigate the ways in which hegemonic narratives of the past—including masculinist, absolutist, and fundamentalist interpretations of Islamic texts as well as an Islamophobic and Orientalist depiction of Islam—are mobilized to justify the order of things in the present. In her view, "L'historie est toujours une langue de groupe" (History is always the language of the group) (1987b, 19).

The power and pleasure of Mernissi's work is best shown by bringing to light her examination of the burden of cultural and social inheritance in a postcolonial or neocolonial context. She creates new theories and concepts by reinterpreting the past and present to imagine the future and by spinning more conventional thinking into odd and unexpected patterns that elude normative thinking. To challenge absolutist references to religion, religious texts, or historical events in the representations and interpretations of the past, she uses *jadal*, the art of dialogue and debate (Huff-Rousselle 2003). As Diya M. Abdo notes, "Mernissi's original text is multiply loaded, in that author and text occupy an ambiguous and ambivalent position, both anti-imperialist and anti-fundamentalist. Thus, the comparison is not simply between a text that is patently pro-Western and an alternate that is pro-Islamic, but something considerably more complex" (2010, 176).

For Mernissi, *jadal* is a well-informed, rigorous, witty, bold, and skilled debate that exists at the intersection of knowledge and power. Within the Islamic context, both *kalam* (the speech act) and *kalameh* (the word or words) are at the center of religious discourse and Islamic theology.[2] Mernissi emphasizes the importance of different regimes of meaning making in changing and challenging the order of things in the present and the future.

Mernissi refers to four components of her use of *jadal* through words and debates: (1) her engagement with patriarchal and Eurocentric vocabulary through transcoding; (2) her sociological approach, using evidence-based inquiry to interrogate what was said or textualized in a specific historical context; (3) her theoretical and methodological questioning of various interpretations of the sacred text as well as of the hadith by the knowledge elite;[3] and (4) the significance of women as subjects of knowledge, readers and interpreters of the sacred text, as well as storytellers not only in their interrogation of the past but also in their reimagining of the future. The art of *jadal* and the war of words—the debate being artistic but also fiercely adversarial—provide a space where various points of view and interpretations

---

2. *'Ilm al-kalam* in Islamic philosophy refers to pursuing theological knowledge through debate and discussion.

3. The hadith are direct or indirect transmissions of the Prophet's sayings and actions that Sunni Muslims follow as the second source of legislation in Islam. Shi'a Muslims—and many Muslim scholars—are more skeptical about the authenticity of the hadith.

encounter each other with their knowledge of the text, analysis of it, and rhetorical strategies used toward its representation.

For Mernissi, one of the most important aspects of *jadal* is *adab*, or "adding the brains of others to your own" (Leccese 2006, 348). In an interview of her by Francesco Alfonso Leccese, she describes how Prophet Muhammad challenged racist Arabs who considered themselves superior to others and how he destroyed the previous aristocratic systems. She further argues that one of the reasons Islam spread throughout India was the possibility for people to escape the caste system (Leccese 2006, 348). She praises the Abbasids and their rule, which was based on a successful globalization of trade and travel. In other words, in her view the Abbasids' system of government facilitated the movement and knowledge of local customs and cultures in their system of governance by applying the Sufi belief in communication or *adab*, meaning a dialogue with the stranger, through translational practices of trade and travel, but not through military strategies (Leccese 2006, 349). Mernissi consistently criticizes current forms of globalization based on a lack of "global justice" and especially the use of arms to invade another country—for example, in the case of the US occupation of Iraq. She considers globalization essential to shaping a great civilization, yet she interrogates neocolonialism and uneven globalization. She also considers the expansion of the internet and satellite TV as a means of democratization. Of course, Mernissi does not say much about media as a site of reproduction of power relations or as a tool used for surveillance, false news, and propaganda. However, she is cognizant of the "export of democracy" from the global North to the global South. Mernissi challenges the West's simplistic view of Islam, Muslims, and Arabs and constantly reminds her readers of the context within which current forms of globalization are taking place. She also revisits dominant historical narratives to bring to life the lost, forgotten, or suppressed democratic traditions of the Muslim world.

To engage in a debate, one must have two main tools: fierce language and in-depth knowledge of the subject matter. Although there is no writing on Mernissi's pedagogic approach to the transmission of knowledge, her notion of *jadal*, combining both an untamed and forceful language and a deep knowledge of the text and the historical context, offers a powerful pedagogic teaching tool for our times, when there is a need to go beyond the acquisition of knowledge via the internet and scheming through various texts, including the sacred ones. For example, Islamophobic and superficial references to selected passages of the Qur'an obviously lacking a close reading and understanding of the text have increasingly become a site of circulation of either anti-Muslim racism or fundamentalist interpretation of Islam.[4] The power of Mernissi's text is in her ability to engage in debates both critically and rhetorically, using her knowledge of the past and understanding of the present to show how the former is constructed through the latter. Her reading is deeply feminist, prioritizing politics and relations of power over anything else. Several examples demonstrate her advocacy of—or, more accurately, her decolonial gesture toward—restoring the long historical tradition of *jadal* in Arab and Muslim worlds in an era when debates are replaced with polite parallel talks. Mernissi challenges and subverts Orientalist, racist, and masculinist representations of Islam, Muslims, Arabs, and Muslim and Arab cultures either as the "other" of the West or as invested in patriarchal local traditions frozen in time and history.

What is unique about her approach is that not only does she deconstruct representational practices, but she also shows how these portrayals create a privileged position for the male elite to maintain and justify their position of power. Her method of *jadal* calls not only for a reexamination of religious texts through the lens of historical context but also for an interrogation through debate and

4. One could argue that in addition to the imperial and military intervention by the United States and its regional allies, the rise of ISIS (Islamic State of Iraq and Syria) has much to do with the performance of a stereotypical fundamentalist narrative projected onto the Muslim world. In my view, ISIS's televised performance of violence and brutality is more in proximity with Hollywood images of Muslim terrorists than with any interpretation of Islam.

discussion of the omissions of suppressed or concealed text. For her, the gap between the speech acts—what was relayed to Prophet Mohammad through *vahy* (divine revelation through a voice that cannot be attached to any subject) and what was textualized almost a hundred years after the Prophet's life—calls for an interrogation of a patriarchal culture that was interjected historically. These patriarchal cultural practices have prioritized and privileged the male elite's interventions, interpretations, and revisions. Also, the modern colonial and Orientalist depiction of Islam and Muslims as uncivilized and backward have provoked a somewhat more defensive reaction from the local elite.[5]

To challenge and transform patriarchal social practices, on the one hand, and Orientalist and racist ideas about Islam and Muslims, on the other, the synergic complacency of these discourses must be opened and deconstructed. Through the art of *jadal*, Mernissi questions both colonial and patriarchal orders and borders, using different genres of writing, multilingual competency, as well as many points of entry into the world of religious and cultural discourses. She sometimes brings to life women characters who were erased from the hegemonic historical narrative. Other times she questions the representation of a specific narrative or text. For Mernissi, the context, text, and subjects of interpolation or reception were unfortunately folded together and thus thrown into obfuscation.

Language Matters: From Global Harem to Petro-fundamentalism

One of the powerful strategies Mernissi uses in her writing is to decenter the words used in Orientalist discourses—both old and new—either by applying them to new circumstances or by focusing on their political meaning. This form of transcoding puts words

---

5. I have extensively elaborated on the concept of civilizational imperialism and civilizational thinking in the colonial and postcolonial contexts in Moallem 2005 and 2021.

back in circulation in radically new ways.⁶ Also, as a multilingual scholar, Mernissi uses language as a site of resistance and as a means of engaging various audiences. As she addresses different audiences functioning within specific cultural and linguistic infrastructure, she is well aware of the significance of what Gayatri Chakravorty Spivak (2007) calls "deep language learning."

Two examples demonstrate Mernissi's strategy of using language as a site of resistance. The first is the concept of the harem, a favorite notion in Orientalist writing. The second is the concept of fundamentalism. As Sarah Graham-Brown notes, in Orientalist discourse the harem represents Orientalist fantasies about "a forbidden life of women, of sexuality caged and inaccessible, at least to Western men, except by a leap of imagination" (2003, 502). In the colonial era, this inaccessibility mobilized a visual industry—from studio photography to films to advertisement—that seemingly enabled the voyeur's eye to penetrate the impassible.

Mernissi uses several strategies to challenge the notion of the harem. For example, she uses the harem to talk back to power when she refers to a global harem as a way to depict the geopolitical divides of our current world. In another case, she refers to the French colonial quarter as a harem with borders and boundaries. Expanding the harem concept to include the space of the Occident, she challenges the stigma of the harem as peculiar to the disciplining of Muslim women, expanding it to other forms of bordering and ordering. The notion of the harem, in this case, challenges and unsettles the global North's self-image as liberated and free. Indeed, Mernissi turns the concept of the harem into a complex geopolitical and multidimensional signifier that makes its original usage irrelevant.

For Mernissi, the harem is several things. It is about internal boundaries—what she calls "the harem within"—as modes of discipline that displace women and limit them as femininized subjects. It

---

6. Stuart Hall defines transcoding as taking an existing meaning and reappropriating it for new meanings (2013, 259).

is also about an external spatial order (but not the closed door in its Orientalist imaginary) that relegates space to the private or public. In her view, both nation-states and the global world of many borders and boundaries are harems in some fashion, policing the space. In her book *Scheherazade Goes West* (2001), she uses the notion of the Western harem to interrogate the beauty culture and the more visible regimes of disciplining gender performance. Using her experience of looking for clothing in Germany, she challenges the temporal, violent, and more visible systems of gender regulation in the West as forcing women to identify with femininity and an idealized body. In my view, however, Mernissi's concept of Western beauty reinforces the men/women dichotomy by dismissing issues of class and race given that a significant portion of those marketing and selling femininity through consumer goods are women entrepreneurs in the global North.[7] Mernissi is nevertheless able to show how the notion of the harem could be applied to depict consumerist beauty standards in the West.[8]

Thus, the harem is redefined from a physical place where Persian, Turkish, and Arab women are imprisoned along with their slaves to a cultural space of disciplining gender, race, class, and nation since modernity. The vision of a harem as the fantasy land of the Western male imperialist requires the colonial project of "saving Muslim women," a belief that this private space welcomes Western men's intrusion because these women desire to be exposed and free. Mernissi brilliantly turns her gaze inward and challenges the segregation of space and control of the visibility of women as forms of patriarchal containment of women's sexual power. In a robust theoretical and historical effort, she argues that Muslim cultures place restrictions

---

7. For a brilliant analysis of the convergence of corporate practices, consumerism, and women's entrepreneurship, see Kaplan (1995). Inderpal Grewal (1999) also discusses the globalization of the Barbie doll and its marketing in India.

8. Some of the arguments made by pro-veiling Iranian Muslim women also criticize the ways in which capitalism has objectified and commercialized women's bodies for consumerist purposes. See Rahnavard (n.d.).

on women based not on a belief in women's biological inferiority but in recognition of their power: women symbolize *fitna* (chaos) and are thus a dangerous threat to social order (Aït Sabbah 1982).[9]

To elaborate further on this point, Mernissi discusses the historical context within which Islam emerged as a monotheistic religion. What is radically different about Islam and its concepts of sexuality, Mernissi argues, is the historical context within which women had significant power.[10] In her view, the pre-Islamic goddesses Al-lat, Al-Uzza, and Al-Manat were extremely important in the seventh-century Quraysh, where the Prophet Mohammad emerged. Indeed, in Islam, sexuality is not positioned against order but is defined by the relationship between *'aql* (reason) and *shahwa* (sexual desire). Islam's claim to be the religion of reason is based on the regulation and control of desire rather than on its suppression (Aït Sabbah 1984, 110).[11]

As I have argued elsewhere, the woman question under colonial rule relies on the construction of Muslim women as oppressed, silenced, locked up, and imprisoned and thus, it follows, on their liberation from their owners, their family, and their fellow countrymen as part and parcel of the colonial idea of the *mission civilizatrice* (Moallem 2005). Mernissi shows how the notion of the harem as an enclosed space enables the colonial fantasy of penetrating that space. The intrusion into and occupation of colonized locations did not rely

---

9. In *Scheherazade Goes West* (2001), Mernissi goes back to the history of pre-Islamic Mecca and the powerful position of the female goddesses worshipped there (Lat, Menat, and Uzza). In "Women and the Advent of Islam" (1986), Leila Ahmed refers to the powerful position of both pre-Islamic Meccan women and the early Muslim women, including Prophet Mohammad's first wife, who was a prosperous forty-year-old merchant when she married him. He was twenty-five.

10. In her pioneering work on women of the pre-Islamic era and early Islam, Ahmed (1986) makes a similar argument by showing the powerful presence of women in public life, especially in Mecca.

11. Also, through an interrogation of a series of secondary Islamic sources that treat women as the object of love and desire in the Muslim conscious and unconscious, Mernissi illustrates the sexual dynamics that depict women as permanent threats to social order (Aït Sabbah 1984, 34–36).

solely on the colonizer's gaze but, as Malek Alloula has eloquently argued, established a material relation of power between the colonized and the colonizer. In *The Colonial Harem* (1986), Alloula focuses on the role of photography in general and, in the case of French colonial rule in Algeria, of postcards in particular as an intimate and visual approach, arguing that in no other society have women been so excessively represented through photography. "If the women are inaccessible to sight (that is, veiled), it is because they are imprisoned. This dramatization of the equivalence between the veiling and the imprisonment is necessary for the construction of an imaginary scenario that results in the dissolution of the actual society, the one that causes the frustration, in favor of a phantasm: that of the harem" (21).

The representation of veiling and its association with imprisonment continue to be widely appealing even in a postcolonial context. For example, in the context of Iran, where veiling has been mandatory since the Iranian Revolution of 1979, the representation of veiled women has concealed the presence of Iranian women in all social, political, and cultural spheres, including educational institutions, film and media production, and the political arena.[12]

Another example is the notion of fundamentalism widely used in the 1990s to depict Iran and the Iranian postrevolutionary Islamic Republic.[13] Mernissi reminds us of the convergence of imperialism and fundamentalism not in what mainstream discourses portrayed as fundamentalist Islam but in the collaboration and complicity of the local elite in charge of the petroleum industry with Western liberal democracies. She expands the notion of fundamentalism to what she calls "petro-fundamentalism." Using the example of Saudi Arabia, a promoter of intolerance, misogyny, and xenophobia internationally, she describes petro-fundamentalism as liberal democracies' strategic support of conservative Islam as both a bulwark against communism

---

12. For more on the representation of veiled women in Iran, see Moallem 2015.
13. Elsewhere, I have challenged the use of the term *fundamentalism* to depict the Islamic Republic of Iran. See Moallem 2002 and 2005.

and a tactical resource for controlling Arab oil (1996, 251). Mernissi also emphasizes that fundamentalist conservatism's interpretations of Islam display an obsession with women's morality that has much more to do with the crisis of gender and class identities, reflecting the conflict between men of lower classes seeking power through religion and women of the urban upper or middle class who have gained access to the public sphere (Mernissi 1987a).

Mernissi finds a profound contradiction between the mainstream representation of Islamic fundamentalism as an authoritarian ideology and political system incompatible with the West and what she calls "the most puzzling marriage of the century: the bond between a fanatical creed and the most modern liberal states" since the discovery of oil and the reemergence of Wahhabism (1996, 252).[14] She further questions the rationality/irrationality binary, one assigned to Western liberal democracies and the other depicting Islam, by demonstrating the hypocrisy of liberal democracies when it comes to oil and arms sales. Challenging the idea of a dichotomous and separate world, Mernissi advocates an interrogation of oil, arms, and fundamentalism as the point of departure to understand the relationship between the West and the Muslim and Arab worlds.

The Text and the Context

For Mernissi, the text is always located within a historical context and is consequently open to scholarly investigation. She once wrote, "La geopolitique etait une science axe sur la defense du tangible, le territoire, les frontiers et les richesses qui s'y trouvent" (Geopolitics was a science focused on defending the tangible, the territory, the borders and the resources within it) (1987b, 26), in criticizing

---

14. Saudi Arabia's financial backing of the Gulf War and its continuous funding of a war on Iran since then provide ample evidence of the militarist agenda of the petro-fundamentalist elite of Saudi Arabia, their control of the oil industry, and their investment in the global and regional arms market. They also provide evidence for the more disturbing reality of the bonding of petro-fundamentalism and Western liberal democracies.

the multinationals, the corporations, and neoliberalism in the postcolonial era. In her view, "Le nouvel imperialism n'est meme pas economique, il est plus insidieux: c'est une maniere de compter, de calculer, d'evaluer. Finis les cheres vieilles chanson nationalists qui ont 'mis l'ennemi dehors.' L'ennemi est enracine dans notre petite machine a calculer. Il est dans notre tete, it est notre facon de compter, de consommer, d'achetter, de calculer" (New imperialism is not even economic, but, more accurately, it is about calculating, evaluating, and manipulating. It is the end of those nationalist songs that were putting the enemy outside their frame. The enemy is inside the small, the micro calculating machines. It is in our head, in our ways of processing what we buy and consume) (1987b, 37).

The art and the act of reading or text interpretation are crucial for the art of *jadal*. Without a close reading of the primary and secondary religious texts, and without their juxtaposition against the historical context, one cannot successfully engage in debate to counter a biased interpretation of the sacred text. For example, in Mernissi's reference to paradise, she challenges and unsettles both Orientalist and masculinist imagination of the Muslim paradise as a hierarchical and patriarchal utopia. Her reimagination of heaven turns it into a space of equality, with an absence of power. A celestial model is there to inspire terrestrial order in the world of power and privilege.

This historical and ironic methodology enables Mernissi and her interrogation of Islamic discourse, especially within the context of the Arab world, to approach the way Islamic discourse was vernacularized and circulated in the Muslim world. She sometimes uses this approach from within a historical sociology framework and sometimes articulates it in a rather witty and ironic voice, suggesting, given the religious sensitivity around this issue, that the Muslim unconscious is based on the fear of a pre-Islamic matriarchal order.

Mernissi uses hermeneutics to invite a reflection on reading as an openness of the text to the act of reading and on the significant impact of written language on one's ideas of the world. The latter, of course, includes both textuality and intertextuality, or what is being cited and referred to repetitiously. As a feminist sociologist, Mernissi values the significance of writing and educating, the knowledge of sacred texts, and historical context. She has no illusion that knowledge can be detached from the interpreter, the reader, or location within the networks of power and privilege. She uses hermeneutics to show what the text reveals or conceals, recognizing the will to control as well as the historical context within which the author writes about a topic. Methodologically speaking, Mernissi grounds her arguments on evidence-based inquiry. However, as a feminist scholar, she does not hesitate to use her positionality and her experience, along with storytelling, to shed light on our current social and political realities.

Digital Scheherazade and the Art of Storytelling

With the expansion of new media and the internet, Mernissi observes, the critical problem that is creating anxiety in the Arab world for both elites and masses, from heads of state to street vendors, including men and women, is the digital chaos induced by information technologies such as the internet. These new technologies, she notes, have interrupted the *hudud*, the frontier that divided the universe into a sheltered private arena where women and children were supposed to be protected and a public one where men exercised their presumed authority (Mernissi 2006, 121).

According to Mernissi, women have always been our storytellers, and now new media allow their stories to reach multiple audiences in a global context where masses of women have access to the internet. The "digital Scheherazade," whose thousand-and-one stories can now reach beyond national boundaries, makes Mernissi an enthusiastic supporter of cyberspace and its effects. She sees a new venue for feminist interpretation and circulation of knowledge. Uncritical of how cyberspace is subjected to the relations of power and privilege, she focuses on the possibilities for more marginalized voices to be heard.

Furthermore, Mernissi sees a link between the relations of power and the relations of domination of the feminine, something that paradoxically forms and produces both modern Muslim identities and a Muslim identity crisis. She discusses what she calls "cosmo-civics" (a new term that opposes "cosmocrats" [Leccese 2006, 346]) as a new possibility for feminist activism—including a new understanding that women are fighting the same issues and the same causes all over the world—offered by this technological revolution. She asks, Who has access to the religious knowledge? Who can provide interpretation (*tafsir*) of religious sources? And what kind of historical evidence contradicts or reinforces such interpretation of the text? For Mernissi in *Chahrazad n'est pas marocaine* (1988), Scheherazade exploits women's access to power and culture.

The Importance of Media and Popular Culture

Mernissi is one of the pioneer Arab feminists who recognized early on the significance of media technologies in the life of men and women in the Arab world. Indeed, she takes very seriously the new forms of globalization, the expansion of old and new media, and their impact on Arab society—from TV to digital media to the digital divide.

Mernissi's Scheherazade is more than a digital storyteller (Mernissi 2006). She is a political strategist who knows both how to negotiate within the structures of power and how to subvert them through her linguistic mastery of stories, discernment of the context, and deep cultural memory. She is equipped with the art of *jadal*. Mernissi notes with approval that women are increasingly attending Islamic schools and have become the subject of reading and interpreting the sacred text. In her view, to engage in debate one should master the arguments: "Today more than ever before, it is imperative that we increase our knowledge about Islam by mastering its verses, its hadiths, and its history. This must be done for the simple reason that Islam today is being manipulated by conservative authorities to strip us of our rights" (Mernissi 1991, 6).

As Mernissi noted in an interview in 2003, "If this modern-day Scheherazade's stories were heard by today's rulers, they might be enchanted, and, like the cruel ruler in Scheherazade's mythical world, transformed into believers in *jadal* rather than the force and violence used to build and defend the invisible and terrifying frontiers that divide us. Fairytales can come true—when one believes in them" (Huff-Rousselle 2003).

One example of Mernissi's modern Scheherazade is a privately funded TV series in Iran written by Hassan Fathi and Naghmeh Samini and directed by Hassan Fathi. Titled *Shahrzad* (in Farsi), the series became extremely popular among Iranians both in Iran and in the diaspora. It also became internationally famous and has been dubbed in several languages, including Spanish, French, and Arabic. *Shahrzad* takes place after the CIA-assisted coup d'état in Iran that overthrew the national government of Mohammad Mossadeq in 1953. It depicts the convergence of an active mafia-like patriarch, the corrupt local political elite (including the police and the Savak, the secret police), colonial agents, and oppositional groups. The main character, Shahrzad, is a strong-willed female medical student negotiating these networks of power as part and parcel of her family and community life. Shahrzad is depicted as elegant, strategic, and wise, a woman who can play with power, taking it to its limits in a dramatic social, political, and historical context. Part of the series' popularity, in my view, is the representation of Shahrzad and of other influential women figures in the story.

Conclusion

An interrogation of the burden of cultural and social inheritance, on the one hand, and of living a postcolonial or neocolonial moment, as the present is framed, on the other, has been more than an academic endeavor for many diasporic feminists, including me. The possibility of overcoming the modernist moment and its dichotomous investment in modernization/westernization as well as the impasse created by that mode of thinking—both by westernization and modernization as well as by the oppositional movements—has meant an effort to genuinely believe and perhaps live what some scholars call "decoloniality." Decoloniality invests in the aesthetic and political desire to confront a neoliberal world flooded with commodities, both material and symbolic, that occupy the living space of "consumers" and constrain their imaginative and creative potentiality.

Encountering Fatema Mernissi as a Muslim feminist scholar and her texts as pioneering representational practices that challenge both Orientalist traditions and Islamic discourses locally, regionally, and transnationally constitutes a rich tradition of feminism within the Islamic worlds. Mernissi vivifies the dead, the abject, the forgotten, and the absent by tracing them, sometimes a few centuries back and sometimes in the mediatic and cyber spaces where new opportunities are opened up for women to express their concerns. This methodology provides space for putting scholarly inquiry to work to tell a different story about the past and the present. But if the burden of the legacy of the past frames the present, how do we keep open what Mernissi has opened up for us? How do we not fall into the fetishism of "celebrity culture" in the West and refuse to invest more value in capitalist commodification and incorporation of the symbolic capital of the colonized worlds?[15]

Mernissi's notion of unlearning the things that you enjoy, making something scary or painful possible in a postcolonial context, is central to a decolonial move. For her, revisiting the past to interrogate the pleasures of what we call culture, identity, or belonging is crucial, given that the capacity of producing narratives to create other realities for those who are at the bottom of biopolitics has been destroyed. Mernissi's optimism and her idea of a "cosmo-civics" unfortunately dismiss the importance of imperialist feminism and our neoliberal order's increasing funding of and investment in imperialist feminist ideas in the global North. Women and women's issues continue to be used to construct boundaries of civilization and barbarism that justify cybermilitarism, war, and occupation. Indeed, the decision to invade Afghanistan and Iraq was based in part on the old colonial logic of liberating oppressed Muslim women. Mernissi's

---

15. As opposed to some feminists who function as gatekeepers and native informants when it comes to letting in other feminist voices from the global South, Mernissi resisted the cult of celebrity by sending me and other feminist scholars a list of Moroccan feminists who could be invited to give talks in the United States in her place.

uncritical optimism raises essential questions for feminists, including what shape transnational feminist practices should take at a time marked by the entanglement of the geopolitical relations of power and power's regard of the feminine.

References

Abdo, Diya M. 2010. "Chameleonic Text: Peritextual Transformation in Fatema Mernissi's *Dreams of Trespass* and *Nisa' 'Ala Ajnihat al-hilm*." *Life Writing* 7, no. 2: 175–94. At https://doi.org/10.1080/14484 520903082934.

Ahmed, Leila. 1986. "Women and the Advent of Islam." *Signs: Journal of Women in Culture and Society* 11, no. 4 (Summer): 665–91.

Aït Sabbah, Fatna [Fatema Mernissi]. 1982. *La femme dans l'inconscient musulman*. Paris: Albin Michel.

———. 1984. *Women in the Muslim Unconscious*. Translated by Mary Jo Lakeland. New York: Pergamon Press.

Alloula, Malek. 1986. *The Colonial Harem*. Translated by Myrna Godzich and Wlad Godzich. Minneapolis: Univ. of Minnesota Press.

Culler, Jonathan. 2008. *On Deconstruction: Theory and Criticism after Structuralism*. 25th anniversary ed. Ithaca, NY: Cornell Univ. Press.

Graham-Brown, Sarah. 2003. "The Seen, the Unseen and the Imagined: Private and Public Lives." In *Feminist Postcolonial Theory: A Reader*, edited by Reina Lewis and Sara Mills, 502–19. New York: Routledge.

Grewal, Inderpal. 1999. "Traveling Barbie: Indian Transnationality and New Consumer Subjects." *Positions* 7, no. 3 (Winter): 799–827.

Hall, Stuart. 2013. "The Spectacle of the 'Other.'" In *Representation: Cultural Representations and Signifying Practices*, 2nd ed., edited by Stuart Hall, Jessica Evans, and Sean Nixon, 223–90. Los Angeles: Sage.

Huff-Rousselle, Maggie. 2003. "A Contemporary Scheherazade's Tales of a Borderless World." *Cairo Times*, May n.d.

Kaplan, Caren. 1995. "A World without Boundaries: The Body Shop's Trans/National Geographics." *Social Text*, no. 43 (Autumn): 45–66.

Leccese, Francesco Alfonso. 2006. "The New Arab Mass-Media Vehicles of Democracy? Interview with Fatima Mernissi." *Oriente Moderno*, New Series, Year 25, 86, no. 2: 345–56.

Mernissi, Fatema. 1986. *Women in Muslim Paradise*. New Delhi: Kali for Women.

———. 1987a. *The Fundamentalist Obsession with Women: A Current Articulation of Class Conflict in Modern Muslim Societies*. Lahore, Pakistan: Simorgh.

———. 1987b. *Le harem politique: Le Prophète et les femmes*. Paris: Albin Michel.

———. 1988. *Chahrazad n'est pas marocaine*. Paris: Le Fennec.

———. 1991. *Can We Women Head a Muslim State?* Lahore, Pakistan: Simorgh.

———. 1996. "Palace Fundamentalism and Liberal Democracy: Oil, Arms and Irrationality." *Development and Change* 27, no. 2: 251–65.

———. 2001. *Scheherazade Goes West: Different Cultures, Different Harems*. New York: Washington Square Press.

———. 2006. "Digital Scheherazades in the Arab World." *Current History* 105, no. 689 (Mar.): 121–26.

Moallem, Minoo. 2002. "Whose Fundamentalism? A Statement on the Current Events." *Meridians: feminism, race, transnationalism* 2, no. 2: 298–301.

———. 2005. *Between Warrior Brother and Veiled Sister: Islamic Fundamentalism and the Cultural Politics of Patriarchy*. Berkeley: Univ. of California Press.

———. 2015. "The Unintended Consequences of Equality within Difference." *Brown Journal of World Affairs* 22, no. 1 (Fall–Winter): 335–49.

———. 2021. "Race, Gender, and Religion: Islamophobia and Beyond." *Meridians: feminism, race, transnationalism* 20, no. 2 (Oct.): 271–90.

Rahnavard, Zahra. N.d. "The Message of Hijab." Al-Islam.org. At https://www.al-islam.org/beauty-concealment-and-concealment-beauty-zahra-rahnavard/message-hijab-muslim-woman.

Spivak, Gayatri Chakravorty. 2007. "Welcome to Tomorrow's Helpers." Gender and Women's Studies Commencement Speech, Univ. of California, Berkeley, May.

4

The Lionesses

A Film Project (1981)

HAMID BÉNANI, JALIL BENNANI,
and FATEMA MERNISSI
Translated from French by Paola Bacchetta
Produced by Hamid Bénani

Introduction: The Dance of the Lionesses

Moroccan culture projects through its different modes of expression (literature, song, dance, proverbs, etc.) a fairly clear image of its ideal of femininity.[1] This ideal has always been linked to the idea of obedience, fragility, submission, modesty, and restraint.

According to this ideal, a bourgeois woman is naturally a sexual object, passive and above all beautiful and very seriously concerned with being so, thus a pure reflection of men's desires.

The women who dance in Cheikh El Kamel's courtyard on the twelfth of each Rabïi *1st* seem to embody the opposite of this feminine ideal.[2] Disheveled, their eyes lit and their bodies in a trance, the lionesses of the Issawa sect continue a ritual every year that tramples

---

Translator's note: See chapter 5 on the process of translating *The Lionesses*.

1. This text, written in 1981, remains essentially current today.

2. Month of the Muslim period, anniversary of the birth of the Prophet Mohammed.

1. Jamal Mehssani, *Femmes en trance (Maroc)* (Women in Trance [Morocco]). *Source*: Jamal Mehssani. Printed with the photographer's permission.

upon the classic ideal of femininity.³ Mingled with men in a body-to-body ecstatic state, they exhaust themselves in a dance that seems to defy every gesture of female conduct.

This is only one aspect of the ambivalent phenomenon called *zaouias* (sanctuaries of saints for healing).⁴

---

3. *Translator's note*: Throughout the text, I have left italic and bold type and capitalization as given in the French original.

4. *Translator's note*: In *Les Lionnes*, the term *marabout* refers both to a sacred sanctuary where people go for healing and to the religious figure associated with a sanctuary or with a religious following. *Les Lionnes* uses the related terms *maraboutisme* to refer to the sanctuary system and *phénomène maraboutique* to refer to the phenomena. Although the term *marabout* has Arabic origins (مَربوط, *marbut*, or مُرابِط, *murabit*, meaning a person who is garrisoned) and is in daily use in Morocco, when it appears in French-language texts, it is far from neutral. It carries an intense history of its selective deployment in a colonial homogenizing manner in Orientalist

The *Zaouias* Phenomenon

One of the fascinating aspects of this phenomenon is its continuity.

The upheavals that agitate Third World societies in their processes of full economic, political, and social transformation have caused ruptures in certain areas and disintegration in others. The *zaouias* phenomenon seems to have miraculously escaped any rupture and disintegration. Crowds of men and women make long journeys each year to attend the festival of this or that Saint (*Moussem*). Throughout the year, men and women struggling with the problems of daily life, illnesses, family disputes, and marital conflicts go to the *zaouias* to ask for assistance and to offer, according to their

---

discourse to mean a whole range of Muslim religious spaces and kinds of Muslim religious authority. In 1981, when *Les Lionnes* was written, the term *marabout* and its variants were broadly inscribed in French without critique. More recently, they are deemed *colonial-Orientalist* for many reasons. For example, in French two of many synonyms of *marabout* are *sorcier* (male witch) and *homme laid* (ugly man). To respect *Les Lionnes*'s decolonial spirit, and with the support of Mernissi's coauthor Jalil Bennani, for the English translation I decided to replace *marabout* and its variants with more appropriate grounded terms by returning to the Darija (Moroccan Arabic) words that had been repressed, silenced, suppressed in the first place; that is, I return to what I refer to in chapter 5 as a *pretranslation* language. From Darija, I mobilize two words that appear—albeit only once each—in the text: *zaouia* for "sanctuary" and *wali* for "saint." I then use "*zaouia* system" for the system and "*zaouia* phenomenon" for the phenomenon. Throughout *Les Lionnes*, the French words *sanctuaire* and *saint* are also used as synonyms of *marabout*; in those cases, I directly translate them into English as "sanctuary" and "saint." I reflect upon some complexities and difficulties of these choices in chapter 5. In my notes about translating Zhor's words, the reader will see that in an English-language article from 1977, where Zhor's words surface, Mernissi uses the term *shrine* interchangeably with *sanctuary*. In that dialogue, I leave *shrine* exactly as Mernissi had intended, for she is the interviewer there, and the dialogue is a contribution to the coauthorial voice. Elsewhere, I lean toward *zaouia*, which in the other cases seems to best represent the coauthorial voice. I am indebted to Jalil Bennani for his support and help as I was making these decisions. Any mistakes are my own. Jalil Bennani, conversations by phone with Paola Bacchetta, July 21, 2021, and Feb. 21, 2023.

capacities, animal sacrifices, colorful fabrics, candles, and collective meals, to solicit the intervention of the Saint.

Religious associations—Aissaoua, Hmadcha, Jilala, Heddaoua—are experiencing renewed interest and unexpected vigor and recruitment among youth that ensure their practically unperturbed continuity. And in an era of painful acculturations, these groups present themselves as the custodians of a tradition that apparently has not ceased to ensure certain kinds of equilibrium. Their ceremonial practices, collective acts, therapy, dance, and music, transformed into folklore and reduced to fossils in the margins of the European fringe of the Mediterranean Basin, seem to be stabilized in the South of this same Mediterranean. How do we explain this?

It seems that the answer to this question would shed new light not only on the complexity of the phenomenon of social change in general but more specifically on the question of the almost universal phenomenon of unequal and chaotic industrialization.

One of the goals of this project is to incite the spectator to ask the following question:

What does the industrial project, whether it takes place in a capitalist or socialist framework, have to offer as an alternative to popular expression?

Would anything be gained if we were to replace spontaneous popular culture—which revolutionary elites in Third World countries rejected as the opium of the people—with popular culture produced by these same elites through the monolithic mass-media system?

The point here is not to make everything that comes from the people sacred because often the people respond negatively to the repressive conditions made for them, and they create an alienating subculture of the poor that further marginalizes them.

In this film, we propose to follow the itinerary of Moroccan women in their complex relationships to *zaouias*.

Why women?

On the one hand, because we encounter women more often than men in the *zaouias*.

On the other hand, because *zaouias* seem to respond more sensitively and more deeply to women's problematics.

This approach would open our discussion to other questions. For example, are women linked to the *zaouias* in a relationship that is specific to their gender?

Moreover, because of women's conditions of greater subordination, doesn't this raise a broader social problem more acutely?

Such questions lead us to consider the flamboyant role of the *zaouias* system, as a total social phenomenon:

- As a site where conflicts are staged, expressed, spoken to each other under the tutelary gaze of the *wali* (saint) as an intermediary between the subject and God. As a site where suffering is listened to, which therefore lends it a therapeutic role.
- As a site of expression where the playful function arises, subverting the other charismatic and therapeutic functions.
- As a site that is appropriated and re-created as a means of power and self-assertion by subaltern women whose claims to charisma remain their only possibility for social mobility.
- As a site where central political power and the dominant value system are contested.

The film will sketch the profile of four women whose different trajectories illustrate the different functions of the *zaouias*.

Four Profiles of Moroccan Women in Their Relationship with the Sanctuaries

Fatima: Her mental balance tips, and she can no longer cope with the problems that assail her in her daily life. After having been to the psychiatric hospital in her province, she retreats to the sanctuary of Bouia Omar.[5] For this twenty-two-year-old woman, the sanctuary was not a first choice. She first turned to Western medicine, which is common for women of her generation. But under pressure by her

---

5. Village *zaouia* located north of Marrakech.

family and her social milieu, and given the failure of Western therapy, she came to stay in Bouia Omar.

Zhor: She lives in a working-class suburb of Salé and works as a maid for a senior civil servant in Rabat.[6] For her, going to the *zaouia* Sidi Ben Achir in its grandiose location among ramparts and rocks is entertainment. There, she finds everything she lacks: beauty, calm, rest, availability, contact with others, and freedom.

Halima: After a miserable life as housewife, at age forty the *chouaffa* (clairvoyant) Halima re-creates a competing and clandestine "*zaouia*" in the heart of Rabat's central district. She appropriates the ancestral cult of Aïcha Kandicha and uses it to satisfy her will to power: her need for wealth and prestige.

Lalla Aziza: She is a renowned woman who refused the familial and social values of her time, although she was beautiful and widely courted by men. Thanks to her audacity and her followers, she acquired notoriety and power that overshadowed the Sultan. She was sanctified and endowed with the dignity of a Saint. . . .[7]

Fatima: What Kind of Psychiatry in Morocco . . . and Elsewhere?

Fatima is a young woman who is trying to escape her family environment through marriage. Each time, her relations result in failure, and the ultimate solution remains madness.

She has violent crises (screams, agitation) that are attributed sometimes to *jinns*[8] that inhabit her and sometimes to physical disease inscribed in her body.

---

6. A traditional, poor city at the outskirts of Rabat, capital of the Kingdom of Morocco.

7. *Translator's note*: All ellipses given in this translation of *Les Lionnes* are given in the original.

8. *Jinns* are troublesome spirits that disturb the person they inhabit. In accordance with decolonial principles mentioned in note 4, where *colonial-Orientalist* terms are used to designate these spirits, I revert back to the Darija term *jinns*. The instance of its use here is the first in this text.

The first attempt to explain her crises leads her family to have her stay in Bouia Omar. Then, in a second attempt they have her examined by doctors, hospitalized, and have physical exams taken, hoping to find some kind of organic problem so they can prescribe appropriate medication.

This episode of Fatima's life took place in a back-and-forth movement between Bouia Omar and the hospital.

Fatima agreed to accompany us to Bouia Omar to show us where she stayed.

This village is a crossroads for

- magic, witchcraft
- religion
- cultural traditions
- social encounters
- economic impact

Visit to the Zaouias and Description of the Rites. Individuals with mental disorders but also psychosomatic illnesses and even infertile women or women who cannot get married are brought to Bouia Omar.

Patients can spend one or more nights there. Fatima did so when she had seizures. Now healed, she shows a strong belief in the traditions there and participates actively in the ceremonies.

Healing, she explains, is announced when the *wali* visits in the evening (in a dream or hallucination?) and tells the patient that she can leave the village. When the time comes, in honor of the *wali* a black goat or any other black animal is slaughtered. Before that happened, Fatima had undergone a whole series of acts of exorcism with song, dance, flogging, stripping, etc.

Bouia Omar is indeed a social institution since so-called normal people who believe in the Saint, such as women who wish to have a child or to find a husband, go there, too. They are welcomed by women who comb and style their hair with henna, thus announcing happiness, who bathe them, thus a new sign of purification, and who make symbolic gestures that authorize sexual intercourse. This constitutes a lifting of prohibitions and inhibitions, thus a formal assurance of marriage.

Moreover, other facts demonstrate that Bouia Omar, albeit isolated, is articulated with the rest of the social context.

For example, there we find

- the development of trade, the value of money and the power it confers (people are welcomed better when they respect and respond to the demand for money);
- the value that some people associate with speaking French, thus a reflection of Western domination.

Bouia Omar, a Nonalienated Place? What is striking here is the fact that the social collective takes responsibility for treating the disease.[9] The patient is accompanied by her family, and they all believe in the *zaouia*. The family often stays with the patient in this place and even comes on its own to visit the *zaouia* during certain religious periods.

Therefore, everyone has a place in Bouia Omar. Because of this, the mad person is not devalued. On the contrary, each person has a role in this fringe society. This is the case with the caretaker, who shows us around the village and who is respected by all. Everyone there says the caretaker is Bouia Omar's child. Reality or delirium? We are quickly caught up in this statement when the caretaker adds that Bouia Omar has an infinite number of children. Does this mean that all believers in this Saint are his children? From that point onward, this caretaker would play a role as guarantor of this society's integrity.

Bouia Omar is therefore a place where one can experience one's madness. This is also evident in the area reserved for trance states: a woman is lying down, wiggling from time to time, and this does

---

9. *Note by Jalil Bennani*: After numerous complaints that patients suffered mistreatment there, the Bouia Omar *zaouia* was closed in April 2015 by decision of Minister of Health Houcine El Ouardi.

not surprise anyone. We are told that this is where collective trances take place.

Like the caretaker, the woman in a trance has a role. The trance's therapeutic power is conferred on it by the Saint, who inhabits it. The Saint likes a specific kind of music that generates the trance: it is at this moment that the therapeutic capacities unfold. As the woman spits, she extirpates the *jinns* who possess her.[10] She shakes hands or kisses to give a blessing.

This is a place to experience one's madness also because the decision to interrupt or extend the stay is up to the patient, for the patient alone is visited by the *wali*.

The Development of "Alienism." We find it striking to see that some patients have chains on their hands and feet (an aspect that contrasts with the social tolerance we previously described). Chains, we are told, are reserved for the most agitated patients. They are experiencing "alienism," or the repression that is exerted on the mad person. The restless are the most troublesome.

Other facts point in the same direction. Thus, we find that a wall is under construction around Bouia Omar. This is the sad destiny of this community that will find itself surrounded, symbolizing limitation, separation, exclusion.

The chains, like the wall, testify to the fact that this village, too, as a social institution that is not cut off from the rest of society is a place where the repression of madness that exists in other parts of Moroccan society is developing. Can we blame it on the introduction of Western asylum psychiatry, or is it simply a sign of a society that is transforming and leaving its own traditions behind?

What is at question here is not society's evolution but instead one culture's control over another, with a bulldozing effect that represses traditional culture and freezes its development.

---

10. *Translator's note*: Here the term *jinns* appeared in the French text. The translation is throughout informed by the discussion of jinns in the work of Stefania Pandolfo on Morocco. See Stefania Pandolfo, *Knot of the Soul: Madness, Psychoanalysis, Islam* (Chicago: Univ. of Chicago Press, 2018), 89–99.

The Place of Western Psychiatry in Moroccan Society. Fatima's trajectory opens up a transcultural approach to mental illness.

The study of different societies makes it possible to explore the world of madness beyond the given sociocultural conditions and to question the degree of repression or tolerance in these societies.

This theme of the film could give rise to broad debates on mental illness, the role of psychiatric institutions, and Western medicine. It could lead us to explore the fundamental problem of our situation characterized by conflict between Western science and national cultural tradition.

Traditional Moroccan society had its own response to illness. The forgetting and repression of all this traditional knowledge are testimony to and evidence of another kind of alienation.

Zhor: Or the Sanctuary as a Place of Entertainment

To confine this sanctuary to its therapeutic functions, as Fatima's testimony indicates, would be a big mistake.[11]

---

11. *Translator's note*: Mernissi partially reproduced, abridged, and translated the conversation with Zhor from oral Darija into English in her article "Women, Saints and Sanctuaries in Morocco," *Signs* 3, no. 1 (1977): 101–12. The conversation was then reproduced in full in *Unspoken Words: Women's Religious Lives*, edited by Nancy Auer Falk and Rita M. Gross (Belmont, CA: Wadsworth/Thompson Learning, 2001), 144–53. In Mernissi's follow-up interview with Zhor published in an article in 1982, we learn that the initial interview with her took place in 1974. Mernissi records Zhor's narrative beginning with "The next morning I went to see my mother" and ending with "He's a human being like I am." Throughout, there is some discrepancy between the earlier English translation and the later French one in *Les Lionnes*. To respect *Les Lionnes*'s coauthorship, I have translated the dialogue as it appears in French. However, in addition, to acknowledge Mernissi's prior English translation, I include her English translation wherever it corresponds to the French in *Les Lionnes*; prioritize her translation where in English there would be several English possibilities for a same passage in French; and flag her translations by placing them in notes. These differences in the Darija-to-English and Darija-to-French translations are signs of the difficulties of bringing a text into very different language and epistemic systems. Here, when Mernissi uses the term *marabout* in her English translation, I again return to the pretranslation

A sanctuary can also be a simple place of entertainment, a site where one goes to seek basic secular pleasures, such as meeting others, making acquaintances, seeing the sea, and listening to the silence.

Zhor says: "I slept at my boss' house until 10:00 a.m., and then I went to see my mother.[12] I found her about to eat with the children.... She had made some cakes. I ate a little with them, then I went to spend the day at the sanctuary.[13] I lay down there and slept for a long time."

> Question: Do you go to the *zaouia* often?
> Zhor: Yes, quite often. For example, I prefer to go there on the days of Aid (religious festivals). When one has a family as desperate as mine, the shrine is a haven of peace and calm. I like to go there.
> Q: What do you like about the shrine? Can you be more precise?
> Z: Yes. It's very precise. The silence, the rugs, and the clean mats, which are nicely arranged. And then the sound of the fountain in the silence. An enormous silence where the sound of water is as fragile as a thread. I stay there hours, sometimes whole days.
> Q: The day of Aid it must be full of people.
> Z: Yes, there are people, but they are lost in their own problems. So they leave you alone. Mostly it's women who cry in silence, without speaking, each in her own world.
> Q: Aren't there any men at the shrine?

Darija term *zaouia*. In her article "Women, Saints and Sanctuaries in Morocco," Mernissi uses the term *shrine* often and *sanctuary* less often, yet *Les Lionnes* uses *sanctuaire* (sanctuary) frequently and in only one instance *tombeau* (shrine). To respect the coauthorship here and for consistency, I translate *sanctuaire* as "sanctuary," not "shrine." Please note that in that article the conversation is between Q (Question) and A (Answer), whereas in *Les Lionnes* it is between Q and Z (Zhor).

12. *Translator's note*: In Mernissi's article (1977), "The next morning I went to see my mother."

13. *Translator's note*: In Mernissi's article (1977), "I had a snack with her and the children, and then I went to spend the day at the marabout (sanctuary)."

Z: Yes, but it's separate . . . men have their side, women theirs. But, anyway, men come to see the sanctuary and leave very quickly; the women, especially those with problems, stay much longer.

Q: What do they do, and what do they say?

Z: That depends. Some are happy just to cry. Others take hold of the Saint's garments and say, "Give me this, oh Saint, give me that."[14] "I want my daughter to pass her exams" (she laughs). You know the Saints are men, human beings, but sometimes, imagine, the woman gets what she asks for! Then she brings a sacrifice. . . . She kills an animal and prepares a meal of the meat and then offers it to the visitors. But it's a coincidence. Do you know Sid El Gomri (she laughs).[15]

Salé is full of shrines, full, full. You know, there is a proverb: "If you want to make a pilgrimage, just go around Salé barefooted (instead of going to Mecca)" (she laughs). I assure you that they do say that. . . . I was not born in Salé to invent proverbs (she laughs). All of Salé is a shrine. There are so many that some don't have names (she laughs). You know, my father was born in Salé a long time ago.[16] He knows the *zaouias*, and he talks about them a lot.[17] His specialty is when you're separated from someone or when you have a very bad fight. He helps you overcome your problem.[18] When I go, I listen to the women. You see them

---

14. *Translator's note*: In Mernissi's article (1977), *Saint* is not capitalized.

15. *Translator's note*: In Mernissi's article (1977), there is a question mark after "Sid El Gomri," and this sentence is followed by "Q: No."

16. *Translator's note*: In Mernissi's article (1977), "My father is a native of Salé."

17. *Translator's note*: In Mernissi's article (1977), "He knows the shrines and talks a lot about them."

18. *Translator's note*: In Mernissi's article (1977), "The Saint" is given rather than "He."

tell everything to the tomb and mimicking everything that took place. Then they ask Sid El Gomri to help them get out of the mess. They cry, they scream. Then they get hold of themselves and come back, join us, and sit in silence. I like the *zaouia*.

Q: Are you ever afraid?

Z: Afraid of what? In a *zaouia*, what a question. I love them.

Q: And when do you go?

Z: They are shut in the evenings except for those who have rooms, like Sidi Ben Achir, for example. You can rent a room there, and you can stay a long time.

Q: Rent a room for how much?

Z: Oh, fifteen dirhams.

Q: Fifteen dirhams a night?

Z: No, for fifteen dirhams you can stay as long as you wish, even a month.[19] You know, they call Sidi Ben Achir a doctor. Sick people come with their family; they rent them a room and stay until they are well. You know, it's not Sidi Ben Achir that cures them, it's God, but they think it's Sidi Ben Achir.

Q: Can anyone rent a room?

Z: Before, yes; but now you have to have the *Mokkadem*'s permission.[20] They want to know where you live and be sure that you are really sick. Once a woman rented a room and told them she had a patient, but it was her lover. Since then, the *Mokkadem* has made admission more difficult. He makes sure that the person is really sick and not pretending to be sick.

Q: Are there young people your age at the shrine?

---

19. *Translator's note*: In Mernissi's article (1977), "ten dirhams" is given.

20. Local civil servant. *Translator's note*: In Mernissi's article (1977), the translation of *Mokkadem* is given in the text as "local officials"; in the film project, it is given in a footnote in the singular.

Z: Yes, but we realize that they don't come for the *zaouia* but only for the beauty of the site.[21] There are a lot of young men around the *zaouia* during the spring and autumn; they come to have picnics. You should see the *zaouia* at that time; the Hondas, the motors that make noise, the well-dressed boys, the girls wearing short skirts, all made up and suntanned.[22] It's beautiful. It's relaxing, the silence inside of the sanctuary, and life outside. . . . It's full of young people. You know, they have even made a slide in the wall that goes down to the beach. I will show it to you when we go. It goes faster. You jump from the ramparts, go down the slide, and you're on the beach. You know, some people come to the shrine in the summer for their vacations instead of going to a hotel. There, you find people who live outside the city or who come from far away, from north, south, all parts of Morocco.[23] For them, the shrine is ideal for vacations. It doesn't cost as much as a hotel. The old people can pray, and the young can go to the beach. In the summer, I meet people from all over Morocco. It's as if I were in Mecca, but I'm in Salé! You must come and see me.[24] We can go in the summer if you want; it's more pleasant. You don't have to come and pray: you can just come and look. I told you that when I go to the *zaouia*, it's not to pray.[25] I never ask

---

21. *Translator's note*: In Mernissi's article (1977), "They don't come for the shrine; only for the view. A lot of young men from the neighborhood come to the shrine for picnics during the spring and summer."

22. *Translator's note*: In Mernissi's article (1977), "You should see the shrine then: Hondas, the motorcycles roaring, the boys all dressed up, the girls with short skirts . . . it's crawling with young people."

23. *Translator's note*: In Mernissi's article (1977), "It's especially the people who live outside the city and come from far away, the north, the south, from all corners of Morocco."

24. *Translator's note*: In Mernissi's article (1977), "You must come and see it."

25. *Translator's note*: In Mernissi's article (1977), "I told you when I go to the shrine."

for anything. When the moment comes for me to ask for something, I'll ask God directly, but not the Saint. . . . It's a human being, like me.[26]

This conversation reflects the enormous flexibility of the sanctuary and its inexhaustible possibilities. Individuals, depending on their needs, their gender, their age, the questions they are asking, can shape the sanctuary to suit their needs.

Halima: Or the Appropriation of Charismatic Power

Halima is the eldest child in a family of eight children (six girls and two boys). Her father, after leaving the army when his wife died, switched to farming in the Gharb region and continued his life with another woman, who bore him three more children.

Halima and all her sisters married, except one: Nora, who was paralyzed and prone to fits of hysteria. Nora's crises began to manifest on the occasion of an event that marked the whole family: it was the early marriage of one of the sisters. She was married at age seven to a man who swore in the presence of a third party (a woman who lived near the couple) not to deflower her and therefore not to consummate the marriage until after she was ten years old. The third party died, and the man broke his promise and deflowered the child before the agreed term. The child fled with the help of the family and managed to start a new life elsewhere. This event traumatized the whole family and especially Nora, who went from crisis to crisis and renounced marriage.

Halima, married for the first time at age fourteen and the mother of two children, began to question her marriage after five years. The marriage would not last long. The cause of the problems was her husband's resistance to admitting his wife's exchanges with *jinns*.[27] Indeed, Halima, like Nora, was prone to possession crises.

---

26. *Translator's note*: In Mernissi's article (1977), "When I want something, I'll ask God directly, but not the saint. . . . He is a human being like I am."

27. *Translator's note*: Here *Les Lionnes* uses the French term *génies* (genies). I have returned it to the pretranslation Darija word *jinns*. Actually, the Arabic *jinn*,

Halima told us:

My husband was an ordinary man: rigid. He didn't want to recognize anything strange. He didn't believe in *jinns*. We lived on a farm near Sidi Slimane. When I had my seizures and I fell, he was embarrassed. He didn't want people to know. . . . He didn't want people to see me in that state. And yet he respected me and helped me up when I was in a trance. He helped me, protected me, but he was embarrassed in front of others and refused to admit my condition and to accept me as I am. He was not tolerant. You know, these crises started in childhood. It started off in a banal way. My siblings tickled me, and I started laughing like everyone else, but very quickly it got out of hand. My parents protected me by not allowing my brothers and sisters to tickle me. I would completely lose my mind. I would scream until I surrendered my soul. I ran after them. There was something else. . . .

My frog phobia. It was awful. I was totally terrified of frogs. All you had to do was say the word *frog* for me to start punching, screaming. Once, when I was already an adult and a mother, I fell on my own baby and nearly killed him. My father was annoyed and forbade anyone to provoke me.

After her divorce, Halima married a cousin who knew about her condition and accepted it. He was her best ally when, around her menopause, the first hints of her clairvoyance appeared:

How did I become clairvoyant? One day, toward Mouloud on the eve of the feast, I had visions. I saw animals talking to me. I saw a woman with the split hooves of an equine. I had visions of a different kind, too. I could see that the grocery store next door was on fire. I had said it to those around me, and no one paid attention. A few days later, the grocery store burned down. The visions accelerated and increased, and everything I saw came true. I was afraid

---

the root for the Darija *jinns*, is also the root for *genies*. However, because *genies* is saturated with *colonial-Orientalist* fantasy projections, and in light of the coauthors' decolonial impulses, I found it unusable here.

of it myself. I tried to hide this gift from myself, but it came back more violently. One day I had a very clear dream that marked me. I saw *jinns* in the dream. They ordered me to go to the sanctuary of Sidi Ali Ben Hamdouch, where I would be initiated into my new work. The next day I woke up and told my family members about my intention to go to the sanctuary. At first, they were appalled. They knew my limitations. I had never been anywhere on my own. I did not know how to get anywhere by myself. I've always needed a guide. They discouraged me, but after seeing my determination, they gave in. We made the quest to collect the necessary sum for my trip, and for the first time in my life I made such a long trip alone. I was scared. I was very scared, but I was determined. I even accepted the risk of wandering indefinitely from *zaouia* to *zaouia* without perhaps ever seeing my family again.

She left, made the journey in the initiation sense of the term, took part in the rituals, became acquainted with new horizons, entered into contact with other women in the same situation as her, and gathered with them around the Saint's tomb. At the same time, she entered into a relationship with occult forces, the *jinns*, who would henceforth help her and lead her in her new "mission" as a seer.

She created her own *zaouia*, built around a miniature temple of Aïcha Kandicha (one of the most important figures in Maghrebian mythology).[28] Halima currently has as much if not more of an audience, power, and money than a professor or a doctor.

Lala Aziza: Or the Challenge to Central Power

Tradition tells us that many North African women throughout the centuries have refused their domestic status and the secondary social roles to which they have been confined. Some have even sought charismatic power (they have become Saints) or political power. This is the case, for example, with Imma Tiffelent, who literally fled "on wings" to escape her domestic condition.

---

28. *Translator's note: Zaouia* in Darija is already given here.

Legend has it that, not wanting to get married, Imma Tiffelent escaped in the form of a dove and became a prostitute in the mountains. Twenty-seven young people disappeared after loving her. Then she became an ascetic in a hut on top of the mountain. Ragged, shaggy, she preached religion in the valley. She even discarded her rags, lived naked . . . and prophesized. It is forbidden to touch the trees around her grave, to kill the birds, to dig out the partridge eggs.[29]

The same flight from women's condition under patriarchy is illustrated by the Saint Sida Zahra El Kouch, who was both learned and beautiful and refused throughout her life to become a pure sexual object. She specifically resisted Sultan Moulay Zidane's advances and preferred to die a virgin.

The political role of women Saints in North Africa has been the subject of a prolific literature. North African folklore contains myths and legends relating to a number of women Saints who played important roles in the political arena. Certainly, one of the most famous is the Amazigh Lala Aziza Tagurrami.[30] In the film, she will comprise the fourth profile of a Moroccan woman in her relationship with the *zaouias* system.

Lala Aziza played a strategic role in the history of her region. She arbitrated conflicts that arose within and among tribes as well as between them and the central political establishment. On the one hand, these conflicts were focused on the crucial problem of water supply and distribution. On the other hand, they were about the balance between the central authority embodied by the Sultan and the fiercely independent tribes.

---

29. *Translator's note*: This description of Imma Tiffelent appears as a quote attributed to Trumelet, cited in a book by Emile Derminghem, *Le Culte des saints l'Islam maghrébin*, in Mernissi, "Women, Saints and Sanctuaries in Morocco," in *Unspoken Words*, 149, 152.

30. *Translator's note*: Here I changed "Berber" to "Amazigh" for reasons I mention earlier.

Lala Aziza did not get into politics because she was unsuccessful on the domestic front. She was among the most beautiful girls of her tribe. Many suitors proposed to marry her, but she refused them all. It is said that one day she was alone at the edge of a river and was chased by a young man whom she had rejected. She couldn't flee since there was no way out. She was about to be seized when suddenly she disappeared into the mountain before his astonished eyes. The girl's reputation as a Saint grew and spread far and wide. The Sultan wanted to meet Lala Aziza and asked her to come to Marrakech. She went there, and in the city she continued to be renowned for her piety and the good she did around her. She was greatly honored, but her power grew so great that the Sultan decided to end her influence, and he put her in prison. She died of poison.

Conclusion: Why *The Lionesses*?

After having outlined the profile of these four women through their very specific interaction with the shrine, we can finally shed light on the enigma of the title: *The Lionesses*. Lionesses are women like Halima in search of power. They are women who manage to challenge the monopolization of power by the patriarch and try to appropriate it through parallel channels. And *zaouias* are one of those channels.

Fatima, Zhor, each one seeks in the contact with the sanctuaries to find what is missing, to achieve a lost balance, to tend toward a better life.

But the lionesses are not only Halima from Dior Jamaâ or Fatima from Bouia Omar or Zhor from Salé. They are also and above all the women who carved out the role of saints in the past (such as Lala Aziza). They are extraordinary women who are part of our little-known heritage. They are mythical figures who have never ceased to exist in the collective memory.

Each of these profiles (which will be the subject of a sequence of around thirty minutes) introduces a discussion about the complexity of the *zaouias* phenomenon as

- a site for therapy
- a space of entertainment
- a secret space for the appropriation of charismatic power
- a site of contestation of established central political power.

The testimony and the cinematographic reconstruction can shed new light on these questions that are often ignored or misinterpreted.

5

Toward Decolonial Translating

Reflections on "francophoning-anglophoning" "Les Lionnes"

PAOLA BACCHETTA

In an exceptional gesture, along with her immense production of literary and academic texts and her ongoing activist work, Fatema Mernissi cocreated the film project *Les Lionnes* (1981) with the Moroccan psychiatrist Jalil Bennani and the filmmaker Hamid Bénani. Although written primarily in French, *Les Lionnes* is a polylingual, polyvocal text in which differential elements of Darija (Moroccan Arabic) and Amazigh languages live.[1] This chapter reflects on my process of translating *Les Lionnes* primarily into English, thus on accompanying the text into yet other linguistic, epistemic worlds, with attention and concerns about decolonizing translation at the center.

Les Lionnes is distinct in the Mernissian set of oeuvres in that it is her only film project. The project description was previously unpublished, nor has the film ever been made. I only came to know

---

1. In conversations on July 21, 2021, and February 21, 2023, Jalil Bennani confirmed to me that the women are bilingual, mother-tongue Amazigh-speaking subjects and that Mernissi carried out the conversations with them in Darija. The languages of Amazigh peoples (their self-designation) include Tashelhit (Tashelhiyt, Tashelhait, Shilha), Tarifit, Kabyle, Tamazight, and Tamahaq. Amazigh speakers, indigenous to North Africa from Egypt to Morocco, are more numerous in Morocco than anywhere else. Darija, an oral language spoken by 92 percent of Moroccans, has strong Amazigh influences, along with French and Spanish traces.

about it thanks to a chance discussion in 2019 with coauthor Jalil Bennani when he was an invited speaker at a workshop at the University of California, Berkeley, centered upon the work of a mutual friend, the artist and filmmaker Kader Attia.[2]

Les Lionnes tells the story of three contemporary women—Fatima, Zhor, and Halima—and the historical figure Lalla Aziza, all referred to as "lionesses," who through their distinct relations to the *zaouia*, the space of a sanctuary or shrine, create a different kind of life for themselves. For Fatima, the *zaouia* offers a culturally appropriate mode of psychic dealienation. For Zhor, it is a space of beauty, tranquility, and even entertainment that propels her out of ordinary life. Halima develops her own charismatic power as a *wali* (saint) and creates her own *zaouia*. For Lalla Aziza, the *zaouias* system enabled political resistance. She gathered a large spiritual following and was ultimately assassinated by political power. I will not say more so as to leave open readers' experience in their engagement with the script in chapter 4.

Encounters

This chapter might make better sense if I begin by situating myself in relation to *Les Lionnes*. To do so, I point to intense moments of temporal verticality (a dense present that includes past elements) and temporal horizonatality (a kind of simultaneity of presents and presence).

First, prior to encountering *Les Lionnes* I had had other engagements with women *in possession* in film and in the flesh. The earliest and most impressing was in India while I was creating a first draft of the translation into French of Nilita Vachani's remarkable documentary film *Eyes of Stone* (1990), about a woman's spirit possession in a subaltern rural Hindu context in Rajasthan, India.[3] In the film, the

---

2. The workshop, entitled "Tarrying with the Irreparable: Trauma and Kader Attia's Arts of Repair," organized by Stephania Pandolfo, took place on September 20, 2019.

3. The draft was later modified and finalized by other translators.

main personage, Shanta (the name means "peace" in Hindi, Rajasthani, Urdu, and other Indian languages), exhausted by her oppressive mother-in-law and husband, distressed by confinement to her village, becomes possessed by *bhut*s (ghosts) and jinns (spirits, invisible beings, demons).[4] While *in possession*, these spirits direct Shanta to order her mother-in-law around, chastise her husband, and curse at everyone who has harmed her. When Shanta emerges from the possession state, she remembers nothing about her unusual conduct and of course cannot be punished as it was not she but rather the *bhut*s and jinns who did these things. Shanta is suddenly provided with all her favorite foods (as she must remain healthy), encouraged to take rest, and permitted to travel to a nearby *dargah* (Sufi shrine) to be cured. Through a collage of events and speech, through Shanta's multiple voices and modes of embodiment in and out of the possession state, Vachani's film, with precision, with immense sensitivity, invokes the *in-possession* state as a way to exercise a form of agency that otherwise is not available to a woman in Shanta's social position.

During the period of that earlier translation, I was living in Delhi's Nizamuddin neighborhood, only a few yards from the Nizamuddin Dargah. Over several years before doing this translation, I had gone to the *dargah* regularly for peaceful moments of reflection. There, in its large main space, women entered into trance from time to time, albeit rarely. They would groan, twist their limbs and trunks, throw their heads back and forth, side to side, speak in tongues, ever more excitedly until they collapsed. I witnessed such *in-possession* states on several occasions over the course of six years.

Another event that bears upon in my relationality to the translation of *Les Lionnes* is that while working with Mernissi's collective text, I was simultaneously overseeing the translation into French of yet another plurilingual decolonial feminist text, Gloria Anzaldúa's

---

4. The signifier *jinn*, a plural noun in Arabic yet used in India, has the same signified as *jinns*, a plural noun in Darija used in Morocco.

Borderlands/La Frontera: The New Mestiza (1987), for which I also wrote a reflective preface on translation (see Anzaldúa 2022 and Bacchetta 2022). *Les Lionnes* and *Borderlands/La Frontera*, albeit in different genres and across their respective geopolitical, cultural, spiritual, and linguistic differences, share important characteristics. A major point of intersection is that they both are primarily inscribed in a dominant colonial language: for Mernissi and the coauthors, French; for Anzaldúa, English but also Castilian Spanish in relation to subalternized languages such as TexMex, Mexican Spanish, and Nahuatl. Engaging at the same time with each text in its context, its situated (co)authorial inscription, while imagining the translation and considering reception helped me to work out some of the complexities of each.

All of this accompanied me as I sensed, perceived, felt, and tried to understand Mernissi's collective text. I approached *Les Lionnes* with not only all my uncertainties, doubts, hesitations, and limitations but also my wonder, excitement, determination, love, and concentration.

From a *situated planetarity* perspective, thus with attention to the relationality between a smaller localized scale and the entire planetary scale, questions of power are central to any translation (Bacchetta 2020). Relations of power are: the very condition for the formation of the languages implicated and their assemblage in a same text; co-constitutive of the (co)author(s) as speaking-writing subject(s); factors inflecting upon the availability of linguistic and epistemic elements that (co)author(s) and translator(s) can mobilize; and agents that bear upon the reception of the original and the translation (Bacchetta 2020). I address some of these dimensions in some detail later. Here I simply signal the imbalance, inequity, instability in the relations within and across the languages of the source text and translation text.

To begin with, the primary language in which *Les Lionnes* is written, French, is a dominant global northern language spoken by about three hundred million people. The French that is spoken in dominant metropolitan France is the effect of a long struggle in which regional languages were erased. Today, because of the imposition of French under colonialism, half of French speakers are located in Africa, including the Maghreb. French is now an official or co-official language in twenty-nine countries and is widely spoken in many more. In postcolonial sites, French is most often a language of elites and sometimes of the contextual subaltern subjects who work for them. The genealogy of today's usage of French includes its earlier eminent status as the world's most widely spoken language in global northern international organizations and affairs. Today French is the seventh most widely spoken language across the planet, after English, Mandarin Chinese, Hindi, Spanish, Arabic, and Bengali.

Translations involving French are variably faced with French's *in-coloniality* status. The French state is perhaps unique in the world for its long-standing efforts to establish and perpetuate a particular form of French. In 1635, thus from the beginning of French colonialisms, the state created an institution to define and police the linguistic purity of the French language: the Académie française (French Academy). Since then, the Académie française has operated consistently except for a brief suspension during the French Revolution. Its forty members are called "the Immortals." Its motto is "To Immortality." Its secretary is called "the Perpetual." These self-representational elements announce the Académie française's mission with precision.

francophoning-anglophoning

The *in-coloniality* status of French and the French state's purification practices loom large for *Les Lionnes*, a text in and about a postcolonial site, coauthored by postcolonial intellectuals, marked variably by the presence of Darija and the absence-presence of Amazigh languages. *Les Lionnes* in French is an effect of a prior process of transposing subalternized non-French languages and realities into dominant French, a process I call *francophoning*.

Because *francophoning*'s root *francophone* is complex and caught in multiple political and literary debates, I will briefly define what I mean by it.[5] Francophone and francophonie first emerged inside France in *France, Algérie et colonies* (1880) by the geographer Onésime Reclus, a book that was part of a series designed to support Jules Ferry's movement to bolster French colonialism. In 1926, literary francophonie was consolidated in what was initially titled the Association des écrivains coloniaux (Association of Colonial Writers), then Association des écrivains de la mer et de l'outre-mer (Association of Sea and Overseas Writers), thus still referencing colonies. Today it bears the *colonially amnesiac* name Association des écrivains de la langue française (Association of Writers in the French Language). Historically, the organization has been critiqued for solidifying the *colonial-racial* segregation of (post)colonial authors from (presumably white) French authors and for promoting among the former only those who celebrate France. By the 1960s, the term *francophonie* was used in both a colonial and an anticolonial sense by postcolonial intellectuals, with a special issue of the journal *Esprit* on the French language in 1962 serving as a turning point. Another important moment is 1970, when the Organisation internationale de la francophonie (OIF, International Organization of Francophonie) was created to bring together states, regions, associate members, and observer states where French is a first, cofirst, or second language. Today the OIF has separate international agencies for universities, media (TV5), French-speaking politicians, and economic "development."

Most recently, on March 20, 2018, the international day of the French language, in a speech at the Académie française President Emmanuel Macron announced his strategy for the OIF to spread French farther across the globe (see Macron 2018). Months earlier, he had formed a think tank of well-known postcolonial intellectuals around francophonie, with the Moroccan writer Leïla Slimani as

---

5. The terms have a slightly different genealogy and connotations in Canada, but that topic is beyond the present scope.

chair. In a letter published on January 18, 2018, however, the Congolese writer Alain Mabanckou announced his refusal to cooperate (see Mabanckou 2018). A few months later he cowrote with the Cameroonian philosopher Achille Mbembe a critique of how Macron's plan promotes French nationalism and neocolonialism (Mabanckou and Mbembe 2018).

Given how negatively saturated the terms *francophonie* and *francophone* are in ongoing colonial relations of power, the reader may be wondering why I am proposing the term *francophoning*? First, notwithstanding an avalanche of critique, exactly zero postcolonial French-speaking intellectuals are interested in getting rid of French. For instance, Mabanckou and Mbembe wish to reorient French for other means. The Senegalese philosopher Souleymane Bachir Diagne, invoking Léopold Senghor's public love of French alongside the Kenyan author Ngugi Wa Thiongo's position in favor of writing instead in African languages, espouses the possibility of a multilingual francophone world wherein "the Hexagon is not the center, but only a province" (Diagne 2018).[6]

Second, the term *francophone* historically has two aspects and usages: capitalized (Francophone), it signals states, regions, institutions, and other sites of power; lowercased (francophone), it references people and groups of people. Indeed, Mabanckou and Mbembe conclude their letter to Macron by invoking what francophonie and francophone (lowercase) could come to mean: French could become a "common good"; a "means for the circulation and intersection of life forces and openings"; and "a real francophonie of the people" (2018). It is in this (lowercase) spirit that I propose the term *francophoning*.

But also, third, the term *francophoning* brings into relief that the (lowercase) root *francophone*, which functions generally as a noun or an adjective, can become operative as a verb, as ongoing action that is ever unfinished.

6. All translations of non-English text are mine unless otherwise noted.

Finally, fourth, *francophoning* usefully retains the productive density of its colonial genealogy, ambiguous present, and potential decolonial futurity. The notion of francophoning refuses *colonial amnesia*. It rejects the erasure of the relations of power that continue to saturate francophone. This aspect of francophoning is signaled inside *Les Lionnes* as the coauthors remark how in Morocco and for the women it portrays—who are Amazigh- and Darija-speaking subjects—French is an elite language. *Les Lionnes* depends on the prior transposition of the women's Darija into the text's postcolonial coauthorial voices inscribed in French. The *language gesture* required to produce the text is at once horizontal (the coauthors and the women share Darija) and vertical (Amazigh languages disappear as they are translated into Darija, and Darija disappears as the coauthors write in French).

The task of the translator attempting to accompany this plurilayered, productive mess into English can thus be described as *anglophoning*. English is the most widely spoken language in the world. Like French, it was created through violence against regional languages and then in its travels also against global southern languages. English is the official language of multiple settler colonies (e.g., the United States, Australia, New Zealand). It has bulldozed its way via additional forms colonialism across the global South. Yet, contrary to French, there is no one dominant regulatory body to formally police English. There are multiple dominant kinds of English(es). Some forms are associated with global hot spots of power (i.e., the United States, England), others with lesser global powers (New Zealand, Australia), yet others with regional powers (India, Nigeria, South Africa) or with state powers alone (Uganda, Bangladesh). The language's rules and usages are not exactly identical everywhere. Each form of English is differently particularist, situated, local, limited.

In *Les Lionnes* and *The Lionesses*, dominant French and US English respectively override othered languages and the epistemes of which they are a part, but they cannot erase them. Something of the presuppositions, categories, logics, conclusions, lexical indexes, poetry, music, rhythms of the suppressed subalternized languages persist. The French and English also enable some flows of communication—and miscommunication of course—across linguistic divides, including South-to-South flows.

Pretranslations

How can we think about the place and agency of the suppressed subalternized languages that in *Les Lionnes* and *The Lionesses* the dominant languages conceal? Here I propose the notion of *pretranslation* as a way to flag how disparate prior languages continue to assert themselves, discernibly or not, inside and alongside the colonial language that is visible and audible. The *pretranslation* constitutes a layer or layers, a dimension or dimensions, of the postcolonial and decolonial text and its translation.

In a discussion elsewhere from *Les Lionnes* yet directly relevant to it, Mernissi suggests how central what I call "*pretranslation* languages" can be to the postcolonial or decolonial text: "Saints know no French and often no literate Arabic; the language of this supernatural world is colloquial dialects, Berber or Arabic, the only ones the women master" (Mernissi [1977] 2001, 146). Under the sign of Berber, Mernissi is referring to Amazigh languages, and under the sign of Arabic she is referring, of course, to Darija.

Les Lionnes consists of a multilayered *pretranslation*-scape insofar as to speak with Mernissi in Darija the women are already orally translating from Amazigh languages. After the discussion, Mernissi transposes their words in two separate moments into both English and French. To *represence* elements in the *pretranslation* layers, here the initial Amazigh-to-Darija oral rendering, is to understand the text as a much more complex epistemic multiplicity than at first meets the eye and ear (Bacchetta 2018).

Pretranslation languages manifest and act within a dominant language text in many ways. One of the modes is through forms of hybridity that unfold as *decolonial gestures* in the text. In a discussion about Mona de Praconta's translation of the Nigerian author Chimamanda Adichie's polylingual book *Half of a Yellow Sun* (2006) from English into French, Sylvia Ijeoma Madueke (2019) points to three kinds of hybridity relevant here. For Madueke, a first hybridity type is the directly visible form. Adichie includes words, phrases, or sentences from Igbo, along with a sprinkling of Hausa, Yoruba, and "pidgin," thus elements from what I am calling the *"pretranslation* languages." A second manifestation of hybridity is "relexification," "transliteration," characterized by "traces within traces" (Madueke 2019, 51). Here, the author or translator mobilizes the colonial language in a way that retains the *pretranslation* languages' structures and rhythms. Elements from the *pretranslation* languages do not appear directly, but rather they manifest in how a reading of the text sounds and feels. Madueke highlights that Adichie's novel includes "a process of direct translation of the Igbo language into English, the results of which are English sentences that sound like oral Igbo" (51). The third form of hybridization—which according to Madueke stems from the second—is the use of repetition that "introduces" into the colonial language "a rhythmic oral structure" associated with the *pretranslation* language's "oral discourse" in cases where—for the *pretranslation* language—"repetition is an important linguistic element for the placement of emphasis" (51).

All of these hybridity formations live in *Les Lionnes*, albeit to varying degrees. Given the French state's tight control of French, hybridization elements are unsurprisingly often less numerous, less blatant in French than in English yet can have a radical force in the French text. There, the articulation of *pretranslation* elements can signal in intention or in effect direct defiance or decolonial refusal to cooperate with the French state's linguistic *colonial-racial* purification efforts. In my translation of *Les Lionnes*, I worked meticulously to respect and put into relief the coauthors' decolonial gestures, disposition, and spirit.

With respect to Madueke's insights, first, in *Les Lionnes* and *The Lionesses* specific lexical components—words but not phrases or sentences—from Darija clearly enter the pages and refuse to leave. Second, *Les Lionnes* and *The Lionesses* are inhabited by *pretranslation* "traces within traces" that may be imperceptible to the uninformed dominant reader of the colonial languages. These traces are composed of *pretranslation* elements from Darija and farther back, from (doubly silenced) Amazigh languages (that are *voiced-over* first by Darija and then by French). The *pretranslation* languages live in epistemic content such as the text's categories of thought, presuppositions, logics, conclusions. They surface in the women's speech and silence and in the coauthors' narration. Third, the structure of *Les Lionnes*, its assemblage around three contemporary voices and a fourth unarticulated voice that functions simultaneously as ancestral precedent and echo (of the first three), enacts a kind of *repetition with variability* and a sort of chorus within the text.

Here, it seems important to further disclose some aspects of the relationalities of *Les Lionnes*' coauthors and translator to the colonial languages at hand. Mernissi's and my trajectories with French and English take place across different generations, contexts, and points of departure and arrival. Mernissi was born in Morocco, where her first languages were Darija and French. She studied in the United States and became perfectly fluent in academic and literary English. I was born in the United States but came fully into English only after age five and a half. Later, I learned French. I became fluent in French while in exile in Paris, thus immersed in everyday French. My higher degrees are from universities in Paris, thus necessitating fluency in academic and literary French. To reflect with Mandueke (2019), becoming deeply inside other dominant languages certainly left "traces" and "traces within traces" upon both Mernissi and me. Tensions between the dominant colonial and *pretranslation* languages within us, silenced or not, cannot help but be part of our (differential) subjectivities and thus seep into our writing and translation enactments.

I think it matters that Mernissi and her coauthors wrote and that I translate their words in languages that have been made to be our own historically because of colonialism, coloniality, capitalism, racialization, sexism, queerphobia, and displacement. Otherwise, we may not have learned French or English, or we may have learned them otherwise. They are not neutral languages—no language is—but rather have enacted a prior epistemic violence. The entry of

French and English into our lives, albeit in distinct ways, implies an onslaught of presuppositions, categories, concept terms, logics, conclusions, and dominant fields of intelligibility that existed prior to and saturate the scene of thinking, perceiving, feeling, speaking, writing, and translating. In spite of everything, we have made these languages our own. They have become homes. We have come to inhabit them as much as they inhabit us. I do not know with precision how Mernissi and her coauthors experienced the caughtness and the *va-et-vient* inside and between their languages. I do note that Mernissi continued to produce texts in English and French throughout her life.

For me, to carry the coauthors' inscriptions into English required that I listen for the text's (in)accessible *pretranslation* elements; its different and sometimes discordant epistemes; its simultaneous poetry, music, rhythms, intensities, densities, and many kinds of silences. At every turn, I was faced with my own linguistic, personal, and psychic limitations. I still find my translation incomplete. Yet throughout this process I felt accompanied by many beings: Fatema, her coauthors, the four women who are the lionesses across their disparate temporalities, jinns, saints, the sultan, vacationers, the sea, frogs. As translator, I wavered between the forms of rationality that French and English impose and a sense of myself as an always inadequate conduit accompanying the text into yet other epistemic worlds. For me, there is always something out of control in translating, something inexplicable, something that—if we let go, give ourselves to it—takes over and lives through us.

In some ways, a translation is a form of delirium with, inside, and across worlds. It can never be neutral. It is always unfinished. It implicates the translator's whole person as much as the symbolic system/systems that speaks/speak through the translator. The relation to the present and absent languages is corporeal, embodied, fleshy, cellular. We are in the realms of the known and the unknown. The translation process is of the mind but also of the heart, the spirit, the affect that moves or produces stillness or agitation when we inhabit the languages and the bridges between them.

Mary Louise Pratt's work on borders, museums, and heterogeneous collectivities or communities as contact zones is helpful to think about the relationality of languages and bridges. For Pratt, contact zones are "spaces where cultures meet, clash, and grapple with each other, often in contexts of highly asymmetrical relations of power, such as colonialism, slavery or their aftermaths today" (1999, 34). They are also sites where clashes can be resolved and even find harmony. With Pratt, we might consider each body concerned in *Les Lionnes*—the plurilingual women, the coauthors, the translator—as a contact zone wherein languages in conflict do or do not find peace in our flesh.

Much decolonial work performed in a text by its *pretranslation* content can remain invisible to readers. In *The Lionesses*, I often focused on drawing it out from hiding, making it manifest. An example is the dialogue with Zhor. Mernissi recorded her oral dialogue with Zhor in Darija in 1974. She translated parts of it directly into English for an article published in 1977; in 1982, she recorded and translated a follow-up interview; and in 2001, the English translation from 1977 was republished (see Mernissi 1982, [1977] 2001). I stumbled upon these texts while reading broadly for intertextualities between *Les Lionnes* and Mernissi's other works and for insights into my translation process. The English texts of 1977 and 2001 were distinctly unlike other supplemental texts I consulted. They posed an acute problem: I found significant disparities between Mernissi's Darija-to-English and Darija-to-French translations of the same dialogue with Zhor.[7] In this book about Mernissi, I wanted to put into relief Mernissi's relationality to each version. I also desired to respect *Les Lionnes*'s coauthorial voice.

After much consideration and much trial and error, I decided to flag sameness and difference between the two versions. So in *The Lionesses* I reproduced and placed in my English translation of *Les*

---

7. Interestingly, disparity also exists in Anzaldúa's translation of her Spanish poetry into English in *Borderlands/La Frontera*.

Lionnes Mernissi's identical translations (into English and French) of the dialogue with Zhor and placed her discrepant translations in footnotes. I hoped that with the juxtaposition of Mernissi's doubled translation into two colonial languages on the same page, the reader might better understand the challenges (for Mernissi) of translation from a subalternized language into colonial languages—how a voice (in oral Darija) can in transposition and inscription become other to itself and how through translation a text's meaning can be reconstituted when encoded with inaudible earlier and contemporary languages that are (partially) silenced in the colonial language(s).

In *Les Lionnes*, different *pretranslation* languages and voices have distinct weights and functions. We do not hear words in Amazigh languages, yet we know, can feel, their copresence in the text. It just may be that the *pretranslation* defines the postcolonial text, or, albeit distinctly, perhaps any text *in concert* wherein multiple languages—heard, unheard, even unhearable—are speaking or not speaking to each other and to the reader.

Pretranslation elements enabled me to more fully sense *Les Lionnes* and to craft *The Lionesses* as a decolonial text. For instance, in dialogue with Jalil Bennani I mobilized the *pretranslation* to replace some *colonial-Orientalist* terms in the text. A main one is *marabout*. The term *marabout* comes from the Arabic مَربوط (*marbūṭ*) or مُرابِط (*murābiṭ*), meaning "a person who is garrisoned." It is used in the Maghreb to signify the physical space of a sanctuary and the saint associated with it. However, in French Orientalism the term *marabout* came to be used in a colonial homogenizing manner to signal any kind of Muslim sanctuary, shrine, or tomb and any kind of Muslim authority, without distinction. In 1981, when *Les Lionnes* was written, *marabout* was uncritically used in French social sciences and only later became a subject of decolonial critique. For example, in French two of many synonyms of *marabout* are *sorcier* (male witch) and *homme laid* (ugly man). In the translation, in keeping with the coauthors' decolonial spirit, it seemed timely to abandon the term *marabout* and embrace the *pretranslation* Darija term *zaouia* to signify the space of the sanctuary. *Zaouia* appears in *Les Lionnes* only once. *Zaouia* signals the precise kind of sanctuary in question here and, in my view, more than merits the status of "untranslatable" (which I explain later). For the religious authority of the site, again I deserted *marabout* and drew from the *pretranslation* to supplant it with the Darija term *wali*, a word that, again, surfaces in *Les Lionnes*, albeit only once. *Wali* comes from the Arabic وَلِيّ, *walīy*, meaning literally "friend" or "helper" (of Allah), thereby signaling a form of intimacy that is important to this relationality and situation.

In cases where the coauthors used the French terms *sanctuaire* and *saint*, I translated them directly into English (sanctuary, saint). However, in light of Emily Apter's discussion of the possible "deforeignizing" effect of translating Allah as "God" in Islamophobic contexts (2011, 9) (also discussed later) and of the extension of France's colonial "civilizing mission" in assimilation strategies that often perform what Jin Haritaworn, Adi Kuntsman, and Silvia Posocco (2013) call "murderous inclusion," I continue to worry if the term *saint* in *Les Lionnes* and in my translation has a deorientalizing effect or if it comes too close to colonial catholicization and reductive homogenization.

I had recourse to the *pretranslation* for two additional words: *jinns* and *Amazigh*. In one place each, which I signal in separate footnotes in the translation, the term *esprits occults* (occult spirits) and *génies* (genies, also from the Arabic root *jinn*) appear interchangeably with *jinns* in the same sections. Because both *esprits occults* and *génies* have associations with *colonial-Orientalist* fantasies, I returned to the *pretranslation* Darija and replaced both terms with *jinns*. I also substituted the term *Berber*, which appears only once in *Les Lionnes*, with *Amazigh* because the latter is the people's self-designation. Anyway, to think, feel, and work in complicity with *pretranslation* languages and their elements can—and in the case of *zaouia*, *wali*, *jinns*, and *Amazigh* did—enable the translator to respect and retrospectively act in complicity with the coauthors' decolonial desires.

Languages of a *pretranslation* have implications for the genre(s) of the translation, too. Broadly, the overall filmic genre always-already includes many genres that are felt, identifiable: the visual, audio, and so on. Although *Les Lionnes* was never actually filmed, it multiplies these genres because it is co-composed by an interdisciplinary collectivity that is professionally well versed in additional genres: Mernissi the literary author and sociologist, Bennani the psychiatrist, Bénani the filmmaker. In *Les Lionnes*, the plurality of genres they contribute lives in the literary beauty of certain paragraphs, the sociological observations or terminology (i.e., "phenomenon"), the insight into the inner lives of the lionesses, and everything about the temporal-spatialities refined by the filmmaker's vision. Indeed, I write this chapter with Mernissi at the center, but if I were to shift the focus to the other two coauthors, yet other worlds of reflections could unfold.

The *pretranslation* languages implicate other kinds of genres, registers, and mechanisms, too. They may not exist anywhere inside English or French. What to do with the orality, the storying, of Darija? With the *absent-present* Amazigh languages? How to make sense of the temporalities wherein the lionesses who are alive today are presented first and the lioness ancestor, the historical precedent, last? Is there any trace of the simultaneity of the (unseen) movement of the eye in the (unheard and heard) Darija from right to left, in the English from left to right? Indeed, past and present are copresent throughout, and they open up a futurity. In the text, many kinds of dimensions, registers, and layers live.

Translation-Pauses

Another important decolonial dimension of *Les Lionnes* is what I call its *translation-pauses*, defined as kinds of brief haltings of the translation in the text. *Translation-pauses* can be an effect of what Walter Benjamin and others call "untranslatables," or terms in the source language without equivalence in the translation language (Benjamin [1923] 1968), or they may be constituted by one or more kind of silences.

The "untranslatable" has been the object of much scholarly reflection and writing. The term has an interesting history in translation studies. In an early phase, scholars imagined translation as replication and equivalence. In a next moment, translation was thought to be about either reproducing the original text or about poetic license. Walter Benjamin ([1923] 1968) proposed instead that the translation be in harmony with the source's "intentio." Barbara Cassin and coeditors (2014) created a whole encyclopedia of "untranslatables" and proposed—in place of translational sameness and commensurability—difference and commensurability. Emily Apter, drawing on Cassin's work, addresses forms of "nonnegotiated singularity that are negotiated nonetheless" (Apter 2021, 90; see also Apter 2013). Along with "untranslatability," Apter identifies "nontranslation, mistranslation, incomparability" (2013, xxx). With Jacques Derrida's reworking of the Austinian idea of the performative in mind, Apter considers what the "untranslatable" can enact in a text. For Apter, it can either contribute to (decolonial) resistance or reinforce (colonial) power. Her example of the latter is when in US Islamophobic media "Allah" is left in the transliterated Arabic instead of translated as "God," a term that she feels could deforeignize, reconnotate, and resignify the text (Apter 2011, 91).

Here, Lawrence Venuti's writing about the place of "untranslatables" in "foreignization" or "domestication" is very helpful to think with. He points out that foreignization preserves a source text's otherness in translation but can induce exoticization, while domestication of the source text can create intelligibility but also obscure "heterogeneity and hybridity" (2013, 12).

The scholarship on "untranslatables" tells us much about how different source-text words and especially concept terms can operate in a translation. If we reconsider "untranslatables" with *pretranslation(s)* in mind, we can extend the former to include the source text's multiply subalternized epistemes and philosophies. So in *The Lionesses*, to retain the Darija term *jinns*, as the coauthors of *Les Lionnes* did, is to respect the three dimensions: *jinns* as concept term, epistemic element, and philosophical component. For Apter, such use of the "untranslatable" disallows "translational fluency yet enables critical faculties nonetheless" (2013, 138). In *Les Lionnes*, the "untranslatables" drawn from the *pretranslation(s)* are sites of decolonial resistance.

Yet another set of *translation-pauses* that I have in mind are the different *silence formations* within (and outside) *Les Lionnes*. First, a major one is *inadvertent silence*, or silence as the effect of the *pretranslation's* emergence in the translated text. Here a signified appears in the translated text, while its signifier remains absent. In this sense, there is always something archaic and unrepresented in the source text that can be carried into the translation. Understanding this *absence-presence* is made all the more complex by the fact that no spoken language is static; they all are constantly moving, transforming. Thus, the signified that is unattached to a signifier in the source text, or the *unsaid-unwritten* that is nonetheless present, may be seriously multiple and may transmute over time.

To me, a second manifestation of *silence formation* is *inevitable silence*. It is unavoidable. *Les Lionnes* presents three women's recorded and then translated narrations. However, the fourth woman's speech is inside *inevitable silence*, for there is no record of Lalla Aziza's centuries-old voice. Her handed-down actions speak for her. The coauthors narrate her life (with love and immense sensitivity).

A third kind of *silence formation* is what I call *reproductive silence*. It is silence first created in the relations of power that saturate the original text's social context and are carried over into the text itself. For *Les Lionnes*, *reproductive silence* entails the transferred censorship in the French text of what is not permissible to say in Darija and possibly Amazigh languages. Assia Djebar lends insight into this *silence formation* as she reminds us that "from childhood on the little girl is taught 'the cult of silence,' which is one of the greatest powers of Arabic society" (1998, 338–39). Here, as in many contexts across the planet, the social power of voice repression can get automatically reinstated in a text without requiring an agentic stance on the part of speaking subject(s), author(s), or translator(s).

A fourth kind of *silence formation* is *strategic silence*. It entails an agent. In *strategic silence*, the speaking subject actively avoids exposing secrets. The silence can be motivated for many different reasons—for instance, to circumvent the epistemic violence of misinterpretation, to dodge appropriation, to preclude leaving overt traces of one's pain, to produce estrangement that will remind the reader of their nonmastery and thereby demand the reader's respect and efforts (see also Bacchetta 2009).

The Post-translation

How can we create translation that does not lend itself to colonial recuperation and assimilation when colonial and multiple other relations of power saturate the scene of the initial writing and then of the translation and reception? To do so thoughtfully may require understanding not only the challenges the source and translated texts face but also their capacities to overcome them.

A first obstacle for *Les Lionnes* is inequity and violence within and among the languages by which it is composed. Insofar as *Les Lionnes* is a set of prior translations within a (French) translation, we are in the realm of doubleness, of multiplicity, of *pretranslation* dimensions. I addressed earlier how the languages and epistemes that live inside *Les Lionnes* are moved—albeit not eliminated—by internal silencings and pauses and by repressive procedures of dominant French. Talal Asad lends insight into yet another aspect of this relationality in his discussion of how in encounters with a dominant global northern language the "Third World" language is forced to change, not the dominant one (1993, 190). For Asad, there are two main vectors of power at work: political-economic relations and the stronger desire for knowledge produced in the Western language. He points to how Arabic has been transformed since the early nineteenth century by French and English translations into Arabic (191). Some examples are "punctuation, paragraphing, subheadings, new sentence structures, semantic elements and literary styles" (191 n. 3). The changes take place unidirectionally because of "imperialism and capitalism" (191, 199). If we return to Apter and Venuti, we might consider this aspect of relationality as a form of (colonial) domestication. Asad suggests that to prevent this domestication in the translation, the source language "should retain what may be a discomforting—even scandalous—presence within the receiving language" (199). However, with Asad in mind, let us additionally recall Padma Rangarajan's (2006) work on how Indian languages and literatures have influenced dominant English and its literature.

A second obstacle is that the weight of a history of *colonialism-complicit* translations bears upon any present translation of a postcolonial text. We are not in neutral terrain. Edward Said (1979) shows how translation is essential to *colonial orientalization*. Meyda Yegenoglu (1998) reveals translation's operations in the construction of colonial sexual fantasies about Muslim women. Historians and theologians in India have exposed the colonial reconfiguration of Hinduism through the process of selecting only a few Sanskrit texts out of thousands for translation and via translation itself through the mobilization of modes of domestification that do violence to the source. For example, Orientalists selected and domesticated the Bhagavad Gita, which is actually only a small section of one version of the epic Mahabharat, and reframed it as a sort of Bible. I wonder, too, how traces of a subalternized language—such as an "untranslatable"—in a colonial-language translation might be made to function as *colonial foreignization* to signify what the colonizer insists is not part of their culture, to sustain the *colonial-racialized* fantasy of inherent superiority/inferiority. I am thinking, for example, of the signifier *thug* as "untranslatable." The colonial British assigned to *thug* a degrading signification in reference to one "tribe" in Madhya Pradesh, India—the Thuggee people—whom the British fantasized and strategically represented as criminal.

How can we overcome such problems? I want to make three suggestions. The first is that we consider the source text and translation as what we can call, with Ann Laura Stoler's (2011) work on the postcolonial archive in mind, *texts-as-subjects* with agency, not as *texts as (passive) sources*. Second, we can recognize the source *text-as-subject* not in isolation but rather in relation and sometimes in intertextuality with other decolonial texts and actions. Third, we can bring into relief in the decolonial *text-as-subject* its resistant and transformative linguistic, epistemic, and political capacities and enactments. With Frantz Fanon ([1952] 2015, [1961] 2016), who highlights how colonialism is a relation with effects upon both colonizer and colonized (and not upon the colonized alone), we can think about the decolonial *text-as-subject*'s effects upon all parties concerned.

Les Lionnes is part of a vast, planetary history and present of subaltern decolonial creativity. It can be understood, for example, alongside the linguistic agency of youth in France's banlieues (racialized working-class suburbs, with concentrations of Maghrebian and sub-Saharan African families), who invented a *verlan*, a language within and simultaneously beyond dominant French and North and sub-Saharan African languages. With the recent work of Massinissa Garaoun (2022) in mind, we can place the decolonial speaking subjects and coauthors of Les Lionnes in a dialogic relation to the creation of a secret, queer, resistant language within and beyond Maghrebian languages. Les Lionnes can also converse with other subaltern refusals of a colonial episteme via translation. A striking instance is Vicente Rafael's (1993) work on how Tagalog people under Spanish colonial rule resisted Catholic conversion by rearticulating their own religion intact in translation through Christian symbols.

Pretranslation compositional elements position Les Lionnes in defiance of the French state's colonial fantasy of linguistic purity. Les Lionnes stubbornly asserts (articulated and unarticulated) *pretranslation* languages that French cannot fully suppress.

Les Lionnes as a *text-as-subject* epistemically and politically decenters Islamophobic presumptions about Muslim women and Islam. It redefines what constitutes gendered conditions, resistance, and liberation. It preempts *post-translation* co-optation by offering the reader ways to understand the text on its own terms elsewhere from colonial savior narratives, the colonial weaponization of (women's) human rights, and binary discourses of sameness versus difference.

Traces of Mernissi's and the coauthors' awareness of the violence of dominant *readings as reframings* are alive in what Les Lionnes resists and in the coauthors' decolonial work beyond Les Lionnes.

Mernissi was and is often pulled into preexisting polemics that reduce her expansiveness, deform her "intentio," silence her critiques. She has been variably constructed as insulting Islam or as a Muslim fundamentalist saving Islam through a feminist interpretation or as antifeminist or as a westernized feminist or as a saint. She has been made to signify the essence of all that is wrong or, alternatively, of everything that is wonderful and thus beyond critique. Mernissi directly revolted against such fantasies.

A particularly interesting filmic recognition and rendition of Mernissi's resistance is found in Saddie Choua's film *Je crois qu'il y a une confusion chez vous. Vous croyez que moi je veux vous imiter* (I Think You Must Be Confused. You Believe I Want to Imitate You, 2017). Choua's film's striking title echoes Mernissi's own words in an interview by CNN on US television, an extract of which is part of Choua's film. Mernissi was responding to the interviewer's insistence on the *colonial-Orientalist* presupposition that Muslim women are always-already *more oppressed than thou* and his erroneous suggestion that she was promoting women's freedom via westernization.

In her texts, sometimes Mernissi critically inverts readerly entrenched political *colonial-Orientalist* assumptions, as when she writes about *l'harem de l'Occident* (the West's harem). She often directly affronts violent distortions of the *otherwise-awareness* and *otherwise-resistance* that characterize her work. She sometimes flatly refuses her insertion into *colonial-Orientalist* fantasies, projections, and polemics and rejects the epistemic violence upon which they depend. They are cages that confine and destroy the life of her texts. They preclude learning from her work. As Michel Foucault asks, "Has anyone ever seen a new idea come out of a polemic?" (1984, 383).

Concluding Remarks: Beyond francophoning/anglophoning

To create a decolonial translation of a postcolonial text, it seems extremely important to respect the *elsewhere-ing* inside and outside the coauthors' inscription. To listen and to feel in that way are to make translating Mernissi's voice and the collective voice from French to

English in *Les Lionnes* a bit like playing not an out-of-tune musical instrument but rather a musical instrument tuned perfectly otherwise. Its melody, harmony, dissonance can make perfect sense only in its own previously unencountered musical system. I could access Mernissi's voice and the authorial collective voice best when in a quasi–dream state. Translation practice is inside and outside rationality. It can entail a different kind of logic beyond words. From *Les Lionnes* to *The Lionesses*, the instruments and people relating to the text were a bit off key in the dominant (and sometimes in the subaltern normative) scales but perfectly at pitch in their own.

There are risks in the human channeling of any text into another epistemic realm. I hope the translation I created of *Les Lionnes* will not be final, imagined as pure, essentialized, or lend itself to policings of the text's potential transpositions into other English(es), into yet other languages, in the present and the future. Among other things, such closure would problematically reproduce the mechanisms of the Academie française that I critique earlier. I hope there will be many more, many better translations of *Les Lionnes*. I hope they will work to further decolonize the text, give life to the potentialities of *pre-translation* elements, make more evident the activities of the *text-as-subject*, and intervene to circumvent misreadings and unhelpful reframings in ways that—given my many limitations—I could not. The work of translation hails collectivity and can benefit from multiple involvements. I also hope that future translators will love living and dreaming with the words composed by Fatema Mernissi, Jalil Bennani, and Hamid Bénani as much as I did.

References

Anzaldúa, Gloria. 1987. *Borderlands/La Frontera: The New Mestiza*. San Francisco: Aunt Lute.

———. 2022. *Terres frontalières/La frontera: La nouvelle mestiza*. Translated by Nino S. Dufour and Alejandra Soto Chacón. Paris: Cambourakis.

Apter, Emily. 2011. *The Translation Zone: The New Comparative Literature*. Princeton, NJ: Princeton Univ. Press.

———. 2013. *Against World Literature: On the Politics of Untranslatability*. London: Verso.

———. 2021. "What Is Just Translation?" *Public Culture* 33, no. 1: 89–111.

Asad, Talal. 1993. *Genealogies of Religion: Discipline and Reasons of Power in Christianity and Islam*. Baltimore: Johns Hopkins Univ. Press.

Bacchetta, Paola. 2009. "Co-formations: Sur les spatialités de résistance de lesbiennes 'of color' en France." *Genre, sexualité et société* 1, no. 1. At http://journals.openedition.org/gss/810.

———. 2018. "Re-présences: Les forces transformatives d'archives de queers racisé.e.s." *Friction*, May. At https://friction-magazine.fr/re-presence-les-forces-transformatives-darchives-de-queers-racise-e-s/.

———. 2020. "Decolonial Sexualities." In "Decolonial Trajectories," edited by Sandeep Bakshi, Suhraiya Jivraj, and Silvia Posocco. Special issue, *Interventions: International Journal of Postcolonial Studies* 22, no. 4: 574–85.

———. 2022. "'Francophoner' *Borderlands/La Frontera: The New Mestiza* de Gloria Anzaldúa." In Gloria Anzaldúa, *Terres frontalières/La frontera: La nouvelle mestiza*, translated by Nino S. Dufour and Alejandra Soto Chacón, 9–36. Paris: Cambourakis.

Benjamin, Walter. [1923] 1968. "The Task of the Translator." In *Illuminations*, translated by Harry Zohn, edited and introduced by Hannah Arendt, 69–82. New York: Harcourt Brace Jovanovich.

Cassin, Barbara, Emily Apter, Jacques Lezra, and Michael Wood, eds. 2014. *Dictionary of Untranslatables: A Philosophical Lexicon*. Princeton, NJ: Princeton Univ. Press.

Choua, Saddie, dir. 2017. *Je crois qu'il y a une confusion chez vous. Vous croyez que moi je veux vous imiter*. Film. Produced by Saddie Choua.

Diagne, Souleymane Bachir. 2018. "Francophonie en 'guerre culturelle': La liberté de choisir." *Jeune Afrique*, Mar. 1. At https://www.jeuneafrique.com/mag/535698/culture/francophonie-en-etat-de-guerre-culturelle-la-liberte-de-choisir/.

Djebar, Assia. 1998. "Forbidden Gaze, Severed Sound." In *Women, Autobiography, Theory: A Reader*, edited by Sidonie Smith and Julia Watson, 337–42. Madison: Univ. of Wisconsin Press.

Fanon, Frantz. [1952] 2015. *Peau noire, masques blancs*. Reprint. Yaoundé, Cameroon: Kiyikaat.

———. [1961] 2016. *Les damnés de la terre*. Reprint. Yaoundé, Cameroon: Kiyikaat.
Foucault, Michel. 1984. "Polemics, Politics and Problematizations." In *The Foucault Reader*, edited by Paul Rabinow, 381–90. New York: Pantheon.
Garaoun, Massinissa. 2022. "A wīl-i žṛāhīm! An Introduction to a Moroccan Queer Language: Həḍṛāt əl-Lwāba." *Decolonizing Sexualities Network Blog*, Dec. 4. At https://decolonizingsexualities.org/blog/a-wl-i-hman-introduction-to-a-moroccan-queer-language-ht-l-lwba.
Haritaworn, Jin, Adi Kuntsman, and Silvia Posocco. 2013. "Introduction: Murderous Inclusions." In "Murderous Inclusions," edited by Jin Haritaworn, Adi Kuntsman, and Silvia Posocco. Special issue, *International Feminist Journal of Politics* 15, no. 4: 445–52.
Mabanckou, Alain. 2018. "Francophonie, langue française: Lettre ouverte à Emmanuel Macron." *L'OBS*, Jan. 15. At https://bibliobs.nouvelobs.com/actualites/20180115.OBS0631/francophonie-langue-francaise-lettre-ouverte-a-emmanuel-macron.html.
Mabanckou, Alain, and Achille Mbembe. 2018. "Le français, notre bien commun? Par Alain Mabanckou et Achille Mbembe." *L'OBS*, Feb. 11. At https://bibliobs.nouvelobs.com/idees/20180211.OBS2020/le-francais-notre-bien-commun-par-alain-mabanckou-et-achille-mbembe.html.
Macron, Emanuelle, 2018. "Transcription du discours du president de la republique." *Pôle presse*, Mar. 20. At https://www.diplomatie.gouv.fr/IMG/pdf/21_03_transcription_du_discours_du_president_de_la_republique_a_l_institut_de_france_cle8b8911.pdf.
Madueke, Silvia Ijeoma. 2019. "On Translating Postcolonial African Writing: French Translation of Chimamanda Adichie's *Half of a Yellow Sun*." *TranscUlturAl* 11, no. 1: 49–66.
Mernissi, Fatema. 1982. "Zhor's World: A Moroccan Domestic Worker Speaks Out." *Feminist Issues* 1:3–31.
———. [1977] 2001. "Women, Saints and Sanctuaries in Morocco." *Signs: Journal of Women in Culture and Society* 3, no. 1: 101–12. Reprinted in *Unspoken Words: Women's Religious Lives*, edited by Nancy Auer Falk and Rita M. Gross, 144–53. Belmont, CA: Wadsworth/Thompson Learning.
Pratt, Mary Louise. 1999. "Arts of the Contact Zone." In *Ways of Reading: An Anthology for Writers*, edited by David Barthalomeo and Anthony Petrosky, 33–40. New York: Bedford/St. Martin's Press.

Rafael, Vicente L. 1993. *Contracting Colonialism: Translation and Christian Conversion in Tagalog Society under Early Spanish Rule.* Durham, NC: Duke Univ. Press.

Rangarajan, Padma. 2006. *Imperial Babel: Translation, Colonialism, and the Long Nineteenth Century.* New York: Fordham Univ. Press.

Said, Edward. 1979. *Orientalism.* New York: Vintage.

Stoler, Ann Laura. 2011. "Colonial Archives and the Arts of Governance." In *Archives, Documentation, and Institutions of Social Memory: Essays from the Sawyer Seminar,* edited by Francis Xavier Blouin and William G. Rosenberg, 267–79. Ann Arbor: Univ. of Michigan Press.

Venuti, Lawrence. 2013. *Translation Changes Everything: Theory and Practice.* New York: Routledge.

Yegenoglu, Meyda. 1998. *Colonial Fantasies: Towards a Feminist Reading of Orientalism.* London: Cambridge Univ. Press.

Section Two
Family and Kinship

6

Trespassing Queer Kinship with Mernissi's *Dreams of Trespass*

SIMA SHAKHSARI

> The more masters one had, the more freedom and the more fun.
> —Fatema Mernissi, *Dreams of Trespass:
> Tales of a Harem Girlhood*

Mainstream women's, gender, and sexuality studies as well as queer theory often exclude texts from Southwest Asia and North Africa (a vast area with the arbitrary colonial designation of "Middle East") that theorize gender and sexuality. This near absence, including Fatema Mernissi's texts and most other texts by scholars of Middle East studies in North America and Europe, reflects epistemological groundings that canonize Euro-American scholarship and assume works on the region to be nontheoretical, heteronormative, identity bound, and irrelevant to queer studies.[1] To counter assumptions of

---

I wrote the first draft of this article as a tribute to Mernissi for the conference "Mernissi for Our Times," organized in 2016 by Minoo Moallem and Paola Bacchetta at the University of California, Berkeley, Center for Race and Gender. A longer version of this essay was published as "Displacing Queer Refugee Epistemologies: *Dreams of Trespass*, Queer Kinship, and Politics of Miseration," *Arab Studies Journal* 28, no. 2 (2020): 108–33. I am grateful to Minoo Moallem, Paola Bacchetta, Sherene Seikaly, and anonymous reviewers for their feedback.

1. My use of the term *Euro-American* points to the centering of knowledge produced in North America, particularly by US and Canadian scholars of European descent. I am aware of epistemological violence embedded in the use of "America" to

incommensurability, I center the seemingly "unqueer" *Dreams of Trespass* (Mernissi 1994) as a rich text that provides epistemological tools for the study of queer kinship and, subsequently, queer refugee scholarship.

I do not aim to "queer" (as an analytic) and reread kinship theories, Mernissi's *Dreams of Trespass*, or Mernissi herself as transgressive and disruptive of gender, sexuality, or family norms. Nor am I interested in discovering a hidden queer subject, claiming a forgotten queer past, or imposing an intelligible identity or a desire deemed queer on the protagonists in Mernissi's memoir/semiautobiographical text.[2] Rather, I want to encourage thinking about epistemological assumptions in gender studies and queer studies curricula that render Mernissi's *Dreams of Trespass* an impossibility as a teachable text. Many Middle East studies scholars have critiqued Mernissi's scholarship, and I do not seek to lionize Mernissi or her scholarship.[3]

---

refer to the United States and the erasure of eastern Europe in wholesale uses of "Europe." Here, however, I am referring to a geopolitical privileging of queer theory that is produced in North America and Europe, whether by white scholars or queers of color in the United States, Canada, western Europe, and some parts of eastern Europe.

2. In multiple interviews, Mernissi stated that the book is a mix of memoir and fiction. Some of the characters (such as Chama) are fictional, while others are based on Mernissi's childhood. This blurring of autobiography and fiction is why I have characterized this book as "semiautobiographical."

3. Scholars of Middle East studies have critiqued Mernissi for multiple reasons. Basing their criticism on her work on gender and Islam, some critics, such as Anouar Majid (1998), have accused her of not addressing class and global capitalism. These critics, however, often ignore Mernissi's sociological work on Morocco in the 1970s and 1980s in response to the structural-adjustment policies and her late-life Casablanca Dream project with women carpet weavers in the Moroccan High Atlas region, which focused on the impact of development and global capitalism on women living in poverty. Other scholars, such as Mervat Hatem (1987), have critiqued Mernissi's earlier work as unsympathetic to Islam, while a different group has taken issue with her Islamic feminism and her "soft" feminism. For example, Shahram Akbarzadeh and Lorraine Barlow (2006) juxtapose Mernissi's earlier work (such as *Beyond the Veil* [1975], which they consider to be revolutionary) to her later works (such as *The Veil and the Male Elite* [1991], which they characterize as reformist and "soft") and

My objective in focusing on Mernissi's *Dreams of Trespass* is twofold. First, I explore the potential of this text in helping us understand queer kinship through temporal bonds and alliances (not based on assumptions of transnational solidarity among already-existing queer subjects who are linked based on their sexual identities) and

---

critique her later work for attempting to excuse what they consider to be misogynistic and patriarchal verses in the Qur'an. More sympathetic critics such as Margot Badran (2009) and miriam cooke (2000, 2001) have highlighted Mernissi's important contributions to Islamic feminism, while Raja Rhouni (2010) and Lamia Ben Youssef Zayzafoon (2005) have pointed out the contributions by and shortcomings of Mernissi's work in relationship to Islamic feminism. Zayzafoon's astute work examines the category of "Muslim woman" as a plural signifier that challenges both Orientalist/Islamophobic and conservative Muslim positions, and she critiques Mernissi for reproducing Orientalist and conservative discourses by deploying the notion of "truth" and authenticity of originary narratives. Rhouni, in contrast, carefully distinguishes between different phases of Mernissi's scholarship and characterizes Mernissi as a Gramscian "public intellectual" whose oeuvre demonstrates her responsiveness to the temporal and political shifts in her lifetime rather than an investment in a static theoretical framework. Rhouni is right in arguing that many of Mernissi's critics often collapse her scholarly and fiction writing into a single category of "Islam and gender." This conflation of Mernissi's "secular phase" and her "Islamic feminist phase," Rhouni argues, is owed in part to the fact that Mernissi's earlier works were not translated into English until much later (and some never were). In fact, Mernissi's shift from sociological studies of development and class to secular feminism, Islamic feminism, and finally a focus on civil society and human rights in her later years confirms Rhouni's important point about Mernissi's complex intellectual trajectory. Mernissi's position on Islam and feminism drastically changed from *Beyond the Veil* in 1975 to the publication of her trilogy—*Le harem politique* in 1987 (translated as *The Veil and the Male Elite* in 1991), *Sultanes oubliées: Femmes chefs d'état en Islam* in 1990 (translated as *The Forgotten Queens of Islam* in 1993), and *La peur-modernité: Conflit Islam démocratie* in 1992 (translated as *Islam and Democracy: Fear of the Modern World* that same year). Mernissi shifted to fiction with the publication of her first novel, *Dreams of Trespass: Tales of a Harem Girlhood*, in 1994. In 2001, in response to the reception of *Dreams of Trespass* in the West, Mernissi published *Scheherazade Goes West*—a critique of the Orientalist constructions of the harem. As Rhouni (2010) points out, although Mernissi stopped producing work on gender and Islam in the late 1990s, her work remains foundational for Islamic feminism.

therefore move beyond Euro-American theories of kinship, heteronormative bonds of blood, liberal notions of choice, or identity-based renditions of queer attachment. (For some studies of kinship in the Middle East, see Abu-Lughod 1986; Hasso 2010; Hoodfar 1997; Joseph 1993, 2005, 2018; Kholoussy 2010; Kholoussy and Celello 2016; Mir-Hosseini 1993; Sehlikoglu and Zengin 2016; and Zengin 2016.) I read kinship in Mernissi's *Dreams of Trespass* alongside queer theory and the anthropological trajectory of kinship, but without recuperating anthropology's voyeuristic gaze or overlooking its colonial legacy. The model of kinship that focuses on temporal alliances, as is the case in Mernissi's *Dreams of Trespass*, challenges the liberal notion of choice/chosen families.

Second, by theorizing queer kinship and refugee world making through Mernissi's *Dreams of Trespass*, I question the bifurcation of queer studies and area studies. I show how queer theory can center a text such as *Dreams of Trespass* as an epistemological grounding and not an exemplar in the study of sexuality (see Arondekar and Patel 2016). Proposing an unlikely text such as Mernissi's as a point of departure, I suggest that queer theory can learn from texts that are often dismissed for being allegedly outdated or "unqueer" or both.

Kindred Dreams and Estranged Texts

> "The main thing for the powerless is to have a dream," [Aunt Habiba] often told me while I was watching the stairs, so that she could embroider a fabulous one-winged green bird on the clandestine mrema she kept hidden in the darkest corner of her room. "True, a dream alone, without the bargaining power to go with it, does not transform the world or make the walls vanish, but it does help you keep ahold of dignity."
> —Fatema Mernissi, *Dreams of Trespass*

The harem has long occupied Western colonial imaginations, where it is characterized by sexual anxieties and fantasies. The title of Mernissi's semiautobiographical book, *Dreams of Trespass: Tales of a Harem Girlhood* (1994), might give the impression that it is yet another Orientalist depiction.[4] Mernissi, however, employs what miriam cooke (2000) calls "multiple critique," wherein the author comments simultaneously on colonial regimes, patriarchal family, and masculinist interpretations of Islam. In *Dreams of Trespass*, Mernissi also offers possibilities for conceptualizing queer kinship in temporal terms beyond sexual identities and binarized notions of desire. She eschews analyzing the harem as simply a repressive space of patriarchal confinement or a transgressive space where women form egalitarian relationships. Instead, Mernissi draws our attention to alliances that *trespass* (but not transgress) heteronormative forms of nuclear family, even as they *sustain* hegemonic articulations of family, status, desire, and citizenship. This combination of trespassing and sustaining is perhaps the reason why the book is almost never considered to be sufficiently transgressive and queer.

Published in 1994, *Dreams of Trespass* is a semifictional account of Mernissi's childhood in Fez, Morocco, during the 1940s and 1950s. In the story, Mernissi lives in a harem with her mother, father, older uncle Ali, divorced aunt Habiba, charismatic cousin Chama, paternal grandmother Lalla Mani (who is a matriarch), other aunt Lalla Radia, male cousin Samir, other cousin Malika, the doorkeeper Ahmed, and the brave harem slave Mina. In a countryside harem, Mernissi's maternal grandmother, Yasmina, lives with her husband, Tazi, along with his wealthy first wife, Lalla Thor (who keeps a distance from the others); his Amazigh wife, Tamou; and his Sudanese wife, Yaya (who considers Tamou and Yasmina to be her companions). The book revolves around women's and girls' conversations, performances, and transgressions in the harem. Through Mernissi's memories, we learn about the different relationships that women in her childhood had to the harem and to each other. She situates these

---

4. Many thanks to the anonymous reviewer who pointed out that the word *harem* does not exist in Moroccan Arabic. I am using the term as it appears in the title and text of the English version of *Dreams of Trespass*.

relationships in their contentious and contradictory bonds to *hudud* (sacred boundaries), French colonialism, nationalism, and feminism. Mernissi narrates her story in a nuanced manner that depicts the harem neither as a space of pure pleasure (as Orientalist discourses represent it) nor as a site of repression. The harem of her childhood is the embodiment neither of patriarchy and heteronormativity nor of queerness (because of transgressions). Whether she is narrating the defense of the harem by Lalla Mani and Lalla Radia or is recounting the contestations to the harem by her mother, her divorced aunt Habiba, or her (fictional) feminist cousin Chama, she neither idealizes nor condemns harem life. She subtly conveys the contradictions, tensions, and desires that include the idealization of the modern nuclear family, class hierarchies, and conflicts—all through narrating the women's relationships to each other, to the nationalist men, and to the colonizers.

The harem in Mernissi's account is an embodied space where kinship is complicated beyond biological reproductivity. The notion of remembering in *Dreams of Trespass* links bodies in a collective life that is not about procreation but about alliances made between women. Together, the women produce a collective past and imagine a collective and different future, symbolized beautifully through the embroidered bird with one wing: "Aunt Habiba said that anyone could develop wings. It was only a matter of concentration. The wings need not be visible like the birds'[,] invisible ones were just as good, and the earlier you started focusing on the flight, the better" (1994, 204).[5] Embroidery in *Dreams of Trespass* becomes a symbolic act of resistance that draws from "traditional" forms of knowledge transmitted through time, while engendering change quietly and collectively. Although the women transgress in embroidering wings that symbolize the desire for individuality and freedom, the collective act itself is an embodied practice that can be reduced neither to the

---

5. From this point, citations to *Dreams of Trespass* (1994) give page numbers only.

procreative model of kinship nor to the Eurocentric modes of production and transmission of knowledge. Mernissi writes, "Of course, birds appeared in traditional embroidery designs, but they were tiny, and often totally paralyzed, squeezed as they were between gigantic plants and fat leafy flowers. Because of Lalla Mani's attitude, Aunt Habiba always embroidered classical designs when down in the courtyard, and kept her big, winged birds to herself, up in her private room, with its direct access to the lower terrace. . . . She reassured me about the future: a woman could be totally powerless, and still give meaning to her life by dreaming about flight" (153). Stories that Mernissi retells from the past encapsulate alliances that exceed biological notions of kinship and marriage—and build on solidarities across time. One of the most captivating features of *Dreams of Trespass* is the way Mernissi recounts and remembers how the women and children in the harem reenact stories from *The Thousand and One Nights* on the terrace.[6] The narrator is Scheherazade, who tells stories to King Shahryar as a way to defer death. Shahryar, who has killed his unfaithful wife, marries a new virgin each day and

6. Also known as *The Arabian Nights* (*Hezaar o Yek Shab* in Persian and *Alf Layla wa-Layla* in Arabic), this favorite of Orientalists' fantasies of the "East" is a collection of Southwest and South Asian stories of unknown date and authorship. They take place in a vast area stretching from present-day China and India to Central and West Asia and North Africa. The earliest known reference to the stories appears in the tenth century, identifying an alleged Persian book known as *Hezar afsaneh* (The Thousand Stories). Ultimately, they are a cumulative collection of tales (some colloquial) told over centuries (mainly orally and not by canonical writers). The oldest surviving manuscript of the tales is a fourteenth- or fifteenth-century Arabic text known as the Galland Manuscript, named after Antoine Galland, who produced the first European-language version of the collection of stories in 1717. An Arabic translation of Galland's French version was first printed in Calcutta in 1839 and then in Leiden in 1984. Yet the source of most translations is another Arabic version referred to as the "Vulgate text," first published in Cairo in 1835 and reprinted many times since then. See Reynolds 2006. For the significance of *The Thousand and One Nights* in Mernissi's work, see Abdo 2007; Dhar 2006; Gauch 2006; and Rhani 2015.

kills her at night after consummating the marriage. Scheherazade, the vizier's daughter who wants to save her younger sister and other virgins, asks her father to give her hand in marriage to the king. Her plan is to tell a story every night and leave it incomplete to keep the king interested. Storytelling and weaving stories into one another become Scheherazade's strategy of survival and Mernissi's strategy of trespassing.

Mernissi uses Scheherazade's stories not to satisfy Orientalist fantasies but to highlight the messiness and contradiction of women's solidarity and liberation through telling their stories in fabular form. On the terrace of the harem, after the reenactment of the women's street march in 1919 and Huda Sha'rawi's story, the women and children reenact the story of Princess Budur of *The Thousand and One Nights*. Mernissi writes, "Scheherazade's women of *A One Thousand and One Nights* did not write about liberation—they went ahead and lived it, dangerously and sensuously, and they always succeeded in getting themselves out of trouble" (133). Describing the reenactment of the story of Princess Budur, whose husband, Prince Qamar al-Zaman, mysteriously disappears in the middle of the desert, Mernissi writes, "At this point, we children, sitting behind Princess Budur's tent, would make all sorts of noises to indicate that the caravan was waking up. Samir was superb at imitating the horse noises and jumping about, and would only stop reluctantly when Chama, as Princess Budur, started reflecting out loud about the solitude and the powerlessness of a woman who suddenly finds herself without a husband" (140). Mernissi skillfully tells the story within the story: "If I go out and tell the valets," says Princess Budur, "and let them learn that my husband is lost, they will lust after me: there is no help for it but that I use stratagem" (140). We learn through Mernissi that Budur wears her husband's clothes and continues with her entourage until they arrive at the City of Ebony, where King Armanus insists on marrying off his daughter, Hayat al-Nufus, to Budur, now the counterfeit Qamar al-Zaman. Mernissi engages her reader with both stories by relaying the humorous harem reenactment of Budur's dilemma in risking death if she refuses the king's proposition or if Hayat al-Nufus finds out about her lie:

> While Chama paced back and forth, dramatizing Princess Budur's dilemma, the audience split into two camps. The first camp suggested that she tell the King the truth, because if she let him know that she was a woman, he might fall in love with her and pardon her. The second camp suggested that it would be safer for her to accept the offer of marriage and then tell Princess Hayat everything, once in the bridal suite, because that would trigger women's solidarity. Women's solidarity was actually a highly sensitive issue in the courtyard, since the women rarely sided all together against men. Some of the women, like Grandmother Lalla Mani and Lalla Radia, who were in favor of harems, always went along with the men's decisions, while women like Mother did not. In fact, Mother accused women who allied themselves with men as being largely responsible for women's suffering. "These women are more dangerous than men," she would explain, "because physically, they look just like us. But they are really wolves posing as sheep. If women's solidarity existed, we would not be stuck on this terrace. We would be traveling around Morocco or even sailing to the City of Ebony if we want to." (141)

Mernissi describes the joy that women and children in the harem of her childhood share when Budur chooses "women's solidarity" and gets married to Hayat al-Nufus: "We on the terrace celebrated the wedding, with Samir and I handing out cookies. Once, Chama tried to argue that since a marriage between two women is not legal, cookies need not be distributed. But the audience reacted at once. 'The cookie rule must be respected. You never mentioned that the marriage had to be legal'" (142).

Budur's attempts to defer the consummation of her/his marriage with Princess Hayat al-Nufus is playfully described in the young Mernissi's voice: "Samir and I would rush forward to let down the drapes and thereby show that one night had passed. Then we would raise the drapes again and the poor husband would still be praying while Hayat al-Nufus sat waiting to be kissed. We would do this again and again, with the husband always praying, the wife always waiting, and the whole audience roaring with laughter" (142). The frustrated Hayat al-Nufus finally complains to her father about the pious groom. Budur has no choice but to trust Hayat al-Nufus and tell her the whole story and ask her for help. Hayat al-Nufus sympathizes with Budur, and they stage a fake virginity ceremony.

At stake is not whether Budur's drag and the women's reenactment and endorsement of two women's marriage are necessarily transgressive, subversive, or queer. Instead, Mernissi's retelling of this tale and its reenactment in the harem is an example of how women's acts of resistance and their contradictory and contentious alliances in *Dreams of Trespass* complicate biological and heteronormative forms of kinship. As a performance of renewal and generation, the staging of Budur's story on the terrace embodies what Elizabeth Freeman calls "to be long and to belong"—that is, a form of kinship that "encompass[es] not only the desire to impossibly extend our individual existence or to reserve relationships that will invariably end, but also to have something queer exceed its own time, even to imagine that excess *as* queer in ways that getting married or having children might not be" (2007, 299, emphasis in original). Mernissi's stories of the harem and the embodied rituals of storytelling engender forms of attachment and "techniques of renewal" that are sustained over time—a queer kinship that exceeds heteronormative forms of blood kinship.[7] As such, *Dreams of Trespass* can help

---

7. Freeman makes a compelling argument about why, rather than abandon kinship as always-already heterosexual and incompatible with queer theory and politics, we should develop a different sense of kinship as a "technique of renewal"—a process by which "bodies and potential for physical and emotional attachment are created, transformed, and sustained over time" (2007, 298). In contrast to state recognition based on a legal identity that grants personhood, designates legibility and illegibility, and relegates the needy to abstract structures of privilege and abjection, Freeman argues, renewal is a bodily practice that is temporal and grants a future with "uninevitable form" (299).

us rethink queer in order to move not only beyond sexual identities but also beyond the analytical marriage and coupledom between queer and antinormativity. Just as Scheherazade perpetually defers her death through "being long" and by enabling a future through longing, Mernissi tells stories of the past, of the "forgotten queens of Islam" (see Mernissi 1993), through *doing* kinship and being long.

Unlike Orientalist depictions of it, the harem in Mernissi's fabular articulation is neither a valorized space of polyamory and polygamy where anything goes nor a repressive space where women's creativity and freedom are curtailed. It is where women *do* kinship through both *repeating* codes of conduct and trespassing those codes through *renewing* alliances across time. Kinship in Mernissi's *Dreams of Trespass* is a "technique of renewal" and a cultural force that recharge bodies toward love, play, and even violence. Her account of the harem is filled with women's homosociality. Therein, divorced women, former slaves, cowives, and children rehearse techniques of renewal, which include observing codes of conduct, whether the invisible rule, or *qa'ida*, as Yasmina teaches or *hudud*, as Mernissi learns in her Qur'an school. They also feature the trespassing of those codes in corporeal practices on the rooftop, in makeshift theater and games on the terrace, and in embroidering, dancing, performing possession, and telling stories.

Mernissi's formulation of kinship in *Dreams of Trespass* also unsettles the biological models of kinship with which anthropology has long grappled. Women's alliance in Mernissi's *Dreams of Trespass* offers alternatives ways of thinking about kinship through stories.[8]

---

8. David M. Schneider writes, "The European and the anthropological notion of consanguinity, of blood relationship and descent, rest[s] on precisely the opposite kind of value. It rests more on the state of being . . . on the biogenetic relationship which is represented by one or another variant of the symbol of 'blood' (consanguinity), or on 'birth,' on qualities rather than on performance. We have tried to impose this definition of a kind of relation on all peoples, insisting that kinship consists in relations of consanguinity and that kinship as consanguinity is a universal condition" (1984, 72).

Much like David Schneider's idea of kinship as "performance, forms of doing, [and] various codes for conduct" (1984, 72), Mernissi's story decenters the Eurocentric obsession with descent, consanguinity, and blood relationships. Instead, it is through *doing* kinship and *repeating and trespassing* the "codes of conduct" that those who occupy Mernissi's harem move beyond the logic of procreation and form kinship alliances. Mernissi does not sketch a romanticized notion of women's solidarity based on transgressions or a shared womanhood. She shows the conflicting and ambivalent relationship of women to each other, to the men in the harem, to the nationalists, and to the colonizers. For Mernissi, these practices of solidarity are not reducible to an idealized notion of egalitarian and horizontal comradeship. Rather, they highlight differences of status, wealth, and power that mark life in the harem. The messy and chaotic configurations of kinship in Mernissi's childhood are captured in techniques of renewal that seek to normalize couple relationships and liberal notions of personhood and choice, while complying with patriarchal notions of family in the harem. The appeal and the romance of the Anglo-European heteronormative family to Mernissi's mother and some of the other women in the harem lie in the ideology of the bourgeois family, where individuals as interest-free humans are to practice citizenship without local attachments and specificities. Mernissi, however, shows that the abstract notion of the individual does not account for the bodily practices of renewal and dependence that exceed the model of the modern heterosexual nuclear family. (For critical studies of the family in the Middle East, see Joseph 2018.) Recounting the harem occupants' staging of the early twentieth-century feminists on the harem terrace, Mernissi writes, "Deep down, though, the problem with feminists' lives was that they did not have enough singing and dancing in them" (132). She quotes Aunt Habiba as saying, "Why rebel and change the world if you can't get what's missing in your life? And what is most definitely missing in our lives is love and lust. Why organize a revolution if the new world is going to be an emotional desert?" (133). Even as Mernissi advocates feminism, she sees the promise of individualism and liberal citizenship to be tied to a lack of sensuality: an emotional desert with no attachments.

Mernissi's childhood life in the harem cannot be reduced to confinement or to reproduction of the laws of gender and/or kinship. Rather, it is through embodied practices and storytelling rituals that women and children forge what Pierre Bourdieu calls "practical kinship," a "field of relationships *constantly* reused and thus reactivated for future use" (1977, 52, emphasis in original). These rituals—whether embroidering or performing on the terrace or doing something else—transmit, transgress, and reactivate codes of conduct through temporal bonds. Even if the harem is also a space of "official kinship" where law (of marriage) or cultural norms are reproduced, the embodied practices and rituals in the harem sustain modes of belonging that exceed the law. To borrow from Freeman, the "substance" of habitus is not visually or spatially structured but rather temporally structured (2007, 308). Kinship as habitus involves practices of honor, cultivated corporeal disposition, and sharing that are transmitted over time. The temporality of modes of belonging, the repetition of performances of kinship, and the deferral and the timing of bodily gestures and rituals, rather than codified formalism, constitute practical kinship. Such kinship is to "hold out a hand across time and touch the dead or those not born yet, to offer oneself beyond one's own time" (Freeman 2007, 299). Mernissi's women transmit *and* trespass codes of conduct not just through codified rules of the harem but also through "cultivated dispositions" fostered over time in their practices of kinship. As such, in its fabular narration of the mundane, *Dreams of Trespass* can offer an epistemological shift in the understanding of kinship within a nexus of nationalism, colonialism, and geopolitics.

Mernissi's characterization of her childhood "harem" allows for articulations of queer kinship and space beyond the binarized constructs of homo/hetero desire. To think kinship through *Dreams of Trespass* is to enable the imagining of queer bonds that exceed modernist sexual identities and challenge transgression as a queer prerequisite. Mernissi provides an epistemological and pedagogical grounding wherein antinormativity and the wholesale dismissal of blood kin are not conditions of queerness. She pushes against the limits of the nuclear family without undermining the significance of blood kin for nonwhite queers who cannot afford to lose family bonds in the face of racism, xenophobia, and Islamophobia. After all, the privilege to leave behind one's biological family to find queer kin in metropolitan gay centers is often not afforded to many nonwhite queer and trans folks for whom maintaining ties to blood kin and family is a strategy of survival.

Epistemological Displacements and Temporal Areas

> Once they looked at that Simorgh
> Without doubt, this Simorgh was the reflection of those thirty birds
> They saw themselves, thirty whole birds
> Thirty birds in totality were Simorgh
> —Farid-ud-Din Attar Nishapuri, *Mantiq ut-Tayr*
> (my translation)

As mentioned earlier, despite its epistemological contributions to theorizing community, homecoming, and kinship, Mernissi's *Dreams of Trespass* is ignored in US academia. The sidelining of texts about gender and sexuality in the Middle East in gender, women, sexuality, and especially queer theory courses in the United States compels us to ask: How do we choose the texts that we in the United States teach as proper objects of study? Why is Mernissi's work fitting for a women's studies class that focuses on the Muslim and Arab worlds but not for a general-education or queer studies course? Is *Dreams of Trespass* irrelevant to queer studies? Is it too dated? Is it too heteronormative? Is it not queer enough? Or is it *too* queer and *too* perverse? Is it too scandalous to teach students in US colleges and universities that "the more masters one had, the more freedom and the more fun" (152)? In compelling us to face the familiar Orientalist and Eurocentric epistemologies that underlie queer contestations to the normative, is Mernissi's *Dreams of Trespass* too uncanny to teach? Or is it not taught because, as Ella Shohat aptly notes, "when gender is invoked outside of 'western spaces' it is often subjected in the academy to an interdisciplinary order that anxiously and politely sends it 'back' to the kingdom of area studies" (2006, 1)?

The omission in queer and feminist studies of texts that center knowledge production from "elsewhere" points to the Eurocentrism of queer and feminist studies in US academia. Epistemologies that inform US queer studies and queer theory generate *proper* texts and *proper* objects of study, wherein only certain texts are seen as properly queer to teach in queer studies courses in the United States. Minoo Moallem has aptly called this epistemological dilemma "emplacement of dismembering"—the dual process of making certain texts canonical and "forgetting the social and historical conditions that lead to this form of memorizing" (2002, 370). This form of canonization, which queer theory purports to undo, often dismisses Middle East women's and gender studies texts as heteronormative, attached to the repressive structure of the family and kin, and too atavistic for queer studies classrooms. In other words, as Anjali Arondekar and Geeta Patel (2016) argue, queer remains squarely the property of the Euro-American traditions. As such, certain theoretical concepts become hegemonic ways to think, write, teach, get tenure, and—ultimately—matter queerly. Queer theory, as such, reproduces its own canons and norms through regurgitating a few fashionable (and marketable) concepts, despite its antinormative and anticanonical claims.

Of course, pedagogical practices are not the only realm in which Euro-American queer theory becomes canonical. The sanctification of queer theory as a Euro-American body of knowledge is equally entrenched in research conventions that include citational practices, critique, and interpretation of texts and ethnographic data that repeat overdetermined articulations of "queer."[9] For those of us whose

---

9. Needless to say, my critique of queer studies is not a claim of my own transcendence of its faults. It is a recognition of my complicity within the academic disciplines and interdisciplinary fields to which I belong. Despite my insistence on undoing queer theory's whiteness and Eurocentrism, I am the first to admit that as a student of anthropology, queer theory, and women and gender studies in the

research is situated at the crossroads of Middle East studies, queer theory, gender and women's studies, and anthropology, navigating epistemological hierarchies in practices of citation, field formation, and site designation cannot be taken lightly. At times, such hierarchies and divisions deem certain forms of interdisciplinary research too diasporic, not area studies enough, not ethnographic enough, not trans enough, not queer enough, or not woman-centered enough. This division where theory is pure and arealess, even as the United States is ubiquitously the area, while the "area" is a special topic and auxiliary, often determines the way that queer studies scholars design curricula. The ghettoization of "area" is unsettling when the traffic in "transnational feminist studies" or "transnational queer and trans studies" is either a multiculturalist gesture that renders transnational as a one-way flow from "the West to the rest" or a reductionist notion of globalization as "Coca-Cola-ization." In such renditions, *transnational* is often a synonym for *international* and *comparative*, a departmental marketing technique in the race for grants and students.[10] The seemingly transnational queer scholarship as such ultimately recenters Euro-American epistemologies by queering the area or adding queer to the area. In such iterations of transnational queer scholarship, area, which is always and necessarily elsewhere, is never studied in relation to "other areas," while American studies as the hub of queer theory becomes "arealess" and the default location from where queer emanates.[11]

United States, I never considered Mernissi's work as significant to my graduate training. Being interrogated about the non-US centered content of my queer theory course for my first tenure-track job by a senior faculty member who asked disapprovingly, "How is this queer theory?," was a sobering moment to realize that a queer theory course with citations and sites that decenter the US queer canon "counts" only as "special topics" and not as theory.

10. Inderpal Grewal and Karen Caplan (2001) have aptly problematized the Eurocentric studies of sexuality and the uses of the term *transnational*.

11. For an excellent analysis of the division between area studies and queer theory, see Arondekar and Patel 2016.

Undermining queer theory that advances from area studies as a special case study is often coupled with the dismissal of this scholarship as unqueer and heteronormative, if not atavistic. For example, when a colleague suggested a certain text by a Middle Eastern scholar in response to my social media call for texts to be taught in a graduate seminar titled "Queer Geopolitics," another fellow anthropologist and queer theory scholar working in the United States objected that said text was good but needed to be "queered." In such queer territorial entitlements, US-centered queer scholars who have laid claim to queer theory often expect that the object of study be transgressions or injuries that center sex, gender, and sexuality, especially in their overdetermined Euro-American articulations that ignore injuries produced by imperial and settler-colonial violence. As Maya Mikdashi and Jasbir Puar argue, an ostensibly arealess queer studies has become the turf of American studies. Mikdashi and Puar aptly point out that "the work of queer theorists in area studies (rarely read by queer theory as 'Queer Theory' and often relegated to 'sexuality studies') is understood as a 'case study' of specifics rather than an interruption of the canonical treatments of the area studies field at large." They ask, "Should we remain wedded to queer theory's general obsession and commitment to the sexualized human form to recognizable 'queer sexualities,' given that the war on terror has thus far killed at least 1.3 million people (a conservative estimate) in Iraq, Afghanistan, and Pakistan alone?" (2016, 216, 220).

To read Mernissi's *Dreams of Trespass* as a valuable text in queer theory and kinship theory, then, is not to present it as an exception or an exemplar. It is to render the estranged and irrelevant as familiar and relevant, while highlighting the uneven geopolitical relations that some of us cannot afford to dismiss in our queer analyses. As Arondekar and Patel aptly point out, critical engagement between geopolitics and queer theory remains limited. They write, "With a few exceptions, the citational underpinnings that provide the theoretical conduit for such explorations were and continue to be resolutely contemporary and drawn primarily from the United States; that is, geopolitics provides the exemplars, but rarely the epistemologies"

(2016, 152). Ella Shohat has also raised this point in her analysis of the disciplinary divides among ethnic studies, American studies, area studies, postcolonial theory, and gender and women's studies (2006, 1–16). Shohat argues that to place gender and sexuality studies (and, I would add, queer studies), American and ethnic studies, area studies, and postcolonial studies in critical dialogue would require a relational approach and a "multichronotopic form of analysis." Such an analysis would "place the often-ghettoized histories, geographies, and discourses in politically and epistemologically synergetic relations" to show how pasts and presents, and the local and the global overlap and compete with one another" (15).

If we are serious about displacing queer theory's Eurocentrism and its geopolitical investments in "the global North," we need to teach and cite gender and sexuality studies texts from the "Middle East" beyond their designation as estranged exemplars or exceptions.[12] This epistemological decentering requires a critical politics of citation and translation that would, instead of reproducing/recentering the Euro-American queer canon through "citing up," take seriously what it currently dismisses as "area studies"—a politics of citation that refuses the normalization of antinormativity, unsettles the epistemological privileging and uncritical deployments of theoretical concepts that overshadow geopolitics, and resists the desire for innovation and neologism that underlies the relegation of texts from "elsewhere" as provincial, temporally lagging, and unqueer. This is not an easy task, given the neoliberal rhetoric of competition that is deeply engrained in the processes of publishing and tenure. Yet making this epistemological shift is what many scholars of gender and sexuality in the Middle East have been doing, even if their

---

12. These epistemological and pedagogical questions are addressed beautifully and lyrically by Richa Nagar in *Hungry Translations: Relearning the World through Radical Vulnerability* (2019). A collaboration with artists, students, and activists, Nagar's text is an embodiment of the work of alliance building and decentering of canonical knowledge.

work is dismissed by the canons of queer theory and Middle East studies. The scholarship on Middle Eastern sexuality and queer theory in multiple languages is vast and far from uniform in approach.[13]

It is only appropriate to end this essay with a story of kinship, immigration, and knowledge production. Those familiar with Mernissi's writing recognize the story of Simurgh in *Mantiq ut-Tayr* (*Conference of the Birds*), a book of poetry by the twelfth-century Persian Sufi poet Farid-ud-Din Attar Nishapuri (see Attar Mishapuri 2009 for the Arabic version and Attar 2011 for the English version). Simurgh, a mythological phoenixlike winged creature in Persian art and poetry, appears in many old Persian texts and is associated with knowledge, life, human–animal kinship, divinity, fertility, and healing. Simurgh's etymology goes back to Middle Persian, and the most

---

13. It is impossible to comprehensively cite the scholarship here, but it is important to point to at least some of it: Abusalim et al. 2018; al-Ali and Sayegh 2019; Allouche 2017, 2019; Alqaisiya 2018; Amar 2011, 2013; Amar and El Shakry 2013; Amer 2008; Atshan 2020; Atshan and Moore 2014; Farsakh, Kanaaneh, and Seikaly 2018a; Georgis 2013; Hasso 2018; Hatem 1987; al-Kassim and Deeb 2011a; Kiani 2019; Kuntsman 2009; Massad 2008; Meem 2009; Merabat 2014; Mikdashi 2013; Moallem 2011; Naber and Zaatari 2014; Najmabadi 2005, 2013; Özbay and Savcı 2018; al-Qasimi 2012; al-Qasimi and Kuntsman 2012a; al-Samman and El-Ariss 2013; Sari 2019; Hochberg 2010; Savcı 2016; El Shakry 2013; Yıldız 2014; and Zengin 2019. There are also special issues of academic journals, including the *Journal of Middle East Women's Studies* (al-Kassim and Deeb 2011b); the *Journal of Middle East Women's Studies* (al-Qasimi and Kuntsman 2012b); the *International Journal of Middle East Studies* (Baron and Pursley 2013), which includes a roundtable with Dina al-Kassim, Maya Mikdashi, Jasbir Puar, Sima Shakhsari, and Wilson Chacko Jacob titled "Queer Theory and Middle East Studies" ("Roundtable" 2013; introduced in Amar and El Shakry 2013); the *Journal of Palestine Studies* (Farsakh, Kanaaneh, and Seikaly 2018b), which also includes a roundtable with Nadine Naber, Sa'ed Atshan, Nadia Awad, Maya Mikdashi, Sofian Merabet, Dorgham Abusalim, and Nada Elia (see Naber et al. 2018). There is also the collection *Bareed Mista3jil* (Meem 2009), writings by queer Arab women. In addition, *Jadaliyya* and *Kohl* have published many articles about queer Middle East authored by scholars and activists, some of whom are cited here.

famous appearance of this mythical creature happens in Ferdowsi's *Shahnameh* (*Book of Kings*) of the eleventh century CE (for the translation, see Ferdowsi 2016). I am more interested in Simurgh's symbolic significance in *Mantiq ut-Tayr*. In his Sufi poetry, Attar plays with the name "Simurgh" (*si* means "thirty" in modern Persian, and *morgh* means "bird") to tell the story of a flock of pilgrim birds searching for Simurgh, a mythical bird that symbolizes truth. At the end of their long journey across seven valleys, which only thirty of the flock survive, the birds look at their reflection in a lake near Simurgh's alleged residence. It is only upon this collective reflection that the birds realize they *are* the Simurgh that they have been seeking all along. Perhaps we do not need to travel seven valleys in search of queer theory. The Simurgh is us!

References

Abdo, Diya M. 2007. "Narrating Little Fatima: A Picture Is Worth 1001 Tales—'Multiple Critique' in Mernissi's *Dreams of Trespass: Tales of a Harem Girlhood*." *Image [&] Narrative* 19. At https://www.imageandnarrative.be/inarchive/autofiction/abdo.htm.

Abu-Lughod, Lila. 1986. *Veiled Sentiments: Honor and Poetry in a Bedouin Society*. Berkeley: Univ. of California Press.

Abusalim, Dorgham, Sa'ed Atshan, Nadia Awad, Nada Elia, Sofian Merabet, Maya Mikdashi, and Nadine Naber. 2018. "On Palestinian Studies and Queer Theory." In "Queering Palestine," edited by Leila Farsakh, Rhoda Kanaaneh, and Sherene Seikaly. Special issue, *Journal of Palestine Studies* 47, no. 3: 62–71.

Akbarzadeh, Shahram, and Lorraine Barlow. 2006. "Women's Rights in the Muslim World: Reform or Reconstruction?" *Third World Quarterly* 27, no. 8: 1481–94.

Al-Ali, Nadje, and Ghiwa Sayegh. 2019. "Feminist and Queer Perspectives in West Asia: Complicities and Tensions." In *"Queer" Asia: Decolonising and Reimagining Sexuality and Gender*, edited by J. Daniel Luther and Jennifer Ung Loh, 243–65. London: Zed.

Allouche, Sabiha. 2017. "(Dis)-Intersecting Intersectionality in the Time of Queer Syrian Refugee-ness in Lebanon." *Kohl: A Journal for Body and Gender Research* 3, no. 1: 59–77.

———. 2019. "Love, Lebanese Style: Toward an Either/and Analytical Framework of Kinship." *Journal of Middle East Women's Studies* 15, no. 2: 157–78.

Alqaisiya, Walaa. 2018. "Decolonial Queering: The Politics of Being Queer in Palestine." In "Queering Palestine," edited by Leila Farsakh, Rhoda Kanaaneh, and Sherene Seikaly. Special issue, *Journal of Palestine Studies* 47, no. 3: 29–44.

Amar, Paul. 2011. "Turning the Gendered Politics of the Security State Inside Out? Charging the Police with Sexual Harassment in Egypt." *International Feminist Journal of Politics* 13:299–328.

———. 2013. *The Security Archipelago: Human-Security States, Sexuality Politics, and the End of Neoliberalism*. Durham, NC: Duke Univ. Press.

Amar, Paul, and Omnia El Shakry. 2013. "Introduction [to Roundtable]: Curiosities of Middle East Studies in Queer Times." In "Queer Affects," edited by Beth Baron and Sara Pursley. Special issue, *International Journal of Middle East Studies* 45, no. 2: 331–35.

Amer, Sahar. 2008. *Crossing Borders: Love between Women in Medieval French and Arabic Literatures*. Philadelphia: Univ. of Pennsylvania Press.

Arondekar, Anjali, and Geeta Patel. 2016. "Area Impossible: Notes Towards an Introduction." *GLQ: A Journal of Lesbian and Gay Studies* 22:151–71.

Atshan, Sa'ed. 2020. *Queer Palestine and the Empire of Critique*. Stanford, CA: Stanford Univ. Press.

Atshan, Sa'ed, and Darnell Moore. 2014. "Reciprocal Solidarity: Where the Black and Palestinian Queer Struggles Meet." *Biography* 37, no. 2: 680–705.

Attar, Farid-ud-Din. 2011. *The Conference of Birds: The Sufi's Journey to God*. Translated by Afkham Darbandi and Dick Davis. N.p.: Aziloth.

Attar Nishapuri, Farid-ud-Din. 2009. *Mantiq ut-Tayr*. Tehran, Iran: Nashr-e Ferdows.

Badran, Margot. 2009. *Feminism in Islam: Secular and Religious Convergences*. Oxford: Oneworld.

Baron, Beth, and Sara Pursley, eds. 2013. "Queer Affects." Special issue, *International Journal of Middle East Studies* 45, no. 2.

Ben Youssef Zayzafoon, Lamia. 2005. *The Production of the Muslim Woman: Negotiating Text, History, and Ideology*. New York: Lexington.

Bourdieu, Pierre. 1977. *Outline of a Theory of Practice*. Translated by Richard Nice. Cambridge: Cambridge Univ. Press.
cooke, miriam. 2000. "Multiple Critique: Islamic Feminist Strategies." *Nepantala* 1, no. 1: 91–110.
———. 2001. *Women Claim Islam: Creating Islamic Feminism through Literature*. New York: Routledge.
Dhar, Nandini. 2006. "Narratives of Everyday Resistance and Politics of Feminist Self-Representation in Mernissi's *Dreams of Trespass*." *Intersections: Women's and Gender Studies in Review across Disciplines* 4:15–33.
Farsakh, Leila, Rhoda Kanaaneh, and Sherene Seikaly. 2018a. "Introduction to 'Queering Palestine.'" In "Queering Palestine," edited by Leila Farsakh, Rhoda Kanaaneh, and Sherene Seikaly. Special issue, *Journal of Palestine Studies* 47, no. 3: 7–12.
———, eds. 2018b. "Queering Palestine." Special issue, *Journal of Palestine Studies* 47, no. 3.
Ferdowsi, Abolqasem. 2016. *Shahnameh: The Persian Book of Kings*. Translated by Dick Davis. New York: Penguin Classics.
Freeman, Elizabeth. 2007. "Queer Belongings: Kinship Theory and Queer Theory." In *A Companion to Lesbian, Gay, Bisexual, Transgender, and Queer Studies*, edited by George E. Haggerty and Molly McGarry, 293–314. Oxford: Wiley Blackwell.
Gauch, Suzanne. 2006. *Liberating Shahrazad: Feminism, Postcolonialism, and Islam*. Minneapolis: Univ. of Minnesota Press.
Georgis, Dina. 2013. "Thinking Past Pride: Queer Arab Shame in *Bareed Mista3jil*." *International Journal of Middle East Studies* 45, no. 2: 233–51.
Grewal, Inderpal, and Karen Caplan. 2001. "Global Identities: Theorizing Transnational Studies of Sexuality." *GLQ: A Journal of Lesbian and Gay Studies* 7, no. 4: 663–79.
Hasso, Frances. 2010. *Consuming Desires: Family Crisis and the State in the Middle East*. Stanford, CA: Stanford Univ. Press.
———. 2018. "Masculine Love and Sensuous Reason: The Affective and Spatial Politics of Egyptian Ultras Football Fans." *Gender, Place, and Culture* 25, no. 10: 1423–47.
Hatem, Mervat. 1987. "Class and Patriarchy as Competing Paradigms for the Study of Middle Eastern Women." *Comparative Studies in Society and History* 29, no. 4: 811–18.

Hochberg, Gil. 2010. "'Check Me Out': Queer Encounters in Sharif Waked's Chic Point: Fashion for Israeli Checkpoints." *GLQ: A Journal of Lesbian and Gay Studies* 16, no. 4: 577–97.
Hoodfar, Homa. 1997. *Between Marriage and the Market: Intimate Politics and Survival in Cairo.* Berkeley: Univ. of California Press.
Joseph, Suad. 1993. "Connectivity and Patriarchy among Urban Working-Class Arab Families in Lebanon." *Ethos* 21, no. 4: 452–84.
———. 2005. "The Kin Contract and Citizenship in the Middle East." In *Women and Citizenship*, edited by Marilyn Friedman, 149–69. Oxford: Oxford Univ. Press.
———, ed. 2018. *Arab Family Studies: Critical Reviews.* Syracuse, NY: Syracuse Univ. Press.
Al-Kassim, Dina, and Lara Deeb. 2011a. "Introduction." In "Middle East Sexualities," edited by Dina al-Kassim and Lara Deeb. Special issue, *Journal of Middle East Women's Studies* 7, no. 3: 1–5.
———, eds. 2011b. "Middle East Sexualities." Special issue, *Journal of Middle East Women's Studies* 7, no. 3.
Kholoussy, Hanan. 2010. "Monitoring and Medicalising Male Sexuality in Semi-colonial Egypt." *Gender and History* 22, no. 3: 677–91.
Kholoussy, Hanan, and Kristin Celello, eds. 2016. *Domestic Tensions, National Anxieties: Global Perspectives on Marriage, Crisis, and Nation.* New York: Oxford Univ. Press.
Kiani, Shahram. 2019. *Barrasi-ye tarikhi-ye na-jonbesh-e koeir-e Irani.* Stockholm, Sweden: Kitab-i Arzan.
Kuntsman, Adi. 2009. *Figurations of Violence and Belonging: Queerness, Migranthood, and Nationalism in Cyberspace and Beyond.* Bern, Switzerland: Peter Lang, 2009.
Majid, Anouar. 1998. "The Politics of Feminism in Islam." *Signs: Journal of Women in Culture and Society* 23, no. 2: 321–61.
Massad, Joseph A. 2008. *Desiring Arabs.* Chicago: Univ. of Chicago Press.
Meem. 2009. *Bareed Mista3jil: True Stories.* Beirut: Meem.
Merabat, Sofian. 2014. *Queer Beirut.* Austin: Univ. of Texas Press.
Mernissi, Fatema. 1975. *Beyond the Veil: Male–Female Dynamics in Muslim Society.* Cambridge, MA: Schenckman.
———. 1987. *Le harem politique: Le Prophète et les femmes.* Paris: Albin Michel.

———. 1990. *Sultanes oubliées: Femmes chefs d'état en Islam.* Paris: Albin Michel.

———. 1991. *The Veil and the Male Elite: A Feminist Interpretation of Women's Rights in Islam.* Translated by Mary Jo Lakeland. Cambridge, MA: Perseus.

———. 1992a. *Islam and Democracy: Fear of the Modern World.* Translated by Mary Jo Lakeland. New York: Basic.

———. 1992b. *La peur-modernité: Conflit Islam démocratie.* Paris: Albin Michel.

———. 1993. *The Forgotten Queens of Islam.* Translated by Mary Jo Lakeland. Minneapolis: Univ. of Minnesota Press.

———. 1994. *Dreams of Trespass: Tales of a Harem Girlhood.* Cambridge, MA: Perseus.

———. 2001. *Scheherazade Goes West: Different Cultures, Different Harems.* New York: Washington Square Press.

Mikdashi, Maya. 2013. "Queering Citizenship, Queering Middle East Studies." In "Queer Affects," edited by Beth Baron and Sarah Pursley. Special issue, *International Journal of Middle East Studies* 45, no. 2: 350–52.

Mikdashi, Maya, and Jasbir Puar. 2016. "Queer Theory and Permanent War." *GLQ: A Journal of Lesbian and Gay Studies* 22, no. 2: 215–22.

Mir-Hosseini, Ziba. 1993. *Marriage on Trial: A Study of Islamic Family Law in Iran and Morocco.* London: I. B. Tauris.

Moallem, Minoo. 2002. "Women of Color in the U.S.: Pedagogical Reflections on the Politics of 'the Name.'" In *Women's Studies on Its Own: A Next Wave Reader in Institutional Change*, edited by Robyn Wiegman, 368–82. Durham, NC: Duke Univ. Press.

———. 2011. "Passing, Politics, and Religion." *The Scholar & Feminist Online* 9, no. 3. At http://sfonline.barnard.edu/religion/moallem_01.htm#text1.

Naber, Nadine, Sa'ed Atshan, Nadia Awad, Maya Mikdashi, Sofian Merabet, Dorgham Abusalim, and Nada Elia. 2018. "Roundtable: On Palestinian Studies and Queer Theory." In "Queering Palestine," edited by Leila Farsakh, Rhoda Kanaaneh, and Sherene Seikaly. Special issue, *Journal of Palestine Studies* 47, no. 3: 62–71.

Naber, Nadine, and Zeina Zaatari. 2014. "Reframing the War on Terror: Feminist and Lesbian, Gay, Bisexual, Transgender, and Queer

(LGBTQ) Activism in the Context of the 2006 Israeli Invasion of Lebanon." *Cultural Dynamics* 26, no. 1: 91–111.

Nagar, Richa. 2019. *Hungry Translations: Relearning the World through Radical Vulnerability*. Champaign: Univ. of Illinois Press.

Najmabadi, Afsaneh. 2005. *Women with Mustaches and Men without Beards: Gender and Sexual Anxieties of Iranian Modernity*. Berkeley: Univ. of California Press.

———. 2013. *Professing Selves: Transsexuality and Same-Sex Desire in Contemporary Iran*. Durham, NC: Duke Univ. Press.

Özbay, Cenk, and Evren Savcı. 2018. "Queering Commons in Turkey." *GLQ: A Journal of Lesbian and Gay Studies* 24, no. 4: 516–21.

Al-Qasimi, Noor. 2012. "The 'Boyah' and the 'Baby Lady': Queer Mediations in Al Qadiri and Khalid Al Gharaballi's WaWa Series (2011)." *Journal of Middle East Women's Studies* 8, no. 3: 139–42.

Al-Qasimi, Noor, and Adi Kuntsman. 2012a. "Introduction." In "Queering Middle Eastern Cyberspaces," edited by Noor al-Qasimi and Adi Kuntsman. Special issue, *Journal of Middle East Women's Studies* 8, no. 3: 1–13.

———, eds. 2012b. "Queering Middle Eastern Cyberscapes." Special issue, *Journal of Middle East Women's Studies* 8, no. 3.

Reynolds, Dwight F. 2006. "*A Thousand and One Nights*: A History of the Text and Its Reception." In *Arabic Literature in the Post-classical Period*, edited by Roger Allen and D. S. Richards, 270–91. Cambridge: Cambridge Univ. Press.

Rhani, Zakaria. 2015. "The Forbidden Orient! Endo-exoticism and Anti-anthropological Nationalism in the Writings of Some Contemporary Moroccan Intellectuals." In *After Orientalism: Critical Perspectives on Western Agency and Eastern Re-appropriations*, edited by François Poullion and Jean-Claude Vatin, 48–63. Leiden, Netherlands: Brill.

Rhouni, Raja. 2010. *Secular and Islamic Feminist Critiques in the Work of Mernissi*. Leiden, Netherlands: Brill.

"Roundtable: Queer Theory and Middle East Studies." 2013. Featuring Jasbir Puar, Sima Shakhsari, Dina al-Kassim, Wilson Chacko Jacob, and Maya Mikdashi. In "Queer Affects," edited by Beth Baron and Sara Pursley. Special issue, *International Journal of Middle East Studies* 45, no. 2: 331–52.

Al-Samman, Hanadi, and Tarek El-Ariss. 2013. "Queer Affects: Introduction." In "Queer Affects," edited by Beth Baron and Sara Pursley. Special issue, *International Journal of Middle East Studies* 45, no. 2: 205–9.

Sari, Elif. 2019. "Lesbian Refugees in Transit: The Making of Authenticity and Legitimacy in Turkey." In "Migrant and Refugee Lesbians: Lives That Resist the Telling," edited by Eithne Luibhéid. Special issue, *Journal of Lesbian Studies* 24, no. 2: 140–58.

Savcı, Evren. 2016. "Who Speaks the Language of Queer Politics? Western Knowledge, Politico-cultural Capital and Belonging among Urban Queers in Turkey." *Sexualities* 19, no. 3: 369–87.

Schneider, David M. 1984. *A Critique of the Study of Kinship*. Chicago: Univ. of Chicago Press.

Sehlikoglu, Sertac, and Asli Zengin. 2016. "Introduction: Everyday Intimacies of the Middle East." *Journal of Middle East Women's Studies* 12, no. 2: 139–42.

El Shakry, Omnia. 2013. "Rethinking Entrenched Binaries in Middle East Gender and Sexuality Studies." *International Feminist Journal of Politics* 15, no. 1: 82–87.

Shohat, Ella. 2006. *Taboo Memories, Diasporic Voices*. Durham, NC: Duke Univ. Press.

Yıldız, Emrah. 2014. "Cruising Politics: Sexuality, Solidarity and Modularity after Gezi." In *The Making of a Protest Movement in Turkey: #occupygezi*, edited by Umut Özkırımlı, 103–20. Basingstoke, UK: Palgrave Macmillan.

Zengin, Aslı. 2016. "Violent Intimacies: Tactile State Power, Sex/Gender Transgression, and the Politics of Touch in Contemporary Turkey." *Journal of Middle East Women's Studies* 12, no. 2: 225–45.

———. 2019. "The Afterlife of Gender: Sovereignty, Intimacy and Muslim Funerals of Transgender Women in Turkey." *Cultural Anthropology* 34, no. 1: 78–102.

7

Boundary Breaking and Boundary Making

Fatema Mernissi's Paradoxical Narratives

SUAD JOSEPH

Fatema Mernissi ended her boundary-breaking book *Dreams of Trespass: Tales of a Harem Girlhood* (1994) by quoting an explanation she heard as a child as to why boys and girls are different:

> But why? . . . Why can't we escape the rule of difference? . . . Mina replied . . . it all starts when little girls are separated from little boys in the *hammam*. Then a cosmic frontier splits the planet in two halves. The frontier indicates the line of power because whenever there is a frontier, there are two kinds of creatures walking on Allah's earth, the powerful on one side and the powerless on the other.
>
> I asked Mina how would I know on which side I stood. Her answer was quick, short, and very clear: "If you can't get out, you are on the powerless side." (242)[1]

It is this imaginary of crossing frontiers, of trespass, that the memoir positions as its narrative center. She is the little girl who wants to wander into and past the courtyard, play with the boys, speak up at the family gatherings when there are guests, comment on the radio

---

1. Subsequent citations to *Dreams of Trespass* (Mernissi 1994) give just page numbers.

programs, ask questions when adults say things that are confusing or contradictory. That narrative center directs our gaze beyond the harem walls to the horizon, to the "over there," to someplace where we are not or not supposed to go.

It is the imagined "other space" that attracts; that queries and challenges the present space; that makes her wonder: Why the barrier? What is she missing by not being allowed to enter? What would she have or be enabled to do if she could "go there"? What is she disabled from by being closed out? The narrative directs us to consider her exclusion and the cosmic frontiers of power—as well as the structural and psychodynamic conditioning of having to stay within the boundaries.

I would like to suggest there is a paradoxical narrative center in the memoir that is shadowed in the title and might be seen as driving the discourse of the young Fatema's dreams: Mernissi's dream is about dismantling frontiers, breaking through boundaries, knocking down walls, rendering the world penetrable and accessible. Paradoxically, for those boundaries to fall, other boundaries must be built. The constant advice of the mentors she listens to and innocently follows is to stand up, to yell, to scream, not to give in or give up, not to allow herself to be pushed or bullied or trampled upon—not to rely on her male cousin Samir to protest for her but to protest on her own behalf, to put up her own defenses, to build her own shield—indeed, to erect her own self-boundary.

It is the building of the self-boundary that shadows the narrative—a boundary that is unspoken, unnamed with any specificity, but constantly struggled about and fought over by everyone around her. The shadow frontier that is fought over, I might suggest, is not only the visible material harem walls but also the personal boundaries of the self.

In the nine years of her life that Mernissi intimately describes in *Dreams of Trespass: Tales of a Harem Girlhood*, she explores the span of possibilities that her conflicted extended family members permit or promise for her. To a large degree, the men—her father, her uncle Ali, and her grandfather, Tazi, joined by Lalla Mani (her paternal grandmother), Lalla Thor (her maternal grandfather's first wife), and Lalla Radia (her cousin Chama's mother)—stand holding up the exterior walls and reinforcing the interior walls. Ahmed, the gatekeeper in Fez, is the largely reliable and dutiful enforcer. Walls are firm in their dwelling in the city of Fez, where they live most of the year with her parents. It is her family, her paternal grandmother, her uncle Ali, and his family of nine who are the players within the walls. Yet those exterior walls are not always firm; the interior walls can be porous. The times are changing.

Born in 1940, just sixteen years before Moroccan independence, Mernissi narrates critical aspects of the closing chapters of an era. The period 1940–49 is a period of tumult throughout Africa, the Middle East, and the world. That decade covers the upheavals of World War II, the national independence struggles of many African and Middle Eastern countries, the emergence of new regional politics and cultures, and a global economic and social transformation.

The end of World War II signals the end of the nineteenth- and early twentieth-century colonial empires; the rise of new nation-states throughout Africa, the Middle East, and the world; the global expansion of education; the transformation of economies; the coming explosion of populations; the massive migrations to cities and to the colonial metropole; the escalated incorporation of the grinding world markets. The Arab literary and scholarly renaissance had emerged, and pan-Arab nationalism was on the horizon. The worldwide movement of feminism had circulated throughout the region, and the precipice of its second wave was only a decade or so ahead. By 1956, Mernissi's mother was marching in an independence-day celebration. She returned with her hair exposed, never again to wear that scarf she did not want her daughter to wear.

The women of Mernissi's harem are already tuned into the possibilities that lie ahead. A number of them hunger for the external frontiers to collapse. Within themselves and with their children, some of the women lay the foundation for erecting different boundaries—the boundaries of the self. They live this making of the self particularly in the countryside home of Mernissi's maternal grandmother, Yasmina;

her maternal grandfather, Tazi; and his nine wives and their families. In the countryside, there are no walls, there are no gates, the frontier is harder to identify. The frontier can even be frightening because it is not material or visible.

The advocates for the self-making boundaries are her mother, her maternal grandmother, Yasmina, and her cousin Chama (Lalla Radia's daughter). The personification of these self-making projects include a host of women who pass by the country home of Mernissi's maternal grandparents: Tamou, the Riffan who rides into their lives on horseback as a war heroine; Asmahan, the Lebanese singer who serenades them on Radio Cairo and whose life is continually staged for the women by cousin Chama; and the iconic Scheherazade, whose stories are told and enacted over and over as morality plays about women, words, and power.

Mernissi's maternal grandfather, Tazi, does not appear to stand in the way of the women who persist and argue logically (and Islamically) against the frontiers. Mernissi's father frequently relents to her mother's negotiations. Her male cousin Samir is her partner in every transgression—even stands in for her and her wishes by undertaking the protests on her behalf—until they have a parting of the ways at the end of the narrative when they are nine.

How do these paradoxical narratives of boundary breaking and boundary making unfold in Mernissi's telling of her childhood tales? How are the transparent tales of frontiers that must be torn down undergirded by the shadow stories of borders that must be built up? Mernissi deploys the voice and vision of her unformed child self to ask questions, to puzzle out, to prod the adults to speak clearly and consistently. Through the questions of innocents, she draws out the confusing, contradictory, illogical, unjustifiable world of walls. She articulates, through the voices of dreamers like herself, the vision and will for an unwalled world.

Ever present though less clearly signaled are the urgent instructions from the dreamers around her that to be free of the harem walls, she must build interior walls. In this chapter, I explore the intimate relationalities that invent spaces and facilitate the invention of spaces as sites of trespass, as pathways to the journey of boundary-breaking and bound-making selving. To consider these intertwined narratives, I explore a few of the tales Mernissi shares to excavate the landscape of frontiers she draws from her harem girlhood.

Tales of Learning Frontiers

Much of the first part of Mernissi's book of tales lays out the frontiers that she must not cross in her harem girlhood. "Education is to know the *hudud*, the sacred frontiers," she quotes her Qur'an teacher, Lalla Tam, as instructing her and the other children (3). Mernissi elaborates, "To be a Muslim was to respect the *hudud*. And for a child, to respect the *hudud* was to obey" (3). She talks about the happiness of her early childhood because the frontiers are crystal clear: she cannot go into the courtyard before her mother woke up (3); she cannot go into the men's salon; she cannot get to the radio, which is in a locked cabinet; she cannot go onto the terrace; she cannot go beyond the courtyard gate, which is guarded by Ahmed, the gatekeeper; and so forth. She learns that there are *hudud*—frontiers, borders—that she, as a good girl, a good daughter, a good Muslim, cannot cross.

In Mernissi's paternal home in Fez, Lalla Mani, her maternal grandmother, barricades herself with silence. She does not want to hear the sound of children splashing their feet in the courtyard. The carpet is a frontier—no wet feet on her flowered carpet (6–7). The children can see her twice a day—in the morning to kiss her hand and in the evening to kiss her hand.

The men's dining room is another frontier (7). Only men can use it. Only men have the keys to the cabinet with the radio. When her father learns, accidentally from Mernissi, that the women listen to the radio while the men are gone, he laments, "If they made a copy of the radio key, soon they'll make one to open the gate" (8).

When the women learn that Mernissi's father knows about their listening to the radio, they tell the children that the children have to keep secrets from the men; they cannot tell the "truth" if it hurts someone. The children become *"khai'n"*—traitors—for exposing the secret of the radio. Words become another boundary (8).

In Fez, women and children cannot step out of the gate without multiple permissions. The gate is guarded by Ahmed, a full-time gatekeeper. Ahmed chases after Chama when she escapes to accompany her brothers to the movies. He catches her and brings her back to the courtyard (21).

The women themselves are divided—they are never united against the men. Lalla Mani (Mernissi's paternal grandmother), Lalla Radia (Cousin Chama's mother), and Lalla Tam (the Qur'an teacher) are pro-harem. They want to hold up the walls (40). Lalla Thor, Mernissi's maternal grandfather's first wife, insists on hierarchy. She complains to her husband, Tazi, that Yasmina, Mernissi's maternal grandmother, does not respect hierarchy (31).

The women fight over putting either birds or traditional design in their embroidery. Mernissi's mother wants to put birds in the design. Lalla Mani wins the argument, and all have to do traditional design. Chama says the issue is not about the birds; it is about the women themselves: they want wings. Anyone should be able to have wings.

Fatema's father opposes his wife's wearing the lighter, more manlike djellaba; he wants her to wear the heavier haik. Mernissi's mother wants to live alone with just her nuclear family. Against his wife's wishes, Mernissi's father continues to make his family live in the communal home. He is worried that women are behaving like men, that men and women are becoming like the French and losing their cultural identity. He thinks that Qasim Amin, who wrote *Liberation of Women* in 1885, is destroying the harmony of the Arab marriage. Fatema's father does not want Fatema to become fluent in French or code-switch between French and Arabic or smoke cigarettes (like the French) (180). He says the "frontier protected cultural identity" (180). He does not want to lose Arab culture or have it become one culture with French.

Around her, Mernissi sees walls, frontiers, boundaries, barriers. She is constantly being taught to observe and obey the rules, to stay within the *hudud*—the frontiers.

Breaking Boundaries

Yet the young Mernissi has around her numerous boundary-challenging women and even some boundary-challenging men. Her maternal grandmother lives in the country, where there are no walls, no gates, no frontiers. At Yasmina's farm, they can ride horses, swim, climb trees—even though this place, too, is called a harem (39). Mernissi is at first afraid to sleep at the farm because the frontiers are not clear enough. Yasmina tells her it was Allah's original earth that had no frontiers (24–25). Yasmina, her daughter (Mernissi's mother), Mernissi's cousin Chama, and Aunt Habiba (abandoned by the husband she loved)—all are antiharem and speak ardently against it.

Mernissi's mother hates communal life (6). She wants a tête-à-tête with her husband. She insists that there should be no distinctions between wives in the harem based on age and wealth. Her husband's brother (older and wealthier than her husband) accepts her call for no distinctions—at least visible distinctions. Mernissi's mother sleeps late into the morning, has a late breakfast, and misses lunch—even though these acts are in violation of the house discipline and rhythm that Lalla Mani insists upon. Her husband breaks the discipline by providing his wife with whatever she wants to eat whenever she wants it. Mernissi's mother rejects male superiority as anti-Muslim. Mernissi and her cousin Samir were born the same day, one hour apart. Her mother insists on the same celebration for her daughter as for Samir. The men grant her wish (9).

Yasmina is critical of King Farouk because he threw out his wife, Princess Farida, when she did not produce a boy. She explains to Mernissi that only God determines the sex of a child (33). Yasmina explains to Mernissi that rules are unfair because they are not made by women (63). She teaches her that the way to know a rule is after the fact—when you violate it and suffer the violent consequences.

Even Mernissi's uncle Ali tells her father there is nothing wrong with taking a little girl to the mosque on Fridays in Fez. All her young male cousins dress themselves and cut their hair like the French (90), even though her father fears they are losing their cultural identity.

Yasmina names a duck "Thor" to mock her husband's authoritarian first wife (39), further challenging male authority and "tradition."

Mernissi hears and tells the story of Tamou, who, a Riffan and war heroine, arrives at the country house of Grandfather Tazi on horseback. Tamou has been traumatized by the killing of her husband, father, and two children, whom she buries on Tazi's farm. Tazi marries Tamou to give her a home. Yasmina, Mernissi's grandmother, helps Tamou through the trauma and even encourages her husband to invite Tamou to his bed to see if she wants to stay with them (51). Tamou can ride a horse fast, do acrobatics, swear in several languages (53). She is wild and free, and all the women love her, Mernissi fondly observes.

Yasmina, Mernissi's maternal grandmother, climbs trees and hangs out there for hours. Sometimes other women join her and have tea in the trees. She violates hierarchy, washes dishes in the river, insults her husband's first wife, and makes fun of men's whims and fantasies. Mernissi, the child, sees this violation of frontiers but also sees that Yasmina makes her husband laugh. That is what saves Yasmina (30).

Mernissi, Yasmina, and Tamou plant a banana tree to make Yaya, Tazi's Sudanese wife, feel at home in their country (55). Mernissi's takeaway from the planting is that "there was no limit to what women could do on the farm. They can grow unusual plants, ride horses, and move freely about, or so it seems. In comparison, our harem in Fez was like a prison" (54).

Making the Self-Boundaries

Surrounded by frontiers yet embraced by a band of women who constantly mock and challenge the frontiers (and by men who give in enough to undermine the frontiers), Mernissi has a houseful of models to follow. The derision of the harem's bounded culture is internally explicit and unequivocal in Mernissi's storytelling. Less clearly articulated and not named as such, though, are the implicit instructions to create self-boundaries to combat the social boundaries. Mernissi's tales are a running story of self-making. She is taught and given stories and examples to create her own self-frontiers, her own boundaries, to invent her self as a bounded person whose frontiers cannot easily be violated. The relationships she has in the harem allow her to develop the frontiers of her self.

Chama's stories tell her how harems came to exist as a result of men competing with each other for power (44–45). Chama adds that while men's power is no longer measured by the number of women they can imprison, nevertheless the Arab world is stuck in the days of Harun al-Rashid in the eighth century CE. Chama weaves stories of women's resistance to men's competition with each other by repeatedly telling the Scheherazade story as a story of women using words to protect themselves from men with power, such as King Shahryar. Chama reads that women, by withholding themselves sexually and withholding their words, can control men's violent wishes and desires (15–16). By withholding herself, she explains, a woman can even show a powerful man that he is locked in his own prison. The lesson is that being with the woman is what frees him.

Mernissi's mother constantly tells her not to cry or to let Samir do the protesting for her. She has to yell and scream and protest for herself whenever anything annoys her (although her mother admonishes her that she should not protest against her mother because that would lead to chaos) (9).

Grandmother Yasmina tells Mernissi to learn to be responsible for other children. Responsibility, more than just protest, will give her power. She teaches her to control herself as a way to achieve power (9). She tells her to chew her words and roll them over her tongue seven times before she lets them out. Power comes from self-control, is Grandmother Yasmina's message.

Aunt Habiba tells her stories about a woman with wings who is free to fly and roam (22). Mernissi's lesson from Aunt Habiba is that roaming freely in the streets is every woman's dream.

Mernissi's tale of her paternal grandmother, Lalla Mani, could also be read as a story of a woman creating her self-boundaries. Lalla Mani surrounds herself with silence. She wants to be left alone. She wants to stare out the window for hours. She does not want the sounds or presence of children. She builds a boundary around her self (6–7).

Mernissi observes that Grandfather Tazi has to bribe Grandmother Yasmina with a bracelet to get her to change the name of the duck from "Thor" (his first wife's name). She observes Yasmina refusing to change the name but agreeing to call the duck that name only privately in her mind—he gives her a bracelet for this. Tazi lets Yasmina and the women wash the dishes in the river when their argument to do so is logical. He excuses himself by gratefully acknowledging that in Islam responsibility is individual (69). The boundaries are negotiable, Mernissi learns from Yasmina and Tazi. One's boundaries are one's own responsibility—even according to Islam.

Yasmina tells Mernissi never to accept inequality. It is not logical, she argues (26). Yasmina rejects all inequality—whether based on wealth, hierarchy, or power (35). She tells Mernissi that even Yazi's rich first wife, Thor, is the same as the rest of the women because she, too, is stuck inside a harem. She gives Mernissi direct instruction on standing up to authority by standing up for herself, by not obeying, by always looking for where power is located, and by not conceding to it.

Yasmina teaches Mernissi that the harem is about private space and that the rules regulating it do not need walls. "Once you knew what was forbidden, you carried the harem within. You had it in your head, 'inscribed under your forehead and under your skin'" (61). The danger and the power of the harem, Yasmina warns her, are that the frontiers seep inside your mind.

"Wherever there are human beings, there is a qa'ida, or invisible rule. If you stick to the qa'ida, nothing bad can happen to you." Every space has its *qa'ida*, Yasmina instructs her. She cautions Mernissi that most of the *qa'ida* are against women (62), so Mernissi has to prepare herself for knowing where power is and where the rules are.

Mernissi observes all of her paternal uncles, except Uncle Ali and her father, moving out of the family compound in Fez. Their wives want private space, to be alone with their husbands and families. While her father wants to keep the large family together and to live with the family elders (77), her mother does not. She wants to be alone with her husband. In a harem, you have to live according to the group's rhythms. Her mother yearns for privacy, her right to establish her own frontiers, to live according to her own rhythms. She wants to get up late for breakfast and eat her own food. She does not want to eat lunch at Lalla Mani's time; she wants to listen to music and dance. Even her husband acknowledges the need for privacy and the occasional tête-à-tête dinners on the terrace at night.

Mernissi recounts how the women import their Muslim feminists from the East—Asmahan, Scheherazade, Aisha Taymour, Zaynab Fawwas, Huda Sha'rawi—women who toss their veils, make their own choices, and stand up (128). Princess Budur from *Thousand and One Nights* fools men by wearing men's clothing after her husband disappears. She journeys to try to find him. When another king likes her so much that he wants to marry her to his daughter, Princess Budur gives Mernissi another feminist lesson: Princess Budur tells the daughter of the king that she is a woman. The daughter protects her by marrying her, and they rule together (137). This, for the young Mernissi, is a true lesson in women's solidarity.

Asmahan is the most beloved figure to the women of the harem. Asmahan dresses in European clothes and dances and hugs men and loves elegance and is free and sensual and happy and frivolous. Om Khalthum is proper, wears long dresses, and sings only songs of the nation and noble things (104). Mernissi finds that Asmahan is the dream of individual happiness, of a self-indulgent life, oblivious to the demands of the clan and its codes (106). Through the stories of Asmahan, Mernissi and the women of the clan dream of individual boundaries—held firm against the clan, the extended family, and the society. Mernissi wants to grow up in the imaginary of Asmahan and reclaim her as someone who lives through her own choices (111).

Mernissi recounts Aunt Habiba telling her that when you are trapped and powerless in the harem, you dream of escape. Everyone has magic inside them and can bring it out to change their world. Aunt Habiba makes the children feel it is up to them to let that magic out, that they have choices (114). The harem is not their destiny.

Her mother is even more direct: "A happy woman was one who could exercise all kinds of rights, from the right to move to the right to create, compete and challenge, and at the same time could feel loved for doing so. . . . Happiness was also about the right to privacy, the right to retreat from the company of others and plunge into contemplative solitude" (80).

The lesson learned is that obedience is a violation of the boundaries of selving—power is creating one's own boundaries. There are boundaries everywhere. A woman protects herself from the social boundaries, from the hierarchal boundaries, from the patriarchal boundaries by growing her own internal boundaries, her self boundaries.

The more masters there are, the more freedom there is, Yasmina explains to her. Subversive revolutionary that she is, Yasmina instructs her to figure out who has *sulta* (power) and then shuffle the cards and confuse them (152). Even Mina, the escaped slave, tells Mernissi to look up to the sky, look up and surprise your master. You always have a choice to obey or to look up (171). Her mother tells Mernissi: "You are going to transform the world, aren't you? You are going to create a planet without walls and without frontiers, where the gatekeepers have off every day of the year" (201). In some ways, Yasmina, the grandmother, has more freedom than her daughter, Mernissi's mother.

The need for drawing self-boundaries and the cost of drawing self-boundaries come home to Mernissi at the end: Samir is no longer willing to play with her if she insists on taking time away from him to take care of her skin. He wants more of her; she wants more beauty. He makes her choose—him or the skin. "Skin first, Samir," she shouts, losing Samir and choosing the self-making boundary (219). Shortly thereafter comes the day when Samir is thrown out of the *hamman*, bathhouse, because he has "a man's stare" (239). Samir tells Mernissi that men do not need skin treatments because they have skins that are different from women's. They are nine years old. The difference is asserted. A boundary is created.

Boundaries, Relationalities, Connectivities

How are we to make sense of Mernissi's unloading and loading of boundaries? She does not tell us. She does not tell us because her narrative is one of trespass, of boundary crossing, of violation. She does not tell us because she sees her story is one of taking apart. The putting together—the doing, the making, the inventing—of boundaries is shadowed in her text, hidden behind the stories told to her by her mother, maternal grandmother, aunts, and cousins and faintly gestured to by the actions of her maternal grandfather, father, cousin Samir, and even uncle. It is the subtext of the stories of Asmahan and Scheherazade and Aisha Taymour and Zaynab Fawwas and Huda Sha'rawi. Without this subtext, the telling of the tales of a harem girlhood, I would argue, would not have been possible.

How do we make sense of the paradoxical relationship between boundary unmaking and boundary making? I would suggest that the dynamics entailed in *Dreams of Trespass* are the dynamics of patriarchal connectivity. I have theorized family relationships in Lebanon as an intersection of love and power, connectivity and patriarchy. Connective relationships in which each person feels very much a part of the other such that their boundaries are fluid and their interests and desires intimately inform each other are very common in the Arab region. Among the families in which I did extensive, long-term fieldwork in Lebanon, connectivity is understood as love (Joseph 1994). Patriarchy, the gendering and aging of power moralized and framed in kinship terms, is similarly common in the Arab region. Connectivity and patriarchy intersect to support relationships in which not only boundaries are highly fluid, but the power embedded in those relationships is also gendered and aged (Joseph 1994).

The relationships Mernissi describes in *Dreams of Trespass* very much resemble relationships that I encountered in both urban and village settings in Lebanon and that I consider expressions of patriarchal connectivity. The shadow text manifested subtly throughout Mernissi's text, I would argue, tells a story of challenging patriarchal connectivity. It reveals the dilemmas of love understood as the embedding of selves undergirded with gendered and aged power dynamics. It tells a story of a young child who is always taught she can make that challenge. That young child, Mernissi, ultimately chooses "skin first"—the primary boundary of the body.

References

Joseph, Suad. 1994. "Brother/Sister Relationships: Connectivity, Love, and Power in the Reproduction of Patriarch in Lebanon." *American Ethnologist* 21, no. 1: 50–73.

Mernissi, Fatima. 1994. *Dreams of Trespass: Tales of a Harem Girlhood*. Cambridge, MA: Perseus.

8

Fatema Mernissi's Situated Perspective
The Mirror Effect

FATIMA AIT BEN LMAMDANI
Translated from French by Paola Bacchetta

As a sociologist, a novelist, a fervent activist, and a woman, across all her writing, talks, and interviews, Fatema Mernissi tried to trespass borders imposed by the majority and to blur established disciplinary lines. Whether in her research on working-class Moroccan women (Mernissi 1986) or her novels that highlight Moroccan women's resistance strategies (Mernissi 1994, 1996) or her courageous questioning of the sacred texts of Muslim canonical law (Mernissi [1992] 2010) or her activism on behalf of women, Fatema Mernissi deeply influenced contemporary and future feminist research and women's struggles.

In this chapter, I seek to outline the contours of this Moroccan scholar's complex thought about how systems of power intersect and about her own situated perspective. This chapter is also an attempt

I am grateful to Nasima Moujoud and Meriem Rodary for introducing me to Fatema Mernissi's work during my doctoral research period. My sincere thanks also go to Zakia Salim and Houria Alami M'chichi for our dialogues, which helped me to understand Mernissi's thought more deeply. I thank Paola Bacchetta for the translation. Finally, I thank Paola Bacchetta and Minoo Moallem for moving me to reread Mernissi's work and rediscover it anew when they invited me to the conference they organized on Mernissi in 2016.

to link with current discussions on the concept of intersectionality in the French-speaking academy. Therein, intersectionality is used as a methodological tool to analyze social groups that are crisscrossed by multiple relations of power. Patricia Hill Collins defines intersectionality thus: "Intersectionality is an analysis claiming that systems of race, class, gender, sexuality, ethnicity, nation, and age form mutually constructing features of social organization, which shape Black women's experiences and, in turn, are shaped by Black women" (2000, 299).[1]

The concept of intersectionality is equally useful to processes of objectivation insofar as it enables the scholar to reflect upon their positionality as a researcher within the structure of academic knowledge production. However, although a portion of French-speaking academic feminists are convinced that intersectionality is a useful way of rethinking power,[2] very few consider how intersectionality can be useful in the process of objectivation. French-speaking researchers have advocated for intersectionality without questioning the absence of research produced by racialized minority scholars in the French-speaking context. In a critical text about this situation, Nasima Moujoud and I explain that according to French norms of theoretical writing, authors do not provide details about their positionality, thereby circumventing discussion about how their perspective and approach are particularist and "probably simplistic, ethnocentric, culturist, hetero-centrist, masculine or linked to class" (Ait ben Lmamdani and Moujoud 2012, 15). As Sirma Bilge rightly points out, dominant French-speaking feminist scholars use intersectionality in ways that paradoxically contribute to "the whitening of intersectionality" by erasing race and racism (2015, title and passim).

---

1. *Translator's note*: Quoted in English in the original.
2. Among the French publications that refer to Black feminism starting from 2000, we can cite the journals *Genre* (issue 39 [2006]) and *Nouvelles questions féministes (Sexisme, racisme, et post-colonialisme* [2006]) as well as the volume *Black Feminism: Anthologie du féminisme africain-americain (1975–2000)* (Combahee River Collective 2008).

In sum, the majority of French-speaking academics who have adopted intersectionality as an approach avoid considering their own positionality within the academy and society and its effects on the kind of knowledge they produce.

Two factors help explain this phenomenon in the French-speaking academy. The first is that intersectionality has been partially emptied of its political content in that academy, steered away from its activist implications, and reduced to a simple methodological tool. The second factor, which is linked to the first, is that in the context of coloniality, scholarship by women of color and (post)colonialized women researchers on migrant and formerly colonized populations is ignored.

With this situation in mind and in light of Fatema Mernissi's multifaceted work, I propose to address the following two questions:

1. What does it mean for academics to claim intersectionality as an approach to studies of "the other," while neglecting or overlooking their own positionalities as writing or thinking subjects?
2. How can we highlight situated knowledge in a (post)colonial and transnational context?

To answer these questions, I first discuss Fatema Mernissi's critique of colonialism and the patriarchal system. Then I engage with how she deployed her own situated perspective to resist oppression. Finally, I address Mernissi's activist engagements and their effect on her academic and literary work.

Fatema Mernissi, Colonialism, and the Patriarchal System

Although Fatema Mernissi never used terms such as *intersectionality* and *interconnection* that today help us to define how multiple systems of power interact and overlap, her publications and interviews demonstrate an acute awareness of the need to combat multiple relations of power at once. This is clear in how she critiqued colonialism, patriarchy, and class together. For instance, Mernissi strongly rejected colonial and Orientalist discourse about Maghrebian women. She fought against the literatures that represented the harem as central and that projected fantasies of exotic femininity onto Muslim women.

In *Le harem et l'Occident* (2001), Mernissi challenges the colonial notion that according to the norms of Muslim societies, Muslim women are supposed to be confined in closed spaces and that they are mere objects of masculine desire. Albin Michel, Mernissi's publisher in France, made the following comment that reveals contradictory representations of "the harem in the West" and "the harem in the East":

> In the West, the *harem* is represented as a place of pleasure where naked and lascivious women indulge themselves, thus the odalisques of Ingres and Matisse, Scheherazade in a Hollywood version.
>
> On the contrary, in the East the *harem* is a place of confinement where women can only dream of using their talent and their intelligence to get free, whether they lived during the Khalif Haroun al-Rachid's time or in the domestic *harem* of the 1950s in Fès.[3] (Mernissi 2001, back cover)

Albin Michel's comment, which limits the harem to confined space, doesn't do justice to Fatema Mernissi's thinking. She brings the concept far beyond physical space, whether considering women located in the West or women located in the East. Indeed, Mernissi insists that the notion of the harem refers to any kind of binary unisex spaces (for women or for men) wherein the genders do not mix. In the book *Dreams of Trespass* (1994), she refers to the French Senate as a harem because it included so few women at the time.

In her consideration of the notion of the harem, Mernissi was very concerned about the borders that mark the symbolic contours

---

3. Although most of Mernissi's work was published in English, I refer to the French-language versions of her works and quote from them except where otherwise noted. This choice is related to this chapter's aim, which is to understand how the French-speaking world received and framed Mernissi's work. In addition, a focus on Mernissi's French-language interviews has allowed me to grasp the nuances of her thinking.

of feminine space. In an analysis of the notion of a border, *ḥudud*, in Mernissi's novel *Rêves de femmes* (Mernissi 1996, a translation of *Dreams of Trespass* [Mernissi 1994]), Nouzha Guessous (n.d.) identifies elements that constitute the main thematics of Mernissi's research. For example, Mernissi discusses women's power that prevails despite their confinement and illiteracy. This thread is widely documented in Mernissi's sociological work. One of her first books, *Le Maroc raconté par ses femmes* (1986), traces the political engagements that working-class women have within the labor force notwithstanding their overwhelming lack of access to education.[4] At the same time, the heroines of *Rêves de femmes* do not exercise power frontally or directly. They adopt techniques of circumvention so as to transgress the norms established by men. Sexuality is an example of such resistance. Although women's bodies are objects of male domination, women also deploy their bodies as instruments of resistance through the game of seduction. This form of resistance is criticized by some feminists, who perceive it as a way of "softening and even embellishing injustice towards women" (Guessous n.d., 3).

While Fatema Mernissi energetically critiques how Muslim women are represented in colonial discourse, she equally negatively assesses Moroccan nationalists, who, she sustains, have maintained women's subordinate position. She puts into relief the contradictory attitude of Moroccan nationalist men who even while challenging colonialism still consider women as minor subjects. Consequently, Moroccan men do not question the patriarchal order that governs gender relations in Maghrebian societies. For Mernissi, men's ambiguous and conflicted attitude leads to a kind of split conduct: they want to lock up their wives, but they push their daughters to study and to leave the private space. Mernissi identified this conduct in

---

4. I should underscore that the surveys and fieldwork that constitute the data for the book were collected in the 1970s before they became the subject matter of the book published in 1986. This untranslated book's title translates literally as "Morocco Narrated by Its Women."

her own father: he contested colonial domination politically but encouraged his wife to use French products while rejecting local Moroccan ones.

Mernissi illustrates this contradiction in a scene in *Dreams of Trespass* where the narrator's mother reacts against her husband's offer of beauty products from Paris:

> She [Fatema's mother] turned to Father and asked him a question he did not expect. "Who made these products?" He then made the fatal mistake of telling her that they had been created by scientists in clinical laboratories. Upon hearing that, she picked up the perfume and threw everything else away. "If men are now going to rob me of the only things I still control—my own cosmetics—then they will be the ones who have power over my beauty. I will never allow such a thing to happen. I create my own magic, and I am not relinquishing my henna." (Mernissi 1994, 205)[5]

As a feminist intellectual, Mernissi critiqued the national movement for not recognizing women's worth, just as she critiqued French colonizers and their ongoing colonial and Orientalist discourse on Muslim women. She rejected both positions. For her, Muslim men seemed to experience virile power by making women veil, while westerners seemed to experience it by making women take off the veil (Mernissi 2001).

Mernissi's acute awareness of a dual struggle against two systems that reduce women to minor roles while pretending to contribute to their emancipation reveals that her way of thinking about power and about her own positionality is akin to what today is called "intersectionality." It is difficult to hold this position in a university system and political context that require contemporary scholars to adopt a distinct and differentializing attitude toward the Muslim and Western systems. Mernissi actively worked to deconstruct stereotyped images of Moroccan women. The knowledge she produced implies an

---

5. *Translator's note*: The author here quotes from the English version of the book, *Dreams of Trespass*, in her original text.

understanding of her privilege as a Moroccan intellectual who could study in universities in France and the United States. From such a positionality, she questioned women's place as well as her own as a woman scholar. Thus, the reader can identify the recurrent use of "I" in some of her books and interviews.

The Fictionalized Use of "I," or How to Situate Oneself as Resistant

The intersectional approach that underlies Fatema Mernissi's work is not limited to her dual critique of colonialism and the patriarchal system. It is also apparent in her use of the autobiographical "I." Samira Farhoud (2008) emphasizes that the first singular pronoun *I* that Mernissi uses in her writings, especially in the novel *Rêves de femmes*, is not simply a narrative "I" but also a collective "I" that represents a plurality of women's voice(s). "Fatema" the child tells stories from all the other women's viewpoints and, according to Farhoud, puts into relief women's sisterhood:

> Oh, yes, Aunt Habiba, I thought, I will be a magician. I will cross past this strictly codified life waiting for me in the narrow Medina streets, with my eyes fixed on the dream. I will glide through adolescence, holding escape close to my chest, like the young European girls hold their dance partners close to theirs. Words, I will cherish. I will cultivate them to illuminate the nights, demolish walls and dwarf gates. It all seems easy, Aunt Habiba, with you and Chama going in and out of the fragile draped theater, so frail in the late night, on that remote terrace. But so vital, so nourishing, so wonderful. I will become a magician. I will chisel words to share the dream and render the frontiers useless. (Mernissi 1994, 107)[6]

Mernissi's frequent use of the pronoun *I* is emancipating not only for her as an individual but also for women collectively. Mustapha Sami points out how Mernissi's narrative mode makes use of her cultural

---

6. *Translator's note*: The author here quotes from the English version of the book, *Dreams of Trespass*, in her original text.

heritage, combining stories, legends, and historical facts (2013, 124). Here, the narrational "I" is fictional. It is within a novel that is not meant to be autobiographical. Farhoud explains that *Rêves de femmes* situates Mernissi in a fictionalized autobiography. Mernissi's approach has been critiqued by some contemporary scholars—such as Hassna Lebbaady—who consider Mernissi's recurrent use of the term *harem* to reflect "a will to increase exotism around this term" (Farhoud 2008, 141). Perhaps such reactions would be slightly attenuated if the authors considered Mernissi's own clarification in a footnote in the later French version of *Dreams of Trespass*, *Rêves de femmes*, where she emphasizes the fictional character of the book: "If I had tried to tell you the story of my childhood, you wouldn't have finished the first two paragraphs because my childhood was dull and tremendously boring. So, this book is not an autobiography but a type of fiction that is presented in the form of tales told by a seven-year-old child" (Mernissi 1996, 234–35n2). When Le Fennec republished *Rêves de femmes* (in French) in Morocco in 2023, the word *roman* (novel) appeared on the cover.

Earlier, I tried to connect Mernissi's double relation to colonialism and the patriarchal system and to her fictionalized autobiographical "I" as expressive of her situated perspective. Indeed, it seems that Mernissi's works, notwithstanding the catchy titles assigned to some of her books, which in my view are made to comply with commercial editorial policy,[7] demonstrate her resistance as a woman, a Moroccan, a Muslim from the bourgeois class, from the global South, from a formerly colonized country. Using the master's tools (Lorde [1979] 1984; Mathieu 1985), Mernissi, like many feminists throughout the world, reacts, modifies, and resists rules and contours of thought imposed by the dominant. Thus, instead of asking whether Mernissi

---

7. Such titles include *Les sultanes oubliées* (1990, Forgotten Queens of Islam); *Le harem politique: Le Prophète et ses femmes* (1989, The Political Harem: The Prophet and His Women); *Shahrazade n'est pas marocaine, autrement elle serait salariée* (1988, Shahrazade Is Not Moroccan, Otherwise She Would Be Salaried).

fell into the trap of the Orientalism that she critiqued, in my opinion we should ask ourselves what kind of real room she had to maneuver inside multiple structures of domination. Mernissi was aware of this narrow margin and played with it. Her consciousness about power and her resistance to it are perceptible in her presentation on the back cover of her book *Êtes-vous vacciné contre le harem? Texte-Test pour les messieurs qui adorent les dames* (1998, Are You Vaccinated against the Harem? Text-Test for Gentlemen Who Adore Ladies), where she writes: "As a Moroccan, making fun of the arrogant West has always been one of my most delicious fantasies. I started to enjoy it by writing this book in which I dissect the archaisms of our European neighbors. Archaisms, carefully hidden behind their myth of western modernity. The Europeans tell us that they are modern, but . . . they dream of *harems*, like the worst despots of the Stone Age. Well, you see what I mean."

In Mernissi's irony and humor we can sense her acute awareness of relations of power and of the subordinate position to which she is assigned as a writer from the global South. In *Êtes-vous vacciné contre le harem?*, she emphasizes westerners' attitudes toward Muslim women. The harem in this sense is a projection of the West's fantasies and an Orientalist reading of women's position in the Muslim world rather than a description of the reality of Muslim women in postcolonial societies. In her back-cover description of *Êtes-vous vacciné*, she emphasizes that the researcher should respect distance from the object of her research by being playful. She explains that making fun of oneself or others is also a way of resisting capitalist globalization, which exacerbates competition:

> Another reason incited me to write a book that will make Moroccans laugh. According to psychiatrists in Rabat, whom I listen to religiously, laughter is one of the most efficient and economical therapies to uplift the spirits and reinforce self-confidence. It is self-confidence that we need so as to jump into the competition that globalization requires. However, what will happen if my book does not make you laugh? Well, try to resell it in the closest *Joutiya*

[flea market]. Recycling useless things and ideas is yet another kind of therapy, precious for training oneself to surf on the waves of this disturbing globalization that threatens us.

"The Border Is Just an Imaginary Line That Exists Only in the Minds of Those Who Have Power"[8]

The self-reflexive approach or the situated perspective in Mernissi's work also appears in her political practice. It can be presented at two main levels: the first related to her status as a woman writer, the second to her fervent activism.

First, Mernissi's political practice as a woman writer is clear in her frontal challenge to the silence that men impose to inhibit any slight hope that women might have for speech. Also, as Mustapha Sami explains, "Women's writing [in Morocco] has surely been both an act of rebellion against archaism that hinders women's emancipation and a way to counterbalance the vision of Moroccan society provided by literature created by men. In their work women writers set the scene for protagonists who testify about their struggles and their hopes. They engage in unveiling various mechanisms of oppression that subjugate women. Today, women writers' voices are asserting themselves increasingly and have become a piercing cry of speech that has long been confiscated" (2013, 133).

Sami insists on Moroccan women writers' difficulty in being heard. As he demonstrates, the act of writing is an act of unveiling in the symbolic sense. Fatema Mernissi is among those who as early as the 1980s were aware of this border that they had to trespass to become autonomous. As Mernissi underscores about her controversial book *La femme dans inconscient musulman* (1982, published under the pseudonym "Fatna Aït Sabbah"), writing is a way of going beyond the border of masculine exclusivity (Guessous n.d.). It is another way of fighting oppression, of rearranging the elements that the adult order fixes in its own distinct assemblage, and of otherwise

---

8. The quote in the subhead for this section comes from Mernissi's book *Rêves de femmes* (1996, 7).

providing a different and more egalitarian interpretation of women's place in Muslim societies.

To Mernissi, writing is a tool that needs to be shared with other women to struggle for their human rights. After a trip to India, where she met Devaki Jain, Ritu Menon, and others, she created writing workshops in Morocco. She explained her endeavor in an interview by Fatiha Amellouk, presented on the Fondation Hassan II (Hassan II Foundation) website for expatriot Moroccans: "I have been politically active as an organizer of writing workshops to suggest writing as a weapon to make activists who want to change Morocco visible, via a collective book. These actors were political exprisoners and women who founded groups and organizations in working-class districts" (Amellouk 2015).

Parallel to her writing career, Mernissi led a struggle to improve conditions for the most deprived people in her country. She created the Civic Caravans, a network of international relations to give a voice to artists, intellectuals, and unschooled people in the most remote regions of Morocco. Similarly, she founded the group Women, Families, Children to aid the most deprived women and children (Van der Poel 2006). Through her activism and intellectual curiosity, Mernissi ensured that all her work addressed current problems from new perspectives rooted in the reality of the people she engaged with and for whom she opened up the possibility of being heard. In *Le Maroc raconté par ses femmes* (1986), Mernissi proactively adopted "an affective relation in which she implicated herself as a Moroccan woman while opening up a space for the voices of those who are not used to being listened to" (Van der Poel 2006).

In an interview by Maria-Àngels Roque at the European Institute of the Mediterranean in Barcelona in 2014, Mernissi praised the dynamism of youth: "Imagine that those shrewd Amazigh Sinbads of Morocco of 2004 have an overwhelming advantage over the heroes of *The Thousand and One Nights*. While the Sindbad of Baghdad navigated the Indian Ocean with fragile boats with primitive technology, young people in the High Atlas and Zagora discover the world with neither a visa nor a passport, just by surfing skillfully on the internet and by becoming activists in the most dynamic civic organizations" (Roque 2014, 1).

The perpetual curiosity that animated Mernissi and her rootedness in reality, contrary to what some of her work might leave people thinking, have had the effect of putting into perspective "ideology's importance in placing into relief the role that access to school and the labor market play in desegregating women" (Guessous n.d., 3). This is one more reason why she insisted on political engagement as the road to emancipation. In the same interview, she stated: "You are in a *harem* when the world does not need you. You are in a *harem* when your contribution is considered so insignificant that nobody will ask you for it. You are in a *harem* when what you do is useless. You are in a *harem* when the planet turns and you are buried to the neck in contempt and indifference" (Roque 2014, 1).

Mernissi's main objective here is the same as in much of her other work: to reveal the fruits of this Moroccan culture that has been misunderstood and concealed for a long time and to demonstrate that Moroccan women's desire for liberation is endogenous to Moroccan societal dynamism, not something that has been or must be imported from foreign countries.

Mernissi was a researcher-weaver and a border crosser. Whether we consider her work, her writings, or her passionate activism, she spent her life like her young narrator of *Rêves de femmes*, looking for *hudud* (borders) so as to transgress them: "But since then, looking for the border has become my life's work. Anxiety eats at me whenever I cannot situate the geometric line that organizes my powerlessness" (Mernissi 1994, 15).

As Guessous (n.d.) highlights, Mernissi distinguished herself according to three permanent features: (1) her exigency about knowledge, documentation, and expertise within a pluridisciplinary approach; (2) freedom of research without any prohibition or self-censorship; (3) freedom of expression and the duty to ensure that all men and women have the right to speak. These three principles are the foundation of her research ethics, which in my understanding are based in the intersectional approach that I used as a point of departure in this chapter. Many academics also deem Mernissi to be one of the pioneers of Islamic feminism, even if she did not claim to be part of such a movement. Across her writings and her interviews from the mid-1980s, Mernissi campaigned for an Islam where women speak out for the right to interpret Muslim law.

Moreover, Mernissi insisted upon the importance of an intercultural approach to the production and reception of representations of Middle Eastern women by the West and to tackle the binary concept of "tradition/modernity" in a different and original manner (Bernardi 2010, 412). Her reading emphasizes the cultural complexity that she herself embodies through her desire for dialogue between civilizations and to go beyond borders. In *Islam et démocratie* ([1992] 2010), Mernissi invites us to adopt a process of renegotiation of the truth between East and West by deconstructing stereotypes in the media and in the field of education (412). Without being recognized by any movement and by refusing all the labels and the limits that go with such recognition, Mernissi proved the ability of subaltern postcolonial subjects to escape the role of passive subjects that Western hegemony has assigned to them. Thus, subaltern "natives" can become active subjects in knowledge production not only about their own situation but also about that of dominant subjects ([1992] 2010, 413).

Conclusion

Fatema Mernissi's research highlighted issues that were on the agenda of feminist debates in her times and are still being discussed today. Among the most current debates, at least in the French-speaking world, we can cite the questions of intersectionality and the place of the minoritarian writing subject in the academic world. Mernissi intervened with great humor in these conversations that are often deemed troublesome because they question the legitimacy and neutrality of the dominant subject. In addition to this humor, which Mernissi claimed as a tool of resistance, she chose activism, which she considered more effective in the fight against women's domination. Thus, for her, opening a space for women to speak instead of just being an object of research is a way to transgress the borders imposed by both Moroccan men and westerners. For Mernissi, Moroccan men are as responsible for the domination of women as westerners who chose/choose to lock them into stereotypical images while denying them a voice. In the same spirit, she participated in creating the first feminist structures and organizations in Morocco that continue to actively struggle against all forms of gender discrimination, such as the national Democratic Association of Women in Morocco and the Center for Listening and Psychological and Legal Accompaniment for Women Victims of Violence in Casablanca (Guessous n.d.).

Mernissi's writings, especially those on Islam, where she adopted a subversive approach to the interpretation of Muslim law, inspired a whole generation of Moroccans and led the way to an Islamic feminism that was later claimed and animated by authors such as Asma Lamrabet and other critical theologians. These authors "produce a religious hermeneutic from a critical, creative, and innovative intellectual position, most often based on a direct reading of Islam's only sacred text, the Qur'an, informed by Tradition (the sayings and life of the Prophet)" (Latte Abdallah 2013, 219). At the same time, Mernissi conducted research-action on current topics such as women in the media, the use of social networks by young people, and women weavers. Her work allowed a new generation of young Moroccans to recognize themselves in her writing and to refer to it. We can see the present recognition of her academic heritage symbolically in the Fatema Mernissi Chair at the Free University of Brussels, created in January 2016. It was established on the initiative of Le collectif du vivre ensemble (Living Together Collective), founded in 2012 by Fatema Mernissi, Asma Lamrabet, Farid Merini, Farida Belyazid, and Driss Ksikes. The topics chosen for this chair are society, gender, and democracy; media and culture; and globalization, youth, and local dynamics. They indicate continuity with Mernissi's thought. By transgressing all the borders imposed by dominant, male, Western, and bourgeois subjects, the heroine of *Rêves de femmes* managed to pass the torch to a new generation of scholars who, even as they critique her, claim her heritage.

References

Ait ben Lmamdani, Fatima, and Nasima Moujoud. 2012. "Peut-on faire de l'intersectionnalité sans les ex-colonisé-e-s?" *Mouvements* 72, no. 4: 11–21.

Aït Sabbah, Fatna [Fatema Mernissi]. 1982. *La femme dans l'inconscient musulman*. Paris: Albin Michel.

Amellouk, Fatiha. 2015. "Rencontre avec Fatima Mernissi: Site de la Fondation Hassan II pour les Marocains Résident à l'Etranger." At https://www.e-taqafa.ma/dossier/rencontre-avec-fatima-mernissi.

Bernardi, Floriana. 2010. "Gazes, Targets, (En)Visions: Reading Fatima Mernissi through Rey Chow." *Social Semiotics* 20, no. 4: 411–23.

Bilge, Sirma. 2015. "Le blanchiment de l'intersectionnalité." *Recherches féministes* 28, no. 2: 9–32.

Collins, Patricia Hill. 2000. *Black Feminist Thought: Knowledge, Consciousness, and the Politics of Empowerment*. New York: Routledge.

Combahee River Collective. 2008. *Black Feminism: Anthologie du féminisme africain-americain (1975–2000)*. Edited by Elsa Dorlin. Paris: L'Harmattan.

Farhoud, Samira. 2008. "Interventions autobiographiques au Maghreb: L'écriture comme moment de transmission des voix de femmes." PhD diss., Université de Montréal.

Guessous, Nouzha. N.d. "Le(s) féminisme(s) de Fatéma Mernissi." *Revue Economia*. At http://economia.ma/content/les-f%C3%A9minismes-de-fat%C3%A9ma-mernissi. Developed out of a talk given at the Sixth Festival Méditérranéen des ecrits de femmes, Le Féminin Pluriel, Rabat, Morocco, Apr. 28–29, 2016.

Latte Abdallah, Stéphanie. 2013. "Féminismes islamiques à l'heure révolutionnaire: Normes, genre et démocratie." In *Normes religieuses et genre: Mutations, résistances et reconfiguration (XIXe–XXIe siècle)*, edited by Florence Rochefort, 217–30. Paris: Armand Colin.

Lorde, Audre. [1979] 1984. "The Master's Tools Will Never Dismantle the Master's House." Comments on "The Personal and the Political" panel, Second Sex Conference, New York, Sept. 29, 1979. Printed in *Sister Outsider: Essays and Speeches*, 110–13. New York: Sister Visions Press.

Mathieu, Nicole-Claude. 1985. *L'arraisonnement des femmes: Essais en anthropologie des sexes*. Paris: EHESS.

Mernissi, Fatema. 1986. *Le Maroc raconté par ses femmes*. Rabat, Morocco: Société marocaine des éditeurs réunis.
———. 1994. *Dreams of Trespass: Tales of a Harem Girlhood*. Cambridge, MA: Perseus.
———. 1996. *Rêves de femmes: Une enfance au harem*. Translated by Claudine Richetin. Paris: Albin Michel.
———. 1998. *Êtes-vous vacciné contre le harem? Texte-Test pour les messieurs qui adorent les dames*. Casablanca, Morocco: Le Fennec.
———. 2001. *Le harem et l'Occident*. Paris: Albin Michel.
———. [1992] 2010. *Islam et démocratie*. Reprint. Paris: Albin Michel.
———. [1996] 2023. *Rêves de femmes: Une enfance au harem*. Reprint. Casa Blanca, Morocco: Le Fennec.
Roque, Maria-Àngels. 2014. "Mes rencontres avec Fatima Mernissi." IEMed (European Institute of the Mediterranean). At https://www.iemed.org/publication/entretien-mes-rencontres-avec-fatema-mernissi/.
Sami, Mustapha. 2013. "L'écriture de l'enfance dans le texte autobiographique marocain: Eléments d'analyse à travers l'étude de cinq récits. Le cas de chraibi, khaitibi, choukri, mernissi et rachid o." PhD diss., Univ. of Florida. At http://ufdcimages.uflib.ufl.edu/UF/E0/04/51/66/00001/SAMI_M.pdf.
Van der Poel, Ieme. 2006. "Féminisme et/ou autobiographie: De Simone de Beauvoir à Fatima Mernissi." Paper presented at "Actes du colloque international 'Ecriture féminine: Réception, discours et représentations,'" Nov. 18–19, Centre de recherche en anthropologie sociale et culturelle (Center for Research in Social and Cultural Anthropology), Oran, Morocco.

Section Three

Feminism and Islam

9

Fatema Mernissi and the Question of Women's Agency and Power in Islam

AZADEH KIAN

The mounting of radical and violent Islamism and the murderous attacks of recent years have popularized a perspective that essentializes the difference between so-called Western values and Muslims' values. The culturalist/essentialist perspective that attributes to culture the status of a major explanatory element in the functioning of societies and for which historical-cultural origins explain historical development is gaining ground. This perspective, which reifies Islam as an objective force independent of any historical, social, political, or economic context, makes a categorical distinction between the Western and Muslim worlds and analyzes the latter in terms of its deviation from Western history. Culturalism draws an analogy between Islam as defined in this way and Muslims seen as beings imbued with cultural traditions and political and intellectual attitudes considered a fortiori antidemocratic (see Kian 2017). From this perspective, which represents Islam through stereotypical and inaccurate images, Muslim women are incapable of resisting their oppression, let alone influencing the process of social transformation. This context imposes a double oppression on these women. On the one hand, gendered Islamophobia (Hajjat and Mohammed 2013) and Muslimophobia (Halliday 1999, 898) have been accentuated, revitalizing Orientalist tropes and representations of Muslim women as victims of Islam, powerless to act, in need of rescue from

Muslim men and Islam.[1] On the other hand, Muslim women are oppressed by Islamists, who, claiming the presumed essential difference between the West and the Muslim East, impose in their often violent speeches and actions significant limitations on women's rights in the name of preserving "Islamic values."

The massive participation of women in the revolutions in the Middle East and the Maghreb in 2011 suddenly led to a temporary change in their image in public opinion and the Western media, which had banked on the victory of liberal democracy in these countries. However, faced with the success achieved by Islamists at the ballot box, particularly in Egypt and Tunisia, these same public and media quickly became disillusioned, pointing once again at those Muslims presumed to be imbued with Islamic values, including the superiority of men over women. The ideological question and the role of Islam in women's lives are thus highlighted as if Muslim women live exclusively in the closed world of religion and ideology. By giving primacy to the religious factor, the neo-Orientalists in fact admit the postulate of the Islamists who essentialize the differences between "the Muslim East" and "the West" as well as between men and women, thus excluding any possibility of achieving gender equality in Muslim-majority societies. This essentialization is accompanied by a self-esteem gained through the glorification of the culture of origin (national/Islamic) and the stigmatization of the other (the West). Armed with a dichotomous vision and in the name of Islam, the Islamists essentialize inequalities between men and women and reinforce the hierarchical social order that they have presented as being of divine will.

Essentialist analyses, both neo-Orientalist and Islamist, also obscure the contestation of social inequalities between women and men by those who not only refuse to accept divine justifications for

---

1. Fred Hallidy (1999) makes a distinction between Islamophobia, which denotes the fear of the religion and of its ideas and practices, and Muslimophobia, which indicates the fear of Muslims. He prefers to use the second term when discussing the racialization of Muslims.

human action but also refuse to become agents of the neo-Orientalist, neocolonial discourse that claims to rescue Muslim women and free them from the patriarchal yoke that oppresses them.

Fatema Mernissi's pioneering work on women and Islam is therefore timely and of great interest in countering these discourses. It combines historical and theological analyses and attempts to historicize and contextualize Islam and Islamic traditions through a feminist, anti-Orientalist critical approach. Admittedly, Mernissi sometimes reproduced binary oppositions between "the West" and "the Muslim world" or used homogenous categories such as "Muslim man," "Muslim woman," "Muslim sexuality," "the Western man," and "the Western psyche" (Mernissi 2001b). Similarly, in some cases, notably in *Beyond the Veil* (1975), one of her early publications, she seems to have been influenced by binary thinking that makes a categorical distinction between the public and private in Islam. She argued that

> strict space boundaries divide Muslim society into two sub universes: the universe of men (the *umma*, the world religion and power) and the universe of women, the domestic, sexuality and the family. The spatial division according of sex reflects the division between those who hold authority and those who do not, those who hold spiritual powers and those who do not. The division is based on the physical separation of the *umma* (the public sphere) from the domestic universe. These two universes of social interaction are regulated by antithetical concepts of human relations, one based on community, the other on conflict. (Mernissi 1975, 138)

Lila Abu-Lughod has highlighted some of these contradictions in Mernissi's work:

Her sophistication, creativity, and political courage are stunning; and yet her work, when it moves between her home in the Arab world and the Western context in which it is so well received, can be troubling. Her 1994 memoir of coming of age is called *Dreams of Trespass: Tales of a Harem Girlhood*. Instead of refusing to reproduce the old Orientalist stereotype of women in harems, she brings to life the world of women and patriarchal authority in the enclosed household of her wealthy Fez family. Conjuring up a rich emotional world and capturing exquisitely family dynamics and women's experiences, she nevertheless anchors the memoir in her "innocent" interrogation of the meaning of boundaries, the invisible rules of space, and sexual difference. In the end, despite her celebration of women's traditional powers of beauty, she unambivalently pits her mother's strong wish for modernity for a little girl dressed in Western clothes who will attend school, learn French, and become liberated—against all the restricting forces of tradition and the harem. Tradition and Modernity. Harems and Freedom. Veiling and Unveiling. These are the familiar terms by which the East has long been apprehended (and devalued) and the West has constructed itself as superior. These are some of what [Edward] Said calls the dogmas of Orientalism, and they are the very terms that feminist scholars like Lata Mani, in her belatedly published book on colonial India, *Contentious Traditions*, have brilliantly called into question. (2001, 108)

In *Scheherazade Goes West* (2001b), however, Mernissi acknowledges the diversity of Muslim societies with respect to women and their status. Similarly, her work on Morocco has drawn attention to the heterogeneity of the notion of "woman" and the diversity of trajectories and experiences of women from different sociocultural backgrounds. She also wrote about the intersection of gender and social class in her analysis of conflicts between "unveiled women" and "fundamentalist men," arguing that the conflict is between newly urbanized middle- and lower-class men who seek power by politicizing religion, on the one hand, and unveiled women mainly from the urban middle class, on the other.

In any case and despite the contradictions that sometimes run through Mernissi's work, her research shows that in the history of Muslim-majority societies since the advent of Islam, women have been subjected to power relations and that some of them also enjoyed authority as a result of their religious, poetic, literary, scientific, political, and military knowledge. They tried to influence, subvert, or challenge the male-dominated social structure that Islamic laws consolidated. Her work has made visible the agility of women, not only famous ones, such as those of the Prophet's family—Khadija, Aisha, Umm Salama, Hind, Fatema, Zeynab, and Sukeina—but also ordinary women (Mernissi 1991).

According to Mernissi, Umm Salama represents one of the most vocal women in early Islam. She belonged to the aristocracy of the Quraysh tribe and already had four children from her first marriage when the Prophet asked her to marry him. She initially refused before accepting. After the marriage, she asked the Prophet why men are mentioned in the Qur'an, but women are not. The Prophet replied, "Allah spoke of the two sexes in terms of total equality, that is as members of the community." He added that "God identifies those who are part of His Kingdom" (Mernissi 1991, 118–19).

According to Mernissi, the question asked by Umm Salama was a sign of the existence of political turmoil, not just the whim of a beloved wife. Later, it was ordinary Muslim women who questioned the Prophet's wives: "Allah has spoken of you (the Prophet's wives) by name in the Koran, but He has said nothing about us. Is there then nothing about us that merits mention?" Mernissi concludes, "The women apparently hoped to see things change with the new God" (1991, 119). The first Muslim women, by raising the issues of inheritance, the right to war and war booty, gender relations, and physical violence, pressed the Prophet to make a declaration on the free will of a woman as a believer in the new community (Mernissi 1991, 148).

For Mernissi, Hind Bint Utba, wife of Abu Sufyan, who played a central role in the Meccan opposition to Muhammad, represents dynamic, influential, enterprising women in public as well as in private life. Hind finally accepted Islam reluctantly. When the Prophet commanded her to swear to "not commit adultery," Hind replied, "A free woman never commits adultery." The Prophet is said to have thrown an amused glance at his companion and father-in-law Umar because he was aware of Hind's love affairs and her relations with Umar before Umar's conversion to Islam (Mernissi 1991, 116–17). When the

Prophet asked the women "not [to] kill their children," Hind pointed out that he, a military leader who originated battles in which blood was shed, was going too far in asking such a thing from women, who are the ones to give birth: "We have brought children into the world and we have raised them, but you have killed them on the day of *Badr*" (Mernissi 1991, 117). The incident with Hind shows not only that the women of the Quraysh aristocracy were highly esteemed as a social group, like the men, swearing allegiance and taking part in the negotiations with the new military leader of the city, but also that they could express a boldly critical attitude toward Islam. They were not going to accept the new religion without knowing exactly how it would improve their situation.

Another dynamic, courageous, rebellious woman in public as well as private Mernissi writes about is Soukeina, the Prophet's great-granddaughter. Soukeina was Imam Hussein's (the Third Shi'ite Imam, the central myth of Shi'ism) beloved daughter. Sukeina was born in 49 AH (671 CE) and was nine and present at the killing of her father, Hussein, at Karbala on Muharram 10, 61 (October 10, 680). Mernissi argues: "That tragedy partly explains her revolt against political, oppressive, despotic Islam and against everything that hinders the individual's freedom—including the hijab" (1991, 194). "Soukeina was a *barza* (remarkable) woman who had sound judgment, was known for her *'aql* (reasoning), and was celebrated for her beauty—an explosive mixture of physical attractiveness, critical intelligence, and caustic wit. She disdained marriage proposals by princes and caliphs for political reasons. She ended up marrying five or six husbands. She quarreled with some, made passionate declarations of love to others, brought one to the court for infidelity, and never pledged *ta'a* (obedience) to any of them. In her marriage contracts, she stipulated that she would not obey her husband but would instead do as she pleased and that she did not acknowledge that her husband had the right to practice polygyny (Mernissi 1991, 192). She made one of her husbands sign a marriage contract that officially specified her right to *nushuz*, rebellion against marital control. Soukeina died in Medina at the age of sixty-eight. It is amazing to note that in Iran, the most important Shi'ite country where the myth of Karbala and Imam Hussein is central and played an important role in the victory of the Revolution of 1979 that toppled the monarchy, Soukeina is barely mentioned. The only female figures who are worshiped in official discourse and popular culture are Fatema (the mother of Imam Hussein) and Zeynab (the sister of Imam Hussein), who was in Karbala. Soukeina's passion, knowledge, independence of mind, and push for freedom do not match with the image of the ideal woman propagated by the Islamic Republic and by Islamists throughout the world, which is characterized by motherhood, obedience to her husband, and the endorsement of gender inequality. Even Ali Shari'ati (d. 1977), an anticlerical Muslim ideologue who studied sociology in France and developed a politicized and modern version of Islam, did not take Soukeina as a model of the fighting Muslim woman. He aimed to transform religion into an ideology of liberation, denounced the shah's policies of cultural westernization, and, following Frantz Fanon, advocated cultural introspection. He also opposed the monopoly of religion by the clergy, whom he accused of alienating Iranian youth from Islam. In his book *Fatemeh Fatemeh ast* (Fatema Is Fatema, 1976), which then became very popular among young, educated, urban, religious women, Shari'ati reconstructed classical female models of Shi'ism through a revolutionary approach to the personalities of Fatema and Zeynab. While their piety and virtue were emphasized, it was their courage and determination, their struggle against injustice, and their political activities against oppression that were valued (Shari'ati 1976 and 1979, 11–12).

According to Mernissi's account, Soukeina qualifies as a pioneer of women's individual and collective aspirations to freedom in the history of Islam.

This critical spirit remained alive during the first decades of Islam. It disappeared only with the onset of absolutism during the reign of Mu'awiya, the son of Abu Sufyan and Hind who became the founder of the Ummayad dynasty (661–750 CE), and with the turning of Islam into a dynastic system. This meant, on the one hand, the disappearance of the tribal aristocratic spirit with the formation of the Muslim state and, on the other hand, the disappearance of Islam as the Prophet's lived experience in which equality, however merely potential it might be, opened the door to the dream of a practicing democracy (Mernissi 1991, 191).

Women and the Quest for Power in Islam

Throughout the history of Islam, as several historians have shown, in many Muslim-majority societies women attempted to influence, oppose, or subvert social structures dominated by men that the Islamic laws reinforced. The main terms of religious discourse were founded at the beginning of Islam. The first is the dominant and hierarchical discourse that marginalized women and led to their social, economic, and legal subordination. The second is the ethical discourse uttered by marginal groups who have challenged political order and its interpretation of Islam, including its conception of gender. They instead underline spiritual and moral equality of all human beings (Abou-Bakr 2010, 136; Ahmed 1992). Against the first type of discourse and in line with the second type, women's authority was acknowledged in religious, jurisprudential, literary, scientific, military, and political spheres.

Women's active presence in domains such as religious sciences and jurisprudence was very important from the tenth to sixteenth centuries (Abou-Bakr 2003). The hadith (words and acts of the Prophet) started to be collected in their written version three to four centuries after the Prophet's death. It is noteworthy to mention that the first hadith were narrated by women from the Prophet's generation. Women were also invited to express their opinion on the question of the Prophet's succession (Kassem 2015, 97). These examples alone show that Islam did not have any problems accepting women's authority. The *muhaddithat* (women specialists in hadith) disseminated the hadith to both women and men; *fiqhat* and *muftiyat* were women specialists in various branches of Islamic jurisprudence and were often consulted on the questions relevant to laws and principles (*ahkam*). As Omaima Abou-Bakr argues, these women muftis possessed religious, cultural, and contextual knowledge to distinguish among the compulsory (*wajib*), the preferable (*mustahab*), the permissible (*makruh*), and the prohibited (haram).

The number of women who possessed religious knowledge and authority is striking. The following list identifies such women from different centuries:

Shaykha Shuhda (d. 1178 CE), whose title was *fakhr al nisa'* (women's pride), lectured before a large public at the mosque in Baghdad. The historian Ibn Khalliqan describes her as "a scholar known by lots of people who had been her students. She had numerous followers beyond Baghdad" (Abou-Bakr 2003, 315–16).

Lella or Saïda Manoubia, whose real name was Aïcha Manoubia, was born around 1180 CE in Manoubia and died in 1257. She was a Tunisian saint (*zaouia*) who studied hadiths and Islamic jurisprudence with Abou Hassan al-Chadhili. She prayed at the Zitouna mosque along with men, became the head of a very important Sufi order called Chadhiliyya, and had a very large audience of both older and younger generations.

Fatima bint Ayyash of Baghdad (d. 1314 CE) had very good jurisprudential knowledge. Ibn Taymiyya (born in Turkey in 1263, died in Damascus in 1328), a very well-known traditionalist theologian, specialist of jurisprudence, and Hanbalite authority, admired her for her intelligence and insights (Abou-Bakr 2003, 318).

Aisha (1359–1436 CE), daughter of Ali ben Muhammad bin Ibrahim, lived in Cairo and taught several imams. She traveled to Palestine and taught hadith to several important personalities.

Sarah (1358–1451), daughter of Umar bin Abdelaziz, taught religion to imams and several religious personalities, including the well-known hadith scholar and historian Sakhawi, who declared having been her student.

Fatima, born in 1451 in Cairo, daughter of Qadi Kamal al-Din, presents an example of an intelligent religious woman who was a specialist in religious knowledge and a literary critic. She was a specialist in hadith, traveled a great deal, and lived near sacred places (*mujawarah*) in Mecca, Medina, and Jerusalem. In this environment, male and female pilgrims as well as specialists in religious sciences interacted with each other (Abou-Bakr 2010, 131).

For religious scholars who shared the ethical vision of Islam, women were not considered inferior to men. Sakhawi, for example, was sensitive toward the question of justice when it came to the distribution of religious compensation. He thought that women who could not pray or fast due to their menstruation were not less dear to God because, he argued, what counts is the intention. He said that "the God of Sha'ban and Ramadan is one" (quoted in Abou-Bakr 2010, 135).

According to Omaima Abou-Bakr, many of these women were given the title *sheykha*, which in the Hanbalite school is used for *alima*. Others obtained titles such as *sitt al wuzara* (minister ladies), *sitt al fuqaha* (jurisconsult ladies), *sitt al-ulama* (erudite ladies), *sitt al quda* (justice ladies), and so on (2003, 318). During the Middle Ages, women were respected in Muslim societies. However, they were absent from official positions in the madrassa (theology schools) and from judicial posts. This absence was not a matter of any religious prohibition or society's refusal but a matter of politics and power (Abou-Bakr 2003, 326).

Under the Fatimid dynasty, several women enjoyed religious, political, and financial power (Cortese and Calderini 2006). The Fatimids were rivals of the Abbasids (750–1258) and ruled over North Africa, Sicily, Yemen, Egypt, and Syria (from 909 and then in the Egyptian period from 969 to 1171). Toward the end of the eleventh century, upon her husband's death Arwa constructed her palace and with her mother-in-law, Asma, constructed two mosques in and near San'a (Masjid al Hurra). Both Arwa and Asma held the title *malika* and enjoyed the privilege of the head of state: the *khutba* (sermon) was recited in the mosques in their names (Mernissi 1990, 192–93). Asma, who died in 1087, led Yemen with her husband, Ali Ibn Mohammad, founder of the Sulayhids. She participated in official meetings unveiled.

Cairo became the royal city under Caliph 'Abd al-'Aziz, with several palaces, mosques, pavilions, roads, bridges, and gardens, and commercial, intellectual, and human exchanges there grew sharply. Sitt al Mulk, born in 970 CE, was the daughter of Caliph 'Abd al-'Aziz and a Christian mother. She benefited from exceptional circumstances and became the caliph after her brother al Hakim became a zealot and imposed crucial restrictions on women. He prohibited women from going out even to public baths or markets. He prohibited shoemakers from making shoes for women. Some women, including his own wives and concubines, disobeyed and went out, so he had them locked in cases and drowned them in the Nile. Finally, Sitt al Mulk overthrew him and ruled over the empire for four years from 1020 to 1024 in the name of her nephew. However, the *khutba* was never said in her name in the mosques (Mernissi 1990, 219–22).

Under the Fatimids, women inherited the same as men; they had contraceptive rights without needing to ask their husbands' authorization. They went to religious judges and even talked about their private lives, including sexual lives, and obtained what their rights allowed them (Cortese and Calderini 2006, 213).

In addition to Fatimid women who practiced power as caliph, sultan, or *malika*, other elite women enjoyed power and authority under the Mamluks, Ottomans, and Safavids (respectively in Egypt, Turkey, and Iran). Mamluks were slaves from Central Asia who rose to power in Egypt and Syria from 1250 to 1517 CE. This period was extremely rich and prosperous. Under the Mamluks, who also ruled over India, Sultana Radia became a very famous woman. She rose to power in Delhi in 1236 and remained in power for several years. Queen Chajarat ad-dur became Egypt's ruler in 1250. She defeated the French army and imprisoned the French ruler Louis IX.

In addition to elite women, ordinary women, too, enjoyed authority in different parts of the Muslim world. The Moroccan/Amazigh traveler Ibn Battuta, who traveled to Central Asia in 1334, was surprised by the high status women held in this region and how they were respected by Mongol and Turkish men. He also reported that Turkish women were not veiled and that husbands usually acted as their servants: "You could often take the husband for the servant" (Mernissi 2001a, 190).[2]

Despite much historical evidence, however, women of power were erased by Arab historians, who, as Mernissi writes, reserved for them only a disdainful silence. But, as she argues, the Arabs have not been the only historians to leave women out of their accounts: "The outstanding British historian Bernard Lewis [who passed away in May 2018] declares with such assertiveness that reminds [one] of the Ayatollahs that there have not been any queens in Islamic history and that the word 'queen' when uttered designates [only] foreign European or Byzantine queens" (Mernissi 1990, 159, citing Lewis 1988, 103).

Muslim Women and Power in the Modern Period

In Iran under the Safavid dynasty (1502–1722 CE), when Shi'ism became the state's official religion, women of the royal court and aristocratic women enjoyed high status. They received a good education, were financially independent, and could manage their wealth, protect artists and architects, and create charity foundations. Several of these women were in positions of power. Some princesses would not marry and were active in politics. This was the case for Princess Mahin Banou (1519–62), known as *shahzadeh sultanum*, "princess sultan," and beloved sister of Shah Tahmasb (1514–76). It was also the case for Pari khan Khanum II (1548–78) and Zeynab Begum (d. 1641). Several daughters of Shah Tahmasb are flagged by bibliographical sources from this period for their knowledge and know-how. Under Shah Tahmasb, who had many women warriors and horse riders, Kheyr ol Nesa Begum (1549–79) took political, administrative, and military decisions and approved royal orders. "No business was conducted without her opinion or advice" (Szuppe 2003, 159). Other women from nobility in Mazandaran and Gilan in

---

2. All translations of non-English source text are mine unless otherwise noted in the references.

northern Iran participated actively in political and military conflicts. Under Shah Abbas I (1587–1629), Zeynab Begum was a very close adviser to the king and in 1606 was the only woman present while military discussions were held in the court. Until 1629, she participated in the management of state policies before Shah Safi (1611–42), the successor of Shah Abbas I, excluded her from the royal court. Under the Safavid dynasty, other educated women were engaged in intellectual activities. According to one source, "In the 16th century the society was ready to grant an important space to women of the royal family or those of the political elite; royal women were considered as partners of the king. The situation started to change from the 17th century onward, when the culture of sedentary people gained importance, assigning women to the harem" (Szuppe 2003, 162). However, other sources show that the harem itself continued to play a role in politics often through a collaboration between royal women and both white and Black slaves, including eunuch slaves, who had become the new elites and had gained crucial importance. The "cage" system contributed tremendously to the empowerment of royal women. Indeed, the rise to power of women (and of slaves and eunuchs) in the Safavid royal court, especially beginning with the reign of Shah Abbas I, can be explained by a change in the system of education of princes with the adoption of the "cage" system, also used in the Ottoman Empire. The "cage" system secluded the prince sons in the harem, thus strengthening the bond between mothers and their sons. It also led to the power of the shah's mother (Babaie et al. 2004). Before this change, the prince sons' predecessors grew up far from their crowned father, far from the capital, under the tutelage of the Qizilbash (literally Red Heads), the Turkmen devoted to Shah Ismail (r. 1501–24), founder of the Safavid dynasty, and became governors of provinces and generals in the army. The fate of the Crown Prince was thus generally linked to his guardian's Qizilbash tribe; the guardian in turn had considerable influence on the reign of the future king. When the "cage" system was adopted, it deprived the Qizilbash of the role of guardian of princes and future kings, which had allowed them to manipulate the princes and sometimes even use them against the king. Parallel to the attempts to extract the princes from the Qizilbash's power, a new system of royal concubinage was adopted whereby, unlike in the past, the shah's wives and concubines were no longer exclusively from the ranks of the Qizilbash. The concubines were also former slaves, some of whom converted to Islam, while others did not. They replaced the princesses and became mothers of the future heirs. After the reign of Shah Safi in 1629–42, power gradually shifted from the court to the more interior parts of the king's house. In the hierarchy of the harem, the king's mother headed the seraglio, followed by preferred wives and high-ranking eunuchs. According to the traveler Jean Chardin, the problem for the shah's ministers was the harem, where the shah held a form of privy council that prevailed over all others. The council was held between the queen mother, the great eunuchs, and the preferred concubines. If the ministers did not adapt their advice to the advice of those close to the king (i.e., those in the harem), with whom he spent much more time, the ministers risked having their advice rejected, which often led to their ruin (Babaie et al. 2004, 45).

Correspondingly, the veil became the symbol of status among Muslim leaders and urban elite under the Ottoman and Safavid rule. Royal women, both Ottoman and Safavid, showed their power, prestige, and piety through the considerable financial means they allocated to the construction of public monuments.

In Iran, the period of the Safavid dynasty corresponds to the Golden Age of the *waqf* (plural *awqaf*), a pious bequest designating property inalienable, the usufruct of which is consecrated to a religious institution or public utility. Some Safavid kings such as Shah Abbas I even designated all their wealth as a *waqf*, drawing a good number of members of their court into this practice. Mohammadreza Neyestani (2017) describes many *waqf* charters preserved in the archive of the Organization and Charities of Isfahan, a *waqf* whose founders were women of Safavid royalty or women from the wealthy classes unrelated to the court.

Construction of schools (madrassas) and educational centers grew significantly not only in the capital Isfahan but also in many cities of the kingdom, large and small: "This proliferation of religious schools transformed Safavid Persia into one of the main learning centers of religious sciences of Shi'ism: a position it would keep until the fall of Isfahan and the end of the Safavid dynasty. The *waqf* played a role in this process of developing the teaching centers" (Neyestani 2017, 14).

The women of the royal court and those belonging to wealthy families built several Shi'ite religious schools, two caravansaries (inns surrounding the court), a mosque, a *hammam* (bathhouse), water fountains, and so on. The majority of these constructions also benefited from a *waqf*. Through the *waqf*, these women gained popular legitimacy and immortalized their names. Delaram Khanom, the wife of Shah Abbas I, built the Jadeh Koochak School in 1645–46 and dedicated a *waqf* to the building's maintenance. Hoori Nam Khanom, another royal wife, built her school, Jadeh Bozorg, in 1647–48. Zeynab Beygom, wife of Ḥakim al-Malik Ardistani, a physician, built the Nimaward School in 1702. Princess Shahr Banoo Beygom had a school and a *hammam* built in her name. Maryam Beygom also built a school in 1703–4, granting a *waqf* to maintain it. Between 1668 and 1692, the women of Shah Soleiman's entourage built several complexes and gave them rich *awqaf* to maintain and run their patronage activities. The majority of these places built by women of Isfahan had a Shi'ite religious function; the schools were indeed used to celebrate and in particular to propagate Shi'ism. This is noteworthy because the second half of the seventeenth century coincided with the spread of Twelver Shi'ism. Women therefore also participated in this movement by building schools and granting *awqaf* to sacred Shi'ite places, such as the mausoleums dedicated to Imam Reza in Mashhad and Imam Hossein in Karbala (Habibi 2017; Neyestani 2017).

Like the Safavid royal and wealthy women, women of the Ottoman imperial harem showed their prestige, piety, and power by mobilizing their considerable financial means to construct monumental buildings, including the ones for public use. The practice dates back to the sixteenth century, when Hurrem Sultan, the Sultan Suleiman's beloved principal concubine, funded the construction of a large mosque and a bathhouse in Istanbul. She also constructed buildings in Jerusalem to serve the poor. But her financial means were not comparable to the huge financial resources and fortune of the queen mother, or *valid sultan* in Turkish, who used them for charity. These activities of the women of the royal harem also promoted the power of the ruling dynasty. Other elite women used the institution of the *waqf* to their advantage, too. In Aleppo, Cairo, and Istanbul, between a third and half of the urban *awqaf* were founded by women. The founders themselves appointed the administrators of the *waqf* property during their lifetime and appointed their descendants as future directors. They also usually appointed women—their daughters, sisters, mothers, or their freed slaves—as beneficiaries of *waqf* property. The women used the *waqf* to ensure their own and their female descendants' control over the property (Tucker 1999, 81).

Women's Property Rights in Islam

In accordance with Islamic law, Muslim women have had the right to possess and control their property, even after marriage. In Aleppo in 1770, for example, women were involved either as buyers or sellers in 59 percent of all property transactions. In 1800, the proportion rose to 67 percent. In Egypt, elite women owned properties, including farms. In Tunisia, peasant women of Mediterranean regions possessed between 10 and 14 percent of olive trees, the main source of wealth (Tucker 1999, 76).

Under Muhammad Ali (1805–48) in Egypt, the centralization project was a detriment to Egyptian women, depriving them of economic independence. Their situation worsened under British colonialism and the influence of the Napoleonic Code of 1804. Muhammad Ali introduced new institutions copied after the European model, which turned out to hurt women. Banks, insurance companies, and the stock exchange in Europe did not recognize women's legal existence, and these financial institutions followed the same strategies in Egypt. Therefore, Egyptian women were not authorized to open bank accounts in their own names or to exchange on the stock market. It was only in the twentieth century that they were again able to participate in some of the activities they had normally conducted until the eighteenth century (Lotfi-al Sayyed Marsot 1996, 45–47).

In the nineteenth century, the fortunes of these rich women, like that of their husbands, diminished considerably with the erosion of the *waqf* in Egypt and the Ottoman Empire owing to the decline in trade controlled by indigenous traders in favor of European control over the import and export of goods. Moreover, as the state became more powerful, economic opportunities for wealthy women became scarcer. However, women from the ruling elite still acquired skills in household and money management, paving the way for a gradual transition to their economic activities prevalent in the twentieth century (Tucker 1999, 82).

Working-class women's economic activity had been supported by wealthier women through local and informal networks, but these networks were largely weakened with the centralizing integration of the Egyptian economy into the European market (Tucker 1985). In Syria and Egypt, for example, women workers lost their jobs in the weaving industry and were forced into domestic service. In Aleppo following integration into the world market, the number of female weavers fell from twenty thousand at the beginning of the nineteenth century to only two thousand in the mid-nineteenth century (Meriwether 1993, 75). In Iran, many women active in carpet weaving and fabric spinning lost their jobs with the country's integration into the international market, which led to Iran's specialization in the production of raw materials and the decline of local industries (Seyf 1994). Following the research of Afaf Lotfi-al Sayyed Marsot (1996), one can conclude that the presumed link (usually made by westerners) among modernization, westernization, and women's emancipation should thus be challenged. In fact, with modernity and European colonization, women's rights deteriorated in the Arab world, and women's reclusion increased in the Ottoman Empire after European intervention. Lotfi-al Sayyed Marsot points out that "although religion plays a role in determining attitudes toward women, there are other, perhaps more powerful considerations" (1996, 50).

Contrary to the common belief that Islam deprived women of their rights and their agency, women, both those who belonged to upper classes and those who were from urban and rural lower classes, could claim their rights by going to a religious judge. They could file for divorce, inheritance rights, and guardianship of their children after divorce and would obtain them. Fathers and husbands did not use women's property without their consent, and women would complain to the court if their husbands did so (Jennings 1975). Lady Elizabeth Craven, who visited Istanbul in the eighteenth century, wrote: "I think I have never seen women enjoying more freedom than in Turkey. Regarding men's attitude toward our gender Turkish men constitute an example for all other nations" (quoted in Jennings 1975, 57).

Women also prayed along with men in the mosque. Julia Pardoe, who visited Istanbul in 1830, was astonished to see women praying in the Haggia Sofia while their children played in the middle of the mosque. "In Europe it was erroneously said that Muslim women did not have the right to go to the mosque or pray in a mosque" (quoted in Katz 2014, 1).

Muslim Women Reinterpret Islam

Contemporary history in Middle Eastern societies shows that the Islamic referent in the field of gender provoked different approaches from Muslim women. In reaction to modernist, secularist, or westernized positions, some women advocated the return to the Golden Age of Islam. Fatima Rashid (d. 1953) was one such woman. She founded an association called Jam'iyyat Tarqiyat al Mar'a (Society for Women's Progress) and its journal in 1908. Along with Sarah al-Mihiyya (who was from a prosperous family) and other women, Rashid advocated women's return to religion, piety, and modesty. Labiba Ahmad (1870–1951), an important political figure who was close to the Watani Party and later to the Muslim Brotherhood, was close to Hassan al-Banna, their founder. She was both a nationalist and a religious person, daughter of a medical doctor and wife of a judge. She founded the Society of Egyptian Women's Awakening and its journal, *Women's Awakening*, in 1921. According to Beth Baron, although Ahmad used conservative language and advocated the return to traditions, her perspectives and practices were anchored in modernity and contemporary political culture (2005, 198). In addition to philanthropic activities, Ahmad stressed the importance of education, called for the boycott of foreign schools, and demanded the enforcement of the use of Arabic and the study of the Qur'an. She also thought that school should be free for both boys and girls, although she did not advocate an identical educational program for both, arguing that boys' and girls' roles in life were not identical. Ahmad "showed that women were not just objects of Islamist discourse but activists in their own right, and her vision promoted an image—that of a modern Islamist woman—that competed with the secular 'new woman' ideal. . . . However, by stressing the Islamic cultural component as integral to nationalism, she limited the possibility of rewriting social relations along more egalitarian lines" (Baron 2005, 213).

Another important example is Zainab al-Ghazali (1917–2005), who became an important figure among conservative Muslim women religious and political activists in the mid-twentieth century. She was at first a member of Huda Sha'rawi's Union of Egyptian Women, a secular feminist organization founded in 1925. She later left the union but, in accordance with Sha'rawi's demand, never acted against it. She founded the Association of Muslim Women but in the 1940s started to work with the Organization of Muslim Sisters—the women's branch of the Muslim Brotherhood created in 1937—and became its leader. The number of its members rose to five thousand in 1948, making it one of the most important women's organizations in Egypt (Hatem 1994, 672–73). During the 1980s and 1990s, the political scientist Heba Raouf Ezzat (b. 1965) represented the public voice of Islamic women. She qualified feminism as a Western construction and attempted to construct an Islamic modernity through a critique of secularism and feminism, which, according to Ezzat, insisted on individual rights to the detriment of family and collective values. She rejected the separation between public and private spheres and demanded freedom of choice for women, the rights she says they had historically enjoyed in Islamic traditions (El-Gawhary and Ezzat 1994). Omaima Abou-Bakr (b. 1957), a professor of English and comparative literature at Cairo University, is a good example of a contemporary Egyptian Muslim feminist.[3] She graduated from Cairo University before pursuing her education in North Carolina. A specialist in medieval Sufi poetry and medieval Arabic and English literature, she is also interested in mystical women, female spirituality in both Christianity and Islam, history of women in Islam, Islamic feminism, and gender questions in religious discourses. She is the cofounder of the Women and Memory Forum, which is composed of scholars, researchers, and both Muslim and secular activists who are concerned with negative perceptions of Arab women. According to its website, "The prevailing cultural images [of] and ideas [about] Arab women represent an obstacle to improving the conditions of women and their obtaining their rights. One of the most important obstacles facing Arab women today is the absence of alternative sources of cultural knowledge regarding the roles of women in history and in contemporary life" (Women and Memory Forum n.d.). The forum created a research group that advocates and promotes gender analyses in both Arab history and social sciences.

In Turkey, the Capital City Women's Platform is an association of Muslim women, many of whom call themselves feminists. Hidayet Şefkatli Tuksal (b. 1963), a reformist theologian and feminist who cofounded the Women's Platform in 1995, is among them. She historicizes and contextualizes Islam and the Qur'an and warns against anachronism, arguing that "to pretend finding in the Koran a contemporary approach to gender equality is illusory. The aim of the verses was to improve the fate of women of that time. I have found such a flexibility in the Koran and for this reason I continue to be a Muslim" (Ortaq 2009). Berrin Sonmez (b. 1961), one of the platform's former presidents, declared that the platform is highly critical of conservative interpretations of Islam and that its aim is to combine feminism

---

3. Abou-Bakr's book *Al-Mar'a wa-al-jindar* (Woman and Gender, 2002) is an example of these intellectual undertakings.

and religion. She asserted in an interview in 2014: "Islam is often considered an obstacle to the empowerment of women; but, in reality, it is not Islam in itself that dispossesses women but patriarchal and androcentric interpretations of Islam. A new interpretation, from the twenty-first century, from the perspective of women, is necessary. What must we and what do we want to change?"[4] This critical approach rejects the supposedly divine nature of the laws and strips Islamic traditions of their sacred status. These contemporary Muslim feminists believe that women should be free to choose to veil or to unveil. They think that this freedom of choice symbolizes an act of resistance, a crucial means to fight for freedom and democracy. They operate within two distinct sociocultural environments: their original circles (the disadvantaged population) and their acquired circles (the educated and professional middle class). For strategic reasons, they mobilize both circles' interactional networks of relations and cultural resources. The question of the headscarf became central in Turkey and among feminist activists. The Kemalist republicans, for example, refuse to collaborate with veiled feminists. The majority of Women's Platform members are practicing Muslims and wear the veil, but the platform does not force its members to veil. "It is a matter of personal choice. Our aim is to establish fundamental principles of women's rights."[5] Nouria Doran (birth date unknown), who once served as the platform's president, is a theologian. She was veiled but decided to unveil, arguing that according to her interpretation of Islam veiling is not compulsory. She then went to Germany to teach Islamic studies (Kian 2019). The Iranian theologian Sadigheh Vasmaghi came to the same conclusion in 2022, during the Women, Life, Freedom movement.

In Iran, Mrs. Alavi Isfahani-Amin (1886–1983), was one of the most learned religious personalities. She received authorization to interpret the Qur'an from the highest religious authorities, including

---

4. Berrin Sonmez, former president of Capital City Women's Platform, interviewed by the author in Turkish through a translator, Ankara, Turkey, Apr. 12, 2014.

5. Fatma Bostan Unsal, former president of Capital City Women's Platform, interviewed in English by the author, Ankara, Apr. 12, 2014.

Sheikh Abdolkarim Haeri, the founder of the Qom religious seminary in 1921, and thus became a source of imitation (*mujtahid*). Later she authorized several outstanding clerics, including Ayatollah Mar'ashi Najafi, to interpret the Qur'an, the hadith, and Islamic traditions. Ever since her death in the early 1980s, Iran has been devoid of female sources of imitation (*mujtahideh*). To educate women to be capable of reinterpreting Islamic laws and traditions, Fatemeh Amini (b. 1934) founded the first religious seminary for women in Qom in 1972 and later three more in different cities, including Tehran, where I met her at her women's theology school, Fatemeh Zahra, on October 6, 1994. She argued that a woman *mujtahid* should be capable of solving a multitude of problems:

> According to the Qur'an, men and women are equal. . . . But they [men] have not wanted to make women believe in themselves. Our main aim here is to form women *mujtahideh*. The society needs women doctors and engineers as well as women *mujtahideh*. But there is an important resistance against women attaining the degree of *ijtihad* [interpretation]. Without these obstacles, which seriously hinder their training, we could have had at least fifty women *mujtahideh* since the revolution. Many young women study at these seminaries, but nobody encourages them. When I came to Tehran, nobody [no religious authority] supported me, either, although they all knew me for years. A *bazari* (merchant) provided me with a basement flat, and a factory owner paid my teachers. We are independent and have over 250 students, many of whom are also university or high school students as well as medical doctors or engineers.

In Iran, the climax of women's rereading of the Qur'an and Islamic traditions occurred in the 1990s and early 2000s. Religious women's mobilization against "the dispossession of women of their power in the realm of the sacred" (Héritier 1996, 5), however, is not limited to training women *mujtahideh*. The authorities justify such prohibitions by referring to the Qur'an, the sharia, the hadith, and Islamic traditions. Therefore, women's challenge has necessarily entailed debates that revisit and reinterpret Islamic principles. Several articles of the Islamic Republic Civil Code (e.g., those on polygamy) find their origins in the Qur'anic verses, especially Surat al-Nisa' (The Women), but women challenge the dominant readings by the clergy, which they consider distorted. Through presenting their own interpretations, they intend to show that Islam accommodates the equality of rights between women and men. Women who have religious training are better equipped to deal with religious issues. For example, the journal *Payam-i hâjar*, edited by Azam Taliqani (d. 2019), the daughter of the late cleric Ayatollah Mahmoud Taliqani, was the first to refute, in 1992, the legalization of polygamy by proposing a new interpretation of the al-Nisa' verse: "The analysis of the Qur'anic verse on polygamy shows that this right is recommended in some specific cases and exclusively in order to meet a social need in view of expanding social justice" (Ebn-Eddin 1992, 28). The specific cases were war periods during which the heads of households were killed, leaving many widows and orphans with no financial resources. According to Forouq Ebn-Eddin, this phenomenon caused enormous problems for the community of Muslims. In the absence of social institutions to take care of widows and orphans, this responsibility was delegated to Muslim men via polygamy. In her *Payam-i hâjar* article, Ebn-Eddin maintained that "God has recommended polygamy only in the case of a social need, and only if men can preserve equity between their wives" (1992, 28). Combining her religious interpretation with the realities of the postrevolutionary Iranian society, she rejected polygamy as a social necessity. "Contrary to the ancient time, the modern state and its social institutions are conceived to assist needy families. Therefore, polygamy has no social function to fulfill" (29). She argued that polygamy, which only well-to-do men can afford (because of the high costs of *nafaqeh*[6]), deprives other men of opportunities for marriage. The author concluded, "It has been shown that in reality it is pleasure rather than charity that motivates men to become polygamous" (29).

6. According to Article 1106 of the Islamic Republic Civil Code, in permanent marriage the wife's maintenance (*nafaqeh*) should be provided by the husband. *Nafaqeh* includes housing, clothing, furniture, and food.

Contemporary Muslim women activists have evolved in a globalized world that has led to a dissociation between religion and culture. They endeavor to preserve the Muslim character of their societies but to reject laws and institutions that are modeled after Islamic jurisprudence. They question religious and national specificities in the wake of unifying globalized gender norms that have transformed their relations and interactions with both the state power and the society. As Alain Roussillon maintains, "The question is not only to know how to reread the Koran, but also to know how to live individually and collectively as Muslims in a world where identities are shaped in a globalized context and can no longer be thought only in religious terms" (2005, 101).

Among the magazines published by Islamic feminists, *Zanan* (Women) occupied a unique position. Shortly after it was launched in 1992, it published a series of articles to demonstrate that the Qur'an does not forbid women to pronounce religious judgments and that women can even undertake religious, legal, and political leadership roles in society. Rejecting laws that strengthened men's superior position in the family, such Islamic feminists made a case for equality under the law and the sharing of responsibilities between the spouses. Their main argument centered on the active role that women played during the Islamic Revolution and continued to play in public life, despite tremendous impediments. In reinterpreting the sacred texts and the Islamic laws, their intention was to confirm the legitimacy of the authority of women in political, religious, and legal institutions (Kian 2010). Obstacles to women's exercise of religious authority were also discussed in a series of articles in the magazine. "In the central Islamic texts," according to one article, "nothing demonstrates or justifies Islam's ban on women from delivering religious edicts or from becoming sources of imitation. In the secondary sources, however, a number of such indications exist" (Yadegar-Azadi 1992, 21).[7]

---

7. The author of these articles in *Zanan*, who adopted the female pseudonym "Mina Yadegar-Azadi," is in fact Hojjat-ol Eslam Mohsen Saidzadeh. In 1998, he

According to this author, there is no consensus among the religious authorities to justify such obstacles. Consequently, "a woman is able to deliver religious edicts . . . and can also lead the people in the religious, spiritual, political, and legal domains" (28).

Islamic feminists' strategy was therefore to challenge power relations in both the society and the state within the context of existing constraints, a version of what Deniz Kandiyoti (1988) called "bargaining with patriarchy." Nevertheless, Islamic feminism, with its claim to multiple affiliations and identities, is often contested by some Western feminists or some Western-oriented feminists from Muslim countries, for whom Islam and feminism are necessarily incompatible. For such feminists, it is inconceivable that women asserting their attachment to Islam could at the same involve themselves with an act of subversion. The analyses they offer define Muslim women as subjected victims of a patriarchy that is supposedly rooted in Islam, and they therefore refuse to concede that Muslim women have the power of "agency," that they can autonomously initiate action and resist power. As Leila Ahmed points out, "Although Western feminists have succeeded in rejecting their culture's myths about Western women and their innate inferiority and irrationality [in comparison to men], they continue to subscribe [to] and perpetuate those [same] myths about Muslims, including about Muslim women, and about harems as well as to assume superiority towards the women within them" (1982, 526). This feminism is sustained by and reinforces the essentialist/culturalist perspectives. "Although religion is seen in Western societies as one institution among many, it is perceived as the bedrock of the societies in which Islam is practiced. . . . The overall effect of this paradigm is to deprive Muslim women of self-presence, of being. Because women are subsumed under religion defined in fundamental terms, they are inevitably seen as evolving in nonhistorical time. They have virtually

---

was summoned before the Clerical Court, stripped of his religious position, and imprisoned for his reformist ideas.

no history. Any analysis of change is therefore foreclosed" (Lazreg 1988, 86).

Muslim feminists' discourse is supported by women with special knowledge of theology who reinterpret the Qur'an and the traditions to the advantage of women. They rebut the Islamic jurisprudence political position that bars women from access to positions of political leadership because of their supposed physical and intellectual frailty:

> The Qur'an mentions only a very few political leaders, yet *Belqeys* (Queen of Sheba) is one of them. Furthermore, she is depicted as one of the most just and rational sovereigns. This is sufficient to show that the Qur'an accepts the natural and intrinsic capacity of women to manage and govern. In fact, *Belqeys* is not exceptional. She represents women as a whole. She has shown that women are not weaker than men in the matter of government and that they can even be better than men, to the extent that the idea of justice was one of the characteristics of the reign of *Belqeys*. (Gorgi 1993, 9)

Conclusion

In societies where Islamic law is enforced, the gender order is at the heart of the hierarchical social order more than is race or class. This order is reinforced by the hierarchical structure of marriage and supported by the dominant discourse of hierarchical Islam, which has elaborated the social, economic, and legal marginalization and subordination of women. As Fatema Mernissi states,

> Muslim jurists, charged with leading the way by drafting a sacred law, have opted for a hierarchical Islam in which the woman represents the inferior element, excluded from power and subject to the will of the one whom the law designates as her custodian: the husband. But in order to succeed in this pyramidal Islam, jurists had to strip women of their privilege as believers, which had immediately set them up as equal to men before God. They elaborate a division of the feminine where sexuality takes precedence. The woman will be first and foremost a sexual object. Her oversexualization masks her dimension as a believer. To master woman is to master desire. To subdue woman is to make reason, the divine will, and order

triumph. The superiority of man over woman is the superiority of reason over unreason. (2016, 202)

Mernissi argues that, contrary to these jurisconsults and guardians of male domination and majority in the Muslim worlds, Ibn 'Arabi, born in Andalusian Spain in 1155, thought that to be satisfied with a literal, jurisprudential interpretation of the Qur'an is to neglect its spirituality. For this Sufi philosopher, described as a heretic by orthodox imams, the feminine can embody harmony and wisdom and be a part of the divine (2016, 12–13).

As the brief historical overview given in this chapter has shown, throughout the history of Islam women have been subject to power but have also exercised various forms of power: religious, political, economic, cultural, and social. They have also mobilized, as have women in other regions of the world, against the social inequalities between women and men. Today in Muslim-majority societies, thanks to women's massive access to education and training, on the one hand, and to their overwhelming presence in the real or virtual public space, as in social movements, on the other hand, men's monopoly over religious discourse and symbols has vanished into thin air. Religious discourse is no longer the prerogative of men, and transnational resistance against the religious order established by conservative and hierarchical readings of Islam is getting organized.

Muslim feminists have challenged not only the masculinized construct of Islamist ideology and essentialist discourses but also gendered Islamophobia/Muslimophobia. In this process, they have contested and reinterpreted Islamic doctrines and laws as well as gendered norms, produced contexts where women can be involved in public debates, interacted with political and religious processes and institutions, and created new meanings. Many Muslim women now refer to Islam and through their own interpretations oppose gendered social relations. Muslim feminisms also challenge the validity of a unitary model of emancipation based on Western history and models.

Mernissi's reflections and ideas can be used both to rescue Islam from its jurisprudential and ideological fixity, or what she calls "orthodox discourse," and to argue against an essentialist perspective that reduces Islam to ideology and jurisprudence. As Mernissi contends, "It remains to be asked why today it is the image of the woman of the 'Golden Age'—a 'slave' . . . who symbolizes the Muslim eternal female[,] while the memory of Umm Salama, A'isha and Soukeina awakens no response and seems strangely distant and unreal" (1991, 195). As a sociologist, Mernissi paid attention to contemporary social and cultural changes, which, she believed, would lead women to participate in discourse making: "In these new Muslim digital societies of the XXI century, women have invaded the media and communication networks, including the internet and satellite channels. Men's monopoly over words and symbols has thus been volatized. The future of democracy in Islam has never been so magnificent as when finally both men and women have the right to speak" (2016, 221).

It is obvious that the imbalance in gender power relations is too staunch to be abolished only through women's better access to education or speech, for they are rooted in social and economic inequalities. However, Mernissi's works have clearly shown that gender social relations, like religion, are not fixed and can and should be changed through women's own struggles in societies where, contrary to essentialist claims, religion is not univocal and has no absolute hold on women.

References

Abou-Bakr, Omaima. 2002. *Al-Mar'ah wa-al-jindar* (Woman and gender. Damascus, Syria: Dar al-Fikr.
———. 2003. "Teaching the Words of the Prophet: Women Instructors of the Hadith (Fourteenth and Fifteenth Centuries)." *HAWWA* 1, no. 3: 306–28.
———. 2010. "Articulating Gender: Muslim Women Intellectuals in the Pre-modern Period." *Arab Studies Quarterly* 32, no. 3: 127–44.
Abu-Lughod, Lila. 2001. "Orientalism and Middle East Feminist Studies." *Feminist Studies* 27, no. 1 (Spring): 101–13.
Ahmed, Leila. 1982. "Western Ethnocentrism and Perceptions of the Harem." *Feminist Studies* 8, no. 3 (Autumn): 521–34.

———. 1992. *Women and Gender in Islam.* New Haven, CT: Yale Univ. Press.

Babaie, Sussan, Kathryn Babayan, Ina Baghdiantz-McCabe, and Massumeh Farhad. 2004. *Slaves of the Shah: New Elites of Safavid Iran.* London: I. B. Tauris.

Baron, Beth. 2005. *Egypt as a Woman: Nationalism, Gender and Politics.* Berkeley: Univ. of California Press.

Cortese, Delila, and Simonetta Calderini. 2006. *Women and the Fatimids in the World of Islam.* Edinburgh: Edinburgh Univ. Press.

Ebn-Eddin, Forouq. 1992. "Lozoum-i eslah-i qavanin-i talaq, t'addud-i zojat va hezanat" (The necessity for the reform of laws concerning divorce, polygyny, and child custody). *Payam-i Hâjar,* Shahrivar 19, 1371 (Sept. 10, 1992), 28–29.

El-Gawhary, Karim, and Heba Ra'uf Ezzat. 1994. "Is It Time to Launch a New Women's Liberation Movement—an Islamic One?" *Middle East Report* 191 (Nov.–Dec.): 26–27.

Gorgi, Monir. 1993. "Zan va zamamdari: Negahi beh hokumat-i malakeh-yi saba dar Qoran" (Women and government: An appraisal of the government of the queen of Saba in the Qur'an). *Farzaneh* 1 (Autumn): 9–29.

Habibi, Negar. 2017. *Ali Qoli Jebadar et l'occidentalisme Safavide: Une étude sur les peintures dites Farangi Sazi, leurs milieux et commanditaires sous Shah Soleiman (1666–94).* Leiden, Netherlands: Brill.

Hajjat, Abdellali, and Marwan Mohammed. 2013. *Islamophobie: Comment les élites françaises fabriquent le "problème musulman."* Paris: La Découverte.

Halliday, Fred. 1999. "'Islamophobia' Reconsidered." *Ethnic and Racial Studies* 22, no. 5: 892–902.

Hatem, Mervat. 1994. "Egyptian Discourses on Gender and Political Liberalization: Do Secularist and Islamist Views Really Differ?" *Middle East Journal* 48, no. 4: 661–76.

Héritier, Françoise. 1996. *Masculin/féminin, la pensée de la différence.* Paris: Odile Jacob.

Jennings, Ronald. 1975. "Women in Early Seventeenth Century Ottoman Judicial Records: The Sharia Court of Anatolian Kayseri." *Journal of the Economic and Social History of the Orient* 18:53–114.

Kandiyoti, Deniz. 1988. "Bargaining with Patriarchy." *Gender and Society* 2, no. 3 (Sept.): 274–90.

Kassem, Moustafa. 2015. "Fatwa in the Era of Globalization." In *Ifta' and Fatwa in the Muslim World and the West*, edited by Zulfiqar Ali Shah, 89–104. Herndon, VA: International Institute of Islamic Thought.

Katz, Marion Holmes. 2014. *Women's Mosque Attendance as a Legal Problem: A History of Legal Thought and Social Practice*. New York: Columbia Univ. Press.

Kian, Azadeh. 2010. "Le féminisme islamique en Iran: Nouvelle forme d'assujettissement ou émergence de sujets agissants?" Translated by Ethan Rundell as "Islamic Feminism in Iran: A New Form of Subjugation or the Emergence of Agency?" *Critique internationale* 46, no. 1 (Jan.–Mar.). At https://www.cairn-int.info/article-E_CRII_046_0045 --islamic-feminism-in-iran-a-new-form-of-s.htm.

———. 2017. "Féminisme postcolonial: Contributions théoriques et politiques." *Revue cités* 4, no. 72 (Dec.): 69–80.

———. 2019. "Globalized Gender and Creative Strategies against Inequalities in Turkey: Capital City Women's Platform (Başkent Kadın Platformu Derneği)." In *The Globalization of Gender: Knowledge, Mobilizations, Frameworks of Action*, edited by Ioana Cirstocea, Delphine Lacombe, and Elisabeth Marteu, 102–22. London: Routledge.

Lazreg, Marnia. 1988. "Feminism and Difference: The Perils of Writing as a Woman on Women in Algeria." *Feminist Studies* 14, no. 1 (Spring): 81–107.

Lewis, Bernard. 1988. *Le langage politique de l'Islam*. Translated by Odette Guitard. Paris: Gallimard.

Lotfi-al Sayyed Marsot, Afaf. 1996. "Women and Modernization: A Reevaluation." In *Women, the Family, and Divorce Laws in Islamic History*, edited by Amira El Azhary Sonbol, 39–51. Syracuse, NY: Syracuse Univ. Press.

Meriwether, Margaret L. 1993. "Women and Economic Change in Nineteenth-Century Syria: The Case of Aleppo." In *Arab Women: Old Boundaries, New Frontiers*, edited by Judith Tucker, 65–83. Bloomington: Indiana Univ. Press.

Mernissi, Fatema. 1975. *Beyond the Veil: Male–Female Dynamics in Muslim Society*. Cambridge, MA: Schenkman.

———. 1983. *Sexe, idéologie, Islam*. Paris: Tierce.

———. 1990. *Sultanes oubliées: Femmes chefs d'etat en Islam*. Paris: Albin Michel.

———. 1991. *Women and Islam: An Historical and Theological Enquiry.* Oxford: Basil Blackwell.

———. 2001a. *Le harem et l'Occident.* Paris: Albin Michel.

———. 2001b. *Scheherazade Goes West: Different Cultures, Different Harems.* New York: Washington Square Press.

———. 2016. *La femme dans l'inconscient musulman.* New and rev. ed. Casablanca, Morocco: Le Fennec. [Originally published under the pseudonym "Fatna Aït Sabbah."]

Neyestani, Mohammadreza. 2017. "Femmes, waqf et droit de propriété en Iran à l'époque safavide." *Hawwa: Journal of Women of the Middle East and the Islamic World* 1515:1–22.

Ortaq, Nukte V. 2009. Interview of Hidayet Şefkatli Tuksal. *Tous les jours toute l'info*, Mar. 23. At https://www.lexpress.fr/monde/une-feministe-relit-le-coran_747735.html.

Roussillon, Alain. 2005. *La pensée islamique contemporaine: Acteurs et enjeux.* Paris: Téraèdre.

Seyf, Asad. 1994. *Iqtisad-i Iran dar qarn-i nuzdahom* (Iran's economy in the nineteenth century). Tehran, Iran: Cheshmeh.

Shari'ati, Ali. 1976. *Fatemeh Fatemeh Ast.* Tehran, Iran: Shari'ati Foundation.

———. 1979. *Red Shi'ism.* Translated by Habib Shirazi. Tehran, Iran: Shari'ati Foundation.

Szuppe, Maria. 2003. "Status, Knowledge, and Politics: Women in Sixteenth-Century Safavid Iran." In *Women in Iran from the Rise of Islam to 1800*, edited by Guity Nashat and Lois Beck, 140–69. Champaign: Univ. of Illinois Press.

Tucker, Judith E. 1985. *Women in Nineteenth-Century Egypt.* Cambridge: Cambridge Univ. Press.

———. 1999. "Women in the Middle East and North Africa: The Nineteenth and Twentieth Centuries." In *Women in the Middle East and North Africa: Restoring Women to History*, edited by Guity Nashat and Judith E. Tucker, 73–132. Bloomington: Indiana Univ. Press.

Women and Memory Forum. N.d. "About WMF." At https://wmf.org.eg/en/about-us/. Accessed Feb. 2, 2023.

Yadegar-Azadi, Mina. 1992. "Qizavat-i zan" (Woman's judgment). *Zanan* 5:17–28.

10

Fatema Mernissi's Heritage and the Pathway for French Muslim Women's Autonomy

HANANE KARIMI

Translated from French by Paola Bacchetta

One of the many contributions of Fatema Mernissi's work is her deconstruction of sacred concepts she felt are caught in manipulation strategies by those who hold religious and political power so they can better conceal the stakes of control and governance in which the concepts are implicated. In this, Mernissi bequeaths indispensable work to the study of Islam as a method for control and governance. Her book *Le harem politique* (1987; translated as *The Veil and the Male Elite*, 1991), in which she analyzes the performative scope of religious and political power, was censored in Morocco for a few decades because of the critical and subversive scope of its content. Mernissi posits boundaries as the central stake of power in *Rêves de femmes: Une enfance au harem* (1996, a translation of *Dreams of Trespass: Tales of a Harem Girlhood* [1994]) and *Le harem politique*.

In this chapter, I propose a sociological analysis of Mernissi's discussion primarily through three of her books—*Le harem politique*,

---

I thank Minoo Moallem and Paola Bacchetta for their careful readings of this text. I owe Paola for the translation of my chapter from French to English, for which I thank her doubly. This chapter also benefited from exigent blind reviews, and I thank the reviewers because they allowed me to enrich this contribution.

La peur modernité: Conflit Islam démocratie (1992b, translated as *Islam and Democracy: Fear of the Modern World*, 1992a), and *Rêves de femmes*. They all address symbolic or political boundaries, whether material or immaterial, that structure the lives of Muslim women in the Maghreb and in the West. In Mernissi's work, borders reveal spaces and configurations of power.

As a point of departure, it is worth positioning these three books in Mernissi's overall written corpus. Scholars identify two stages in Mernissi's academic output: "the 'secularist' one, situated in the 1980s and early 1990s, and the 'Islamic' feminist moments" that began after the 1990s (Rhouni 2010, 2). The trilogy upon which I focus is primarily part of a secularist moment in which Mernissi had an "unsympathetic position toward Islam" (Rhouni 2010, 1). In a later period, Mernissi was said to be "'soft' in contrast to her earlier more radical feminism" (Rhouni 2010, 5). For Raja Rhouni, "the moment of her shift" occurred after *Le harem politique* in 1987, with *Sultanes oubliées: Femmes chefs d'état en Islam* in 1990 (translated as *The Forgotten Queens of Islam* [1993]) and *La peur modernité* in 1992, when Mernissi became more oriented toward fiction writing (Rhouni 2010, 8). Only *Rêves de femmes* is part of the second moment.

The first part of this chapter is based on interviews I conducted with Muslim feminists in France in 2015 during my doctoral research and on readings of Mernissi's books. I address how the women received Mernissi's writings. In brief, I show how for the women, who are caught between two asymmetrical power relations—that is, secularism and religiosity with their analogous logics of subordination but opposite injunctions—Mernissi's work is extremely relevant and finds a home. In France, there is a strong border between the notion of secularism (*laïcité*) and religion. This border is part of what is defined as French exceptionalism. The question of the visibility of Muslim women who wear the hijab is the subject of what I call the *politics of secularism*, in which Muslim women are constantly reminded that their presence is undesirable because they do not correspond to hegemonic femininity (Karimi 2023, 29). There is also the question of the borders of kinds of femininity: *secular femininity* is valued, whereas *religious femininity* (which manifests as Islamic) is considered heretical and thereby is devalued, disqualified, and juridically excluded in accordance with the norms of secularity (Karami 2023, 82).

The second part of this chapter engages specifically with the question of borders in Mernissi's writing. I approach this question through two dimensions: space and time. When we invoke borders, we think of the hijab and the harem, both of which constitute the material border for Mernissi. To contextualize, decipher, or even criticize the hijab either through the hijab's historical arrival in the community of the Prophet Muhammad or through its more contemporary practice in Morocco, Mernissi the sociologist sets the scene. She invites us to "dislodge Islam from clichés, go beyond the idealized imagery of groups in power, scrutinize counter-resistances, study marginal cases and exceptions. This is especially to understand the history of women in Islam, a history that has been condemned like that of the peasants and the poor, to never be reflected in official discourse" (Rhouni 2010, 159). In taking up her own invitation, Mernissi considers relationships of class and gender domination. These aspects enable her analyses to circulate as approaches to social experiences beyond Arab-Muslim borders. To fully account for the fruitfulness of her legacy and the way it has been received beyond the borders of the society it analyzes, I propose to cross geographical and political borders.

Lalla Mernissi's Contemporary Legacy

To analyze the in-between-ness linked to the paradoxical injunctions forced upon Muslim women, I look to a collective of French Muslim feminists whom I met during my doctoral research. I was part of them. We were members of a group called Musulmanes en mouvement (Muslim Women in Movement, hereafter MEM). The group was formed shortly after the publication of the anthology *Féminismes islamiques* (Islamic Feminisms, 2012), edited by the sociologist Zahra Ali. Our group's aim was to provide a space for

Muslim women to think and organize together against both Islamophobia and the sexism that we encountered in Muslim spaces.[1] In 2014, MEM's membership encompassed about twenty women between twenty and forty years old. We were mostly descendants of North African immigrants (from Morocco, Algeria, Tunisia), along with one originally from sub-Saharan Africa (Senegal), one white convert to Islam, and one nonwhite convert. We all were university educated. Some had PhDs in sociology or biology or a master's in psychology. Others were psychologists, nurses, or accounting experts. And still others were photographers, entrepreneurs, or audiovisual technicians. We all desired to change the "order of things" or at least to participate in change in our own way.

To provide religious education to its members, MEM brought in experts on Muslim civilization who were part of our immediate circles (husband, friend, teacher, scholar) and who were sympathetic with the group's questionings. The members studied the history of the advent of Islam; its historical, local, political context; the question of reform; the status of the Qur'an; and so on. At times, members taught themselves and each other as they presented individual critical research on some religious concepts commonly used in ways that discriminate against women within the religious community. For example, a discussion took place about the concept of *qiwama*. In a conservative approach, *qiwama*'s meaning is often reduced to signify the husband's preeminence and power over his wife. But MEM members interrogated that interpretation and redefined *qiwama* more complexly to mean an equitable economic and material duty between the husband and the wife according to a normative conception of the heterosexual couple in Islamic tradition.

Each presentation was followed by discussions that included dissent against the critiques that were sometimes considered too radical

---

1. This dual critique led to, among other things, the formation of yet another group, Les femmes dans la mosquée (Women in the Mosque), in October 2013. For more on this group, see Inge 2013.

and too feminist. During the summer of 2013, veiled Muslim women were regularly victims of physical and verbal violence in the French public space. The pretext was that they were wearing the headscarf. In these circumstances, some group members questioned the mandate of covering oneself according to a hegemonic position on the hijab. The discussion was initiated by Naima, who was inspired by the works of the historian Abul Fadl. His writings are part of a broader analytic that provides social and political context to explain how the hijab emerged historically. Based on her understanding of Fadl's writing, Naima interrogated the cultural, historical, and social relevance of the hijab by recalling that only free women were required to wear it. In fact, Mernissi had argued the same. In light of this scholarship, the women in the group affirmed a need to question the consensual norm of the hijab and to get beyond it. Indeed, the objectives that legitimized the hijab were, at this precise moment of the summer of 2013, counterproductive. To the religious argument of distinguishing Muslim women from other women so that they would not be harassed by men, these women opposed the contextual argument that this distinction put them in physical danger now because of Islamophobia. This moment of collective dialogue did not lead to a consensual vision, especially because of the women's disparate lengths of religious experience. For example, the young white convert in MEM clearly had an idealistic approach to issues of modesty and protection that the hijab represented. Yet other women seemed more worn and tired by the many struggles they have engaged in daily because of how the dominant culture constructs their racialized positionality and racializes their religion—struggles that the recent white convert had not experienced.

Let us return to what Fatema Mernissi says. For her, women were ordered to wear the hijab as a way to solve the situation of their sexual assault in Medina. In her sharp analysis, Mernissi sees the hijab as the counterpart to sexual aggression or, more precisely, its dialogical recognition. She argues that if the hijab "is a response to sexual aggression, in *Ta'arrud* (harassment), it is at the same time its mirror. The *hijab* condenses and reflects this aggression by recognizing that the female body is *'awra*, meaning literally nakedness, a vulnerable body, defenseless" (1987, 254). Mernissi then questions the cognitive association in which appearing in a hijab signifies covering one's nakedness by displacing the analogy to the actual materialization of danger: "Is it by chance that a house without security is called *'awra*, 'naked,' like a woman without a *hijab*?" (1992a, 7). That is, the word that describes an apartment building or a house that is exposed and defenseless is the same word in Arabic that describes a woman who is not wearing a hijab (1987, 129). Mernissi's reasoning is direct. In such a situation, she sees betrayal because enslaved women will continue to be assaulted and abused in the streets. Muslim women will now be separated into two categories by the hijab: free women, against whom violence is forbidden, and enslaved women, to whom *ta'arrud* is permitted.

Mernissi's works, in particular *Le harem politique*, were among MEM's first influential readings because of the language and accessibility of her writings. *Le harem politique* allowed MEM members to engage in anecdotal questioning, for it traces the origins of an apocryphal hadith that has had dire political, social, spatial, and mental consequences for Muslim women. Most MEM members had inherited their religion without extensive knowledge in religious matters, except for two members who had scholarly religious knowledge. Some of the women in MEM had made up for this deficiency by attending classes at religious institutes that most often were part of a traditionalist and conservative Islam. The seed of curiosity and no doubt their social capital led at least half of the women in the group toward a decolonial and feminist political stance. Their first public event was the Social Forum in Tunis in 2013. Later, in October 2013, four of the six women who composed the collective called Femmes dans la mosquée (Women in the Mosque) were from MEM. In 2015, however, MEM fell apart. Today a small group of women have revived it with the help of an earlier MEM member. They wanted to revitalize the group's energy and work, but this was not possible. However, they were able to establish a reading group around Fatema Mernissi's writings. The reading group made central use of Mernissi's deconstructions of misogynist hadiths by revealing their conditions of production and diffusion.

Asma, a mother of two and a psychology student, one of the participants in the reading group and an earlier MEM member, explained that before she had joined MEM, the hijab had been part of the orthodox discipline she observed.[2] Fatema Mernissi's work was far from her reading list. One day she told a friend that she was wondering about her marital relationship, and he advised her to read *Le harem politique*. No doubt Asma had given him some clues that allowed him to connect her situation with the question of domination. Asma's orthodoxy can be understood as a guarantee of conformity to family expectations. She explained to me that she embodied the figure of the "good girl." She was thirty-seven years old at the time of the interview. I asked her to remember her discovery of Fatema Mernissi's work.

Asma told me: "It's a book that I started reading in 2011–2012. And I closed the book for a year; I did not throw it away, I did not sell it. I kept it closed for a year." I asked her why, and she explained: "Because it shocked me too much. There is work behind, about, the false hadiths. It was about the woman's question, but it questioned me too much." Asma felt uncomfortable discovering Fatema Mernissi's work. Precisely, the religious dispositions she had come to embody during her upbringing were in danger. This is what incited her to close the book, to push it away, to forget it. If Mernissi were to demonstrate to Asma that she had gone astray until now, that she had been betrayed by the Muslim clerics, what would become of her? In a convulsion of resistance to change, she pushed back all thoughts about Mernissi, who would reveal to her the epistemic violence with which she had heretofore lived. Yet after this initial response, Asma began to change. She stated: "I first continued reading Fatema. And that was a breath of fresh air, while we were educated in rigidity." Asma had two encounters with *Le harem politique*. The first was

---

2. The interviewee's name has been changed to respect her wish for anonymity.

short, painful, and even violent, probably because she had not sought out the book, but others had arranged for her to read it. The second encounter was free and dynamic. She had solved the problem of her fear of transgressing religious obligations. She explained the fear:

> But I also wondered about my faith. There was something that helped me, that I was attached to my prayers. Maybe I was going to go astray. I was going onto, or I was already on, uncomfortable ground, a minefield. And when I met the [MEM] women, I tried to contact Fatema Mernissi. I had questions to ask her. She did not answer me. I contacted Asma Lamrabet, who put me in contact with Zahra Ali and her sister, and there I discovered a new world. This book, *Le harem politique*, opened me to MEM, to this feminist universe.

Dr. Asma Lamrabet, a Moroccan physician and a well-known Muslim feminist in France, knows progressive Muslim religious thought in France very well. That's why she directed Asma to MEM. This is how Asma joined the MEM collective and took responsibility for her questions about her religiosity. Reading *Le harem politique* was the impetus for a new woman to dare to change because a new world appeared possible. I do not know if Fatema Mernissi knew of MEM's existence, but I can affirm without betraying the members that they are the worthy heirs of her thought.

The example of Asma demonstrates the power of the collective and of individuation in agency. Because such agency necessarily transgresses the rules of the powers that try to silence and invisibilize women, it is discouraged a priori. Mernissi comments thus about Muslim religious discourse: "Individuality in such a system is discouraged, private initiative is *bid'a*," and "the irreducible fortress of sovereign individuality remains the body and its indomitable sexuality" (1992b, 169).

Space: The Hijab or Symbolic Territoriality

In the Arab-Muslim context that Fatema Mernissi analyzes in *Le harem politique*, symbolic territoriality can take many forms. The hijab and the harem are material boundaries that the author experienced. She traces her childhood in Fez and her memories of the circumscribed and constrained space reserved for women in *Dreams of Trespass* (1994). She who dreamed of moving without hindrance remembers this maternal warning about the hijab: her mother asked her never to wear it. This sets the tone. Certainly, this apprehension in her flesh and in her movements within the given geographical confines inspires her analysis of territoriality. But these obstacles are never presented as such. They are bolstered and justified through the standard of modesty that legitimizes the hijab, just as it legitimized the harem in religious or cultural discourses. In *Le harem politique*, Mernissi brings us a radical critique of the religious justification for the hijab. She describes the act of obliging women to wear the hijab as a betrayal of the prophetic project, the goal of which was to form a society of responsible individuals who would be respectful of otherness in all its forms. She analyzes the hijab as a regression to the detriment of women (1987, 260).

To understand this new border imposed on women, Mernissi explores both the symbolism of the hijab in the Islamic unconscious and sexuality in Western psychoanalysis. To this end, she returns to pre-Islamic feminine power that was venerated via statues of female goddesses. According to Mernissi, the legitimate female body in Islam is constructed in opposition to the most common kind of female body in the pre-Islamic period. This oppositionality is revived and transformed into an antagonism focused on the value of Islamic and Western femininity: "Is it possible that the *hijab*, the attempt to veil the woman, which is claimed today as constitutive of Muslim identity, is in fact only the very expression of pre-Islamic mentality, the *Jahiliya* mentality that Islam was supposed to annihilate? What does the *hijab* really represent in its ancient Muslim context? What does this word mean? What are its logic and justification? When was it established, where, for whom and why?" (1987, 114). She finds answers to these different questions in the story of the Prophet and in his words: the Sīrah and hadiths. Mernissi highlights the construction of this reaction through the example of al-Uzza, a pre-Islamic female divinity. After the destruction of the statues, an act that marked the conquest of Mecca by the Prophet of Islam, al-Uzza, the fallen goddess of pre-Islamic Arabia, became synonymous with wandering and polytheism in the new cult. In *Islam and Democracy*, Mernissi analyzes the symbolism of the destruction of the polytheistic divinities by the Prophet Muhammad in these terms: "Islam will break the circle and teach the Arabs to ride the stars and time, and to invent the present. But to do this, it was first necessary to destroy *al-Uzza*, and to erase her from memory: thus, the feminine should never again be visible in the field of power. The time of feminine power will be the end of time, point zero" (1992a, 126). Mernissi thereby analyzes the hijab as an attempt to neutralize women's power, to dispel the memory of the past and the fear that powerful goddesses represented to the new monotheistic cult. Behind the hijab, the negative memory of the goddesses expresses itself. Woman must be veiled, Mernissi says, first and foremost because woman has been identified with the violence of the goddesses (1992a, 86).

Even if her demonstration is seductive, it seems to somewhat contradict the chronology of the hijab's imposition. Indeed, the hijab was introduced nineteen years after the advent of Islam. But this discrepancy does not completely annul the relevance of Mernissi's analysis in *Le harem politique* specifically around the precise circumstances of the hijab's promulgation. In her interpretation, the beginning of women's invisibilization through territorial constraints is based on an attempt to prevent women from activating and spreading their power.

For Mernissi, this distancing of the feminine reveals political Islam's inability to adhere to the principle of equality as an endogenous characteristic (1992a, 66). As I mentioned previously, Mernissi explains that when sexual harassment multiplied in the streets of Medina, the Prophet recommended the hijab to distinguish free women from enslaved women so that the former would no longer be sexually harassed. Relations with time, with power, and with the feminine are then articulated in a discourse on identity, understood here as a religious identity, which because of its patriarchal origin is transformed into a religious and, above all, masculine identity problem. Mernissi writes in *Islam and Democracy* (1992a): "The *hijab* is a metaphor for the *hudud*, the boundaries that separate, order and refer to all others, especially those that delimit *Dar el Islam*, the territory of Islam, and protect it from the rest of the world" (8).

Mernissi's analogies are plural. She finds similarities between the Muslim order and the Freudian order. For her, universalism is a pretext that serves the claim to objectivity. At the same time, universalism is nothing but anthropocentrism and a reflection of its own (Western or Islamic) culture. For Mernissi, these two orders—psychoanalysis and Islam—have in common that they regulate sexualities. They also codify gendered social relations so as to subject individuals, believers or citizens, to these two orders' social and political dimensions. It is for this purpose in particular that the hijab operates as constitutive and representative of the social order. Also, not practicing the code of modesty (that wearing the hijab represents) is identified as a source of *fitna* (disorder) for society as a whole. One of the ways of justifying the hijab religiously is to invoke the danger of *fitna*. *Fitna* not only legitimizes the hijab but also the *ta'ha* (subordination) of the agent who wears the hijab. *Ta'ha* is behavior in keeping with the established order.

Mernissi identifies a typography of the power established by instrumentalizing the *hudud* (borders). The *hudud* operate as a historically and politically sedimented representation and as a *dispositif* of power on bodies, especially on women's bodies. This *dispositif* reveals a symbolic territoriality within the borderlands between public and private space. The domestic and the public, the masculine and the feminine, autonomy and dependence, the visible and the invisible—all are antagonistic pairs that the question of the hijab highlights.

Time: The Importance of Temporality

History transforms territories, and moments of political crisis affect borders by consolidating, creating, or destroying them. The symbolic, material, and immaterial boundaries that Fatema Mernissi analyzes are particularly damaging for women. She emphasizes this with great seriousness as she pays homage to Arab women who go out into the streets when George Bush declares war against Iraq. These women have nothing to lose, she says. They know and anticipate the effects of war in their lives: "The lot of woman in an Arab society that is at peace is precarious enough. But that lot is shaky indeed in an Arab society put to fire and sword by foreign forces" (1992a, 3).

Thus, it is impossible to spread Fatema Mernissi's critique of the hijab without understanding that one is thereby reinforcing certain political discourses of Western intellectuals, especially European and French intellectuals. For the latter, the hijab is a means of stigmatizing women who wear it. The hijab condemns them to social death because by wearing it, they are refusing to conform to the Western social order and especially to hegemonic femininity (understood here as secular). To my mind, the hijab is treated in France as a symbolic marker of antinomy in relation to national purity in its identitary and postcolonial dimension (Karimi 2016). Before this, the banning of Islamic veiling in French schools had materialized what Nasima Moujoud called "the veil of rupture" comprising "intersecting dominations": the racism and sexism at the center of this controversy (2012, 90). This implicates two kinds of femininity and an opposition between them. One form, *hegemonic femininity*, conforms to the Western idea of femininity, while another form, *"Muslim" femininity*, is constructed as heretic and as a threat to hegemonic femininity. Veiled Muslim women in France thereby present what I call a *paradoxical femininity* (Karimi 2023, 90). Feminists in France contributed to visible Muslim women's exclusion by operating a colonial shift, or a "colonial move," as Chandra Mohanty (1988) describes it. A Muslim woman wearing a hijab is perceived as lacking characteristics inherent to the West's hegemonic femininity. Veiled Muslim women in France are denied recognition not only as part of the class of women but also as part of humanity itself insofar as those within this latter category are entitled to dignified and ethical treatment. The racialization of Islam that operates in French society constructs Muslims as a marginal category with cultural and religious attributes that are deemed incompatible with the *laïcité*, or progressive and secular values, of the French Republic. This construction places Muslim women wearing a hijab outside of legitimate femininity.

Fatema Mernissi's writings are anchored in an epistemology of the global South that requires intellectuals to consider both their lack of resources and their privileges so as to avoid having their thought distorted by the coloniality of power (Karimi 2022b). But, in fact, Mernissi's position didn't allow her such an escape from the dualism of Islam versus modernity or, especially, democracy. Lamia Ben Youssef Zayzafoon, who deconstructs the figure of "Muslim woman," points to Mernissi's contributions to that effort. In Zayzafoon's analysis, Mernissi feels caught in a "double bind to reproduce and resist the discourses of both the orientalist and Islamic tradition" (2005, 15). Mernissi approaches borders in their historical, political, and religious dimensions, while exploring what the sacred reveals in this triple dimension. But, for Zayzafoon, Mernissi's assumption "about the territorialized oppressive Islamic culture of the Maghreb . . . is in fact nothing but a current ideological or political invention that masquerades as an authentic Islamic tradition," for "there is no homogeneous or unifying Islamic culture in the Maghreb" (2). Mernissi's early work had been critiqued in the West and among feminist scholars for positing an "East versus West" binary as natural and self-explanatory. However, these oppositions are based on a culturalist reading of Mernissi that positions each side of the binary in a hierarchy according to its culture or its religion. This kind of configuration operates as an obstacle to revealing the almost universal division of space by patriarchy. Men reserve the public space mainly for themselves, while reserving the domestic sphere mainly for women as natural or religious. Powerful men have made such a distinction sacred to justify it and make it immutable: "Male supremacy can exist and consolidate itself only if the division between the public and the private is maintained as quasi-sacred" (Mernissi 1987, 142). Women negotiate the residues of a power that structures this space because the space belongs to the sphere of the invisible and the private (Mounir 2013).

The approach here is to see reality as it is, without romantization, an experience undoubtedly tested in the body and in the spirit, as in Mernissi's case, so as to understand the journeys of women who often take tortuous paths. Also, the context of France transforms the use that can be made of the hijab as a tool in the construction of radical alterity (Karimi 2022a). The hijab shifts from a signifying accessory based in practices, customs, and habits that are relative to statuses assigned by moral and religious power to a means of opposing the diktat of disciplinary hegemony. What a paradox! To use clothing that some people associate with conformity to the model for "good" *religious femininity* as a way to rebel against the codes of what is held up by others as "good" *Western femininity*. Zayzafoon proposes to question the category "Muslim woman" as a semiotic subject. She defines "Muslim woman" as "a subject who is constituted through previous discourses but who is historically situated" (2005, 2). The use of such a category must be resituated in Fatema Mernissi's work. As Zayzafoon reminds us, Mernissi "was formerly a professor at the University of Muhammad V at Rabat, and . . . a member of the United Nations University Council. Because of her dual cultural background, Mernissi's construction of the 'Muslim woman' rests on the double bind to reproduce and resist the discourses of both the Orientalist and Islamic tradition" (15).

The spatial harem of the West, however, exists in other forms. It conditions the presence and appearance of women. In a provocative way, Mernissi points in particular to the aesthetic valuation of tall, slender women, who, according to her, with their emphasis on being only a "size 6," symbolize "the western women's harem" (2001, 208). Mernissi's analogies turn Orientalism back onto the West, orientalizes the West, with the objective of breaking with the constructed "tradition versus modernity" and "East versus West" binaries. Mernissi thereby inscribes her work in a postcolonial feminist approach that targets "the discourse based on the opposition between two sets of societies, whose reference is the colonial context" (Moujoud 2012, 87).

Fatema Mernissi was acutely aware of this culturalist division and throughout her work strives to point out similarities in how power structures act upon women in both the East and the West. She strongly critiques the neo-Orientalist, fantasy-based reading of the harem that describes the harem's hierarchical and segregational function. She demystifies the dominant Western view of the harem by giving an account of that view's social and political character. And we can see in the parallels that she draws between the global South and the global North that she does not wish to spare those in power. Mernissi was very conscious of these parallels and put into relief the fact that the Western powers try to legitimize their colonial conquests in part by invoking colonized men's ostensible bad treatment of women. And we cannot help but notice the resonance of the rhetoric used in France to condemn wearing the veil, where it is associated with a threat to the liberty of all, an argument in continuity with old colonial discourses. It is in this sense that Fatema Mernissi's work spreads Muslim feminist thought and contributes to it.

These pitfalls of the binary vision that in principle opposes Western progressivism to eastern archaism (even if here we speak specifically of Morocco) are an epistemic issue for researchers in the global South, just as they become a political issue for Muslim feminists in the West. For example, the wave of writing under the hashtag #lifeofamuslimfeminist in January 2015 perfectly illustrates the minority and repressive experience of Muslim feminists inside Muslim communities and vis-à-vis the majority feminist group. That writing highlights a double standard. On the one hand, Muslim women are called upon to silence their feminist claims because of the minority status of their religious group and the fear that these claims will be instrumentalized against the community. On the other hand, Muslim women are asked to prove their support for the causes defended by (dominant) feminists because the majority group imagines that the Muslim women's belief in Islam disqualifies them from being feminists. These Muslim women then have no choice but to resist—aesthetically, socially, politically—the paradoxical injunctions of those who want to muzzle them. Mernissi questions this determination to resist in these terms: "Why, I will be asked, did women form this audacious avant-garde? Because we have nothing to lose, except our fears, our masks and all the mutilations that accompany segregation and confinement" (1992a, 150).

The long history of women's invisibilization and silencing has not, however, halted women's determination to fight for their freedom. Mernissi comments on this struggle thus: "Women have never been tamed. Men thought that women could become accustomed to confinement. But women waited for their moment, for the time of difference in dignity, of participation and dialogue" (1992a, 151). These words resonate particularly in the ears of current generations of postcolonial feminists: "Women already began their resolute and perilous match toward the realm of freedom some decades ago" (150).

Concluding Remarks

To highlight the importance of Fatema Mernissi's legacy, I presented a discussion I had with a Muslim feminist whose life was transformed because she encountered *Le harem politique*. Mernissi's writing allowed this woman to move mental boundaries that had been forged in certainty. Mernissi, through her work and her legacy, contributed directly to the path of this woman's emancipation, as she did for so many others. This chapter has explored the temporal and spatial approach of Fatema Mernissi's legacy around the hijab and the harem. For Mernissi the sociologist, both the hijab and the harem constitute material boundaries that are part of a religious moral order. Because of her position as a secular intellectual, her critique of the hijab is rigorous, yet it never falls into the colonial pitfall of blaming women for observing such a practice. On the contrary, Mernissi reminds us of the powerful stakes that shape these borders. Instead of looking at those who make this disciplinary power visible, Mernissi puts into relief the role of powerful men in Arab countries who renounce democracy out of fear of losing control over the morality and sexual practices of their people. She thus demonstrates how the sacred is instrumentalized for political ends, for political Islam.

References

Ali, Zahra, ed. 2012. *Féminismes islamiques*. Paris: La Fabrique.

Ben Youssef Zayzafoon, Lamia. 2005. *The Production of the Muslim Woman: Negotiating Text, History, and Ideology*. Oxford: Lexington.

Inge, Sophie. 2013. "Paris Mosque Sparks Fury over Separation of Sexes." *The Local*, Dec. 27. At https://www.thelocal.fr/20131227/muslim-women-slam-mosques-separation-of-sexes/.

Karimi, Hanane. 2016. "No Liberty, No Equality, No Fraternity: The Death of French Secularism." *Middle East Eye*, Sept. 6. At https://www.middleeasteye.net/opinion/no-liberty-no-equality-no-fraternity-death-french-secularism.

———. 2022a. "Constructing the Otherness of Jews and Muslims in France." *Annual Review of Sociology of Religion* 13:162–82.

———. 2022b. "Overview: Islam and Feminism: Europe." In *Encyclopedia of Women & Islamic Cultures Online*, supplement 23, edited by Suad Joseph. At https://referenceworks.brillonline.com/entries/encyclopedia-of-women-and-islamic-cultures/overview-islam-and-feminism-europe-COM_002215.

———. 2023. *Les femmes musulmanes ne sont-elles pas des femmes?* Marseille, France: Hors d'atteinte.

Mernissi, Fatema. 1987. *Le harem politique: Le Prophète et les femmes*. Paris: Albin Michel.

———. 1990. *Sultanes oubliées: Femmes chefs d'état en Islam*. Paris: Albin Michel.

———. 1991. *The Veil and the Male Elite: A Feminist Interpretation of Women's Rights in Islam*. Translated by Mary Jo Lakeland. Cambridge, MA: Perseus.

———. 1992a. *Islam and Democracy: Fear of the Modern World*. Translated by Mary Jo Lakeland. New York: Basic.

———. 1992b. *La peur modernité: Conflit Islam démocratie*. Paris: Albin Michel.

———. 1993. *The Forgotten Queens of Islam*. Translated by Mary Jo Lakeland. Minneapolis: Univ. of Minnesota Press.

———. 1994. *Dreams of Trespass: Tales of a Harem Girlhood*. Cambridge, MA: Perseus.

———. 1996. *Rêves de femmes: Une enfance au harem*. Translated by Claudine Richetin. Paris: Albin Michel.

———. 2001. *Scheherazade Goes West: Different Cultures, Different Harems*. New York: Washington Square Press.
Mohanty, Chandra Talpade. 1988. "Under Western Eyes: Feminist Scholarship and Colonial Discourses." *Feminist Review* 30:65–88.
Moujoud, Nasima. 2012. "Métiers domestiques, voile et féminisme." *Hommes et migrations* 1300:84–94.
Mounir, Hakima. 2013. *Entre ici et là-bas: Le pouvoir des femmes dans les familles maghrébines*. Rennes, France: Presses universitaires de Rennes.
Rhouni, Raja. 2010. *Secular and Islamic Feminist Critiques in the Work of Fatima Mernissi*. Leiden, Netherlands: Brill.

11

Fatema Mernissi and Animating *The Four Hijabs*

MANAL HAMZEH

In 2016, I collaborated with Jamil Khoury of Silk Road Rising to create an animation film, *The Four Hijabs*, dedicated to the memory of Fatema Mernissi and her groundbreaking scholarship.[1] *The Four Hijabs* is based on my dissertation study and book *Pedagogies of Deveiling: Muslim Girls and the Hijab Discourse* (2012). My research, the book, and the animation are testaments to the endurability and adaptability of Mernissi's feminist scholarship. They continue Mernissi's defiant intellectual work and highlight its tremendous pedagogical potential.

The following excerpt (Hamzeh et al. 2016) opens the film, which brings Mernissi's hijab-related ideas to life:

Friend 1: I want to understand the story of the hijab. The real story.
Friend 2: I feel like the word *hijab* is misunderstood. Like it's been intentionally distorted for ages.
Friend 1: As far as I know, in Arabic the word *hijab* means "to cover" or "protect."
Friend 3: It can also mean a boundary or a barrier.
Friend 1: So, it's not just a headscarf?

---

1. Based in Chicago, the Silk Road Cultural Center is "an interdisciplinary arts organization rooted in Pan-Asian, North African, and Muslim experiences." Its website is at https://silkroadculturalcenter.org/.

Fatema Mernissi and Animating *The Four Hijabs*   235

2. Three friends at the beginning of *The Four Hijabs*. *Source*: Hamzeh et al. 2016. Copyright © 2016 Jamil Khoury.

> Friend 3: No. The headscarf is but one small part of it.
> Friend 2: The hijab is not only about modesty and piety.
> Friend 3: It's actually more complicated than that.
> Friend 1: I know. It's about separating men and women.
> Friend 3: No! The whole gender segregation thing is a big myth.
> Friend 1: But every conversation about the hijab is "to veil or not to veil."
> Friend 2: Which is the wrong question. Certainly, in this story.
> Friend 3: Exactly! The real question is about four distinct hijabs that appear in sixteen Qur'anic verses.
> Friend 1: Just sixteen verses?
> Friend 3: Yep, just sixteen, out of thousands.
> Friend 1: Wait. One, two . . . I know maybe four. The popular ones.
> Friend 2: I know at least six!
> Friend 3: Yes, and those popular verses have been misread. The other ten have been completely silenced.

> Friend 1: Can we read them ourselves? I mean, without Qur'anic scholars?
> Friend 2: Of course. We need to be our own scholars, without mediators! We can interpret the text for ourselves. Let's revisit what the Qur'an says about the four hijabs.
> Friend 1: Wow! Freeing our imaginations and engaging our minds!
> Friend 3: And asking questions about building a gender-just world.
> Friend 1: We can do that?
> Friend 2: We can do that and more.[2]

My journey with Mernissi reflects her work's power, crossing language borders, theories, and time. I began reading Mernissi in Arabic in the 1990s while living in Jordan. I was at the time making sense of my queerness and Arabness alongside Arab and Muslim feminisms. Later, in 2005, while preparing for my doctoral studies, I reread her work in English and with feminist post-structural theories. In the intense Islamophobic context in the United States and Europe after September 11, 2001, I drew on Mernissi's readings of the Qur'an to understand racism against Muslims. I also wanted to expose hijabophobia as a gendered racialized discourse targeting Muslim women who wear an "Islamic" headcover (Zine 2006). I mainly engaged Mernissi's book *The Veil and the Male Elite: A Feminist Interpretation of Women's Rights in Islam* (1991). In this work, Mernissi questions the popular meaning of the hijab as a garment that some Muslim women wear. She expands this popular meaning into four distinct hijabs—the visual, the spatial, the ethical, and the spiritual—by contextualizing the sixteen relevant Qur'anic verses.[3] She defies the dominant androcentric interpretations of the hijab verses and exposes them as distracting controversies of "to veil or not

---

2. Copyright © 2016 Jamil Khoury.

3. The Qur'anic verses for the Ethical Hijab are 33:32, 33:33; for the Spatial Hijab, 19:17, 33:53; for the Visual Hijab, 24:31, 33:59; and for the Spiritual Hijab, 6:25, 7:46, 12:107, 17:45, 18:57, 38:32, 41:5, 42:51, 50:22, 83:15.

to veil" the bodies of Muslim women. Mernissi's rereading of canonical sacred Islamic texts concerning the hijabs and gender is in itself feminist *ijtihad*—intellectual struggle and rigorous theorizing committed to gender justice (Ahmed 2011; Badran 2009; Hamzeh 2012; Mernissi 1991). Her *ijtihad* is a feminist methodology of contextualizing and historicizing Qur'anic hijab verses that aims to create more gender-just understandings of Muslimness. As an Arabyyah-Muslimah feminist, I used Mernissi's *ijtihad* methodology while also drawing on feminist post-structural theories. I wanted to re-expose the heteronormative uses of the first three hijabs and highlight the deployment of a gendering discourse, whether in the United States and Europe or in Islamic nations and Muslim-majority contexts (Hamzeh 2017; Hélie and Hoodfar 2012).

Since 2007, I have had many conversations with my friend Jamil Khoury, a playwright and cofounder of Silk Road Rising, an organization committed to making theater and digital media rooted in Asian, Middle Eastern, and Muslim experiences. We were thinking together to adapt my academic work in *Pedagogies of Deveiling* into a performative piece on stage. Early on, Jamil saw the artistic potential of *Pedagogies of Deveiling*. In his artistic statement on *The Four Hijabs* website, he wrote:

> There's a great deal in Manal Hamzeh's scholarship that motivates me as a playwright. Her book *Pedagogies of Deveiling: Muslim Girls and the Hijab Discourse* introduced me to ideas and paradigms that presented entirely new opportunities for dramatization. By identifying four discernible hijabs . . . [and then] interpreting them through Arab Muslim feminist lenses, Dr. Hamzeh lays bare the reductiveness of a "to veil or not to veil" binary and our obsession with headscarves. Moreover, her intersectional feminism, her anti-racist politics, and her tireless commitment to uncovering truths, in all their complexities, align us as engaged thinkers, creators, and activists. (Khoury 2016)

At some point, Jamil and I were thinking of artistically representing my own story and the stories of young Muslim girls in negotiating access to sports and physical activities. In 2013, we decided to feel the pulse for such an artistic project in the Muslim community in Chicago. I presented Mernissi's ideas in meetings, lectures, and workshops to several Muslim groups in the larger Chicago area, funders and artists, and allies of Silk Road Rising. We wanted to understand how potentially supportive theater audiences would receive my work and Mernissi's daring multilayered meanings of the hijabs, especially in the racist US context. Over two years, the dialogues and workshops reached many people in the Chicago area. Our meetings and workshops opened the space to engage Mernissi's and my ideas in a communal space and with an intentional participatory and art-based approach.

A collaboration among Khoury, animation artists, and me at Valparaiso University Center for the Arts started. We first condensed the complicated ideas in two books, *Pedagogies of Deveiling* (Hamzeh 2012) and *The Veil and the Male Elite* (Mernissi 1991) into a twelve-minute script. My cowriting of *The Four Hijabs* script with Jamil illustrated the adaptability of Mernissi's ideas to an art genre. In 2015, our focus turned to representing Mernissi's hijabs, my theorizing of a gendering discourse, and the community research outcome in the short animation film. To Jamil, this meant that "[in] combining Dr. Hamzeh's scholarship with my playwriting, [in] our shared passion for gender justice[,] . . . we have together created . . . an animated short that challenges conversations about bodies, genders, self-presentation, and the reading of sacred texts" (Khoury 2016).

We hoped that our translation of Mernissi's work into an animation film would be timely and accessible. I wrote for the website, "The Four Hijabs represents our commitment to making critical, cutting-edge academic thought accessible to a general public. . . . [It] brings to the forefront a timely dialogue about the implications [that] out-of-context misinterpretations of the Qur'an have on women's lives and bodies" (Hamzeh 2016).

Adapting the complex ideas required an interdisciplinary and methodological leap between theory and visual art. Jamil dramatized

3. The four hijabs on stage—the visual, the ethical, the spiritual, and the spatial (*from left to right*). *Source*: Hamzeh et al. 2016. Copyright © 2016 Jamil Khoury.

the Qur'anic verses as speaking for themselves, questioning and deveiling their own meanings. The animation artist, Anna Hayden-Roy, symbolized each of the hijabs to signal their dynamic and performative meanings.

> Ethical Hijab: Hello and welcome to all our viewers out there. I am the Ethical Hijab. We have a very special program planned today. One that we have needed for ages. Yes, folks, the wait is over. All four hijabs are together at last!
> Spatial, Spiritual, Visual Hijabs: Woohoo, togetherness! About time, hijabs! Sing it, sister!
> Ethical Hijab: I've convened this here gathering because we four hijabs have been kept apart far too long and because it was the right thing to do. My fellow hijabs, we have suffered, and we have been wrongly accused of making others suffer. Am I right, or am I wrong?

Spatial, Spiritual, Visual Hijabs: Two hundred percent! So right! Estás correcto!⁴

On bridging the theoretical and the visual dramatized representation of Qur'anic text, Jamil wrote, "In developing *The Four Hijabs*, I confronted the challenges of adapting sophisticated theoretical concepts into a character- and dialogue-driven animated short. The source material relates to sixteen Qur'anic verses that have been distorted and appropriated to advance sexist practices.... Our solution was to embody and empower these concepts and verses as self-aware characters, each seeking to undo their misrepresentation. How often does scripture get the chance to resist its appropriators? It's feminist agit-prop meets spiritual reclamation!" (Khoury 2016).

Our animated and dramatized representation of Mernissi's four hijabs was also daring because of her assertions about the covering up of the most crucial hijab, the spiritual, and its importance over the other three hijabs. As a result, Jamil and I risked facing pushback from those who are resistant to questioning the androcentric interpretations of Islamic text, a main call made by Mernissi as well as by *The Four Hijabs*. At the same time, this representation of my theorizing of the hijabs as a gendering discourse brought forth a pedagogical possibility, critical Qur'anic rereading, that could serve all kinds of Muslims and help imagine ways to create gender-justice practices within their lives.

The Four Hijabs was screened on several university campuses in Canada and the United States and in classrooms and art and community spaces in Europe, Jordan, and Egypt. The film is available free online in English, with Arabic subtitles.⁵ It has also been archived on the Anti-Racism Digital Library (Hamzeh et al. 2016) and reviewed by several US media outlets. To dub the film into Arabic, I worked

---

4. Copyright © 2016 Jamil Khoury.
5. The English version is at https://silkroadculturalcenter.org/digital-media/four-hijabs/.

with a producer in Amman, Jordan, who in turn worked remotely with actors who were living the horrifying war in Syria.[6] Moreover, this translating process brought me back to Mernissi and Arabic to speak to a broader audience.

I hope that *The Four Hijabs* will keep Mernissi's work alive and inspire a wide range of audiences who may be intrigued to reread and question the dominant interpretations of the Qur'an, to discuss complex ideas about their own Muslimness, and, ultimately, to imagine a world that exists beyond androcentric historiography.

References

Ahmed, Leila. 2011. *A Quiet Revolution: The Veil's Resurgence, from the Middle East to America*. New Haven, CT: Yale Univ. Press.

Badran, Margot. 2009. *Feminism in Islam: Secular and Religious Convergences*. Oxford: Oneworld.

Hamzeh, Manal. 2012. *Pedagogies of Deveiling: Muslim Girls and the Hijab Discourse*. Charlotte, NC: Information Age Press.

———. 2016. "Creative Team, Theorist/Co-writer, Artistic Statement." *The Four Hijabs*. At https://silkroadculturalcenter.org/related-media/artistic-statement-dr-manal-hamzeh/.

———. 2017. "FIFA's Double Hijabophobia: A Colonialist and Islamist Patriarchal 'Alliance' Racializing Muslim Women Soccer Players." *Journal of Women's Studies International Forum* 63:11–16.

Hamzeh, Manal, and Jamil Khoury (coauthors), Liz Wuerffel (director), and Anna Hayden-Roy (animator). 2016. *The Four Hijabs*. Short animation film, twelve minutes. Originally in English and dubbed in Arabic. Chicago: Silk Road Rising Theater. At https://silkroadculturalcenter.org/digital-media/four-hijabs/ (in English) and https://www.youtube.com/watch?v=XmTFE5rzghU (in Arabic). Also archived in the Anti-Racism Digital Library, July 30. At https://sacred.omeka.net/items/show/136.

Hélie, Anissa, and Homa Hoodfar. 2012. *Sexuality in Muslim Contexts: Restrictions and Resistance*. London: Zed.

---

6. The Arabic-dubbed version is at https://www.youtube.com/watch?v=XmTFE5rzghU.

Khoury, Jamil. 2016. "Creative Team, Adaptor/Co-writer, Artistic Statement." *The Four Hijabs* (website). At https://web.archive.org/web/20180827051613/http://www.fourhijabs.org/co-writer-jamil-khoury/.

Mernissi, Fatema. 1991. *The Veil and the Male Elite: A Feminist Interpretation of Women's Rights in Islam.* Translated by Mary Jo Lakeland. Cambridge, MA: Perseus.

Zine, Jasmin. 2006. "Unveiled Sentiments: Gendered Islamophobia and Experiences of Veiling among Muslim Girls in a Canadian Islamic School." *Equity and Excellence in Education* 39, no. 3: 239–52.

12

Fatema Mernissi

A Personal Memory

AMINA WADUD

I arrived in Rabat after work travel in Europe. I would be returning to Europe, so this break in a predominantly Muslim North Africa was welcomed. My first order of business was a lunch date, when I would finally get to meet Fatema Mernissi, arranged by our mutual friend Dr. Asma Lamrabet.

I could say I had waited more than thirty years for this meeting, but that would not be altogether accurate. Perhaps it would be more accurate to say that Fatema and I had been on our separate paths leading to this. Asma communicated between us. She shared comments about our mutual pleasure at finally having this opportunity to meet face to face. Then Fatema's health took a turn, and she could not breath without oxygen. She sent her regrets that she would not be able to join our lunch meeting. Four days later, she was gone. I would never get to meet her in this lifetime.

This culmination of our life work and this just-missed opportunity to meet indicate some of the fragility in the Muslim women's movements. We are rarely presented with opportunities to form meaningful alliances across differences in this gender jihad. *Jihad* means "struggle." In this case, it refers to the struggle for Muslim women to gain agency and transformation in their own lives, however diverse.

Looking back over fifty years of my engagement in gender justice, I have seen Muslim women enter the new millennium believing that this movement has walked one seamless path. That is the illusion of past reflection. There were many bumps, false starts, and wicked turns on the road, alongside victories and scaled mountain tops. I, too, have lived through some changes without discernment. I never calculated that my own life work would have the impact it has now been allocated. I have been affected by so many others in the work it has taken to travel this road. Most of the names of gender-justice advocates that I have carried with me belong to women I have worked with, exchanged ideas with, and formed alliances with—even across seemingly vast differences. How could I have missed such an opportunity with Fatema Mernissi?

My participation in the gender-justice movement is a faith journey. I entered Islam voluntarily in 1972 at the age of twenty. Two decades later, the dust would settle. On the way, I completed my master's and PhD degrees with a focus on hermeneutics: reading for gender in the Islamic primary sacred text, the Qur'an. I would also live in Muslim-majority, Arabic-speaking North Africa twice.

My dissertation would be edited to become the small book *Qur'an and Woman*, first published in 1992 (and reprinted in 1999). Its publication coincided with the completion of a three-year contract with the International Islamic University in Malaysia (IIU). Malaysia is also a Muslim-majority country but not an Arabic-speaking one. Here I would begin my second career as an activist for reform and justice. Although I spent three prosperous years in Malaysia forming lifetime friendships in the gender jihad, these friendships and justice work were in stark contrast to my relationship to this conservative faux-liberal institution of higher learning where I would never be provided an opportunity to share the important intellectual work initiated by my PhD research. Still, I thrived in this encounter with contradictions. I no longer took for granted that just because some said "Islam" or "Muslim" that they had in mind the same thing as someone else who said these words. Interpretations matter.

Although I was not given a single opportunity to present my work to my university colleagues, I enjoyed a high demand from the larger civil society. Most importantly, I became one of eight founding members of Sisters in Islam (SIS), a nongovernmental organization that is still going strong today. The relationship between my scholarship and the development of SIS was mutually transformative. The scholarship I had done to produce *Qur'an and Woman* was instrumental in increasing both legitimacy and efficacy for SIS. Meanwhile, SIS increased my capacity by providing me opportunities to move outside of academic elitism and come face to face with the lived realities of Muslim women worldwide. Those lived realities would become a part of a new hermeneutical tool for reading gender justice across Islamic texts. It was a matter of context over texts, of aligning the core principles with real women struggling in real communities.

At IIU, I worked with a small research grant titled "In Search for Pro-faith Feminism in Islam." This search was inspired in part by reading Mernissi's work. Sometimes being born into a Muslim culture is not always clear from Islamic constructs based on the classic sources. Culture and ethnicity as Muslim might not bear methodological coherence with Islam's primary sacred sources. These sources have been and still are endlessly debated for meaning and importance. They have tended to operate with an entrenched, gender asymmetry that remains largely uncontested within what is projected as fundamental to Islam.

Fatema Mernissi provided one of the most comprehensive challenges to this gender asymmetry in the 1980s. At that same time, I was working from within the sacred texts to provide justification for the necessity of a critical gender reading of those sources. In the process, I took issue with the way Islam would be collapsed with Arab culture. When Mernissi affirmed her identity as Arab, she did so in tandem with her identity as Muslim. I could find no real distinction between culture and Islam. This is an ongoing concern not limited to Arab culture.

In the Malay language, to convert to Islam is described as *masuk Malayu*, which literally means to "enter (into being) Malay." I had spent two decades searching to find myself: a descendent of enslaved Africans in the Americas who voluntarily entered Islam and then lived in Muslim cultures across Africa and Asia. It would take time to unravel the ways that Muslim societies practice their cultures with no bearing on Islam as referenced within the sacred sources. As a Muslim by choice, I had entered Islam from my own cultural context. I did not see any particular advantage or disadvantage of this context relative to many Muslim cultures. But the tendency to collapse culture with Islam was problematic. In those days, I was often confronted with the idea that "Western" culture would forever be deemed outside and sometimes even estranged from Islam.

In no small way, this idea would lead to a preoccupation with the power to define what Islam is. This project helped me to negotiate globally. Although I was inspired by SIS, a Malaysian organization, defining Islam helped me and was catapulted forward with the launch of Musawah, a global movement for reform in Muslim personal-status laws organized in 2009.

I attended the Beijing Conference on women in 1995 as a member of SIS. From that moment, SIS and I would work to clarify a new voice of Islam and gender reform distinct from the two dominant voices at that forum. One voice was that of secular Muslim feminists. They advocated keeping religion, in particular Islam, out of the debates over gender justice. Religion/Islam was deemed irrevocably misogynistic. The other dominant voice followed from the growing Islamist movement. It opposed any strategy or program of action unless confirmed or originated in a very patriarchal definition of Islam. Both sides agreed on one thing: you could not have both Islam and human rights or feminism. I still identified as pro-faith and pro-feminist, however. That was exactly what I had been looking for in my research on pro-faith feminism.

Over the next decade, a third voice became more coherent. It would wed religion and feminism and become known as "Islamic feminism." If the Muslim women's movement was subject only to existing articulations of the debates' major paradigms, there was no way forward. Islamic feminism took full agency not only in defining feminism and human rights but more importantly also in constructing its own knowledge about what Islam is. Into the next millennium, the Musawah movement for equality and justice in the Muslim family would lead the way in this knowledge construction and advocacy for policy reform.

I came out as an Islamic feminist when it became clear that we can take authority in defining Islam. This authority constructs new knowledge in Islam that is informed by women's lived realities. From my earlier research, it was clear that gender must be established as a category of thought for reading all Islamic intellectual traditions. Because of this critical engagement, as Muslim women we were no longer forced to choose between Islam and human dignity or feminism. Thus, Islamic feminism reconciled the anxiety for many Muslim women who were being forced to choose.

Thinking back on this history, I better understood the journey of someone like Fatema Mernissi and how her work had already made inroads into challenging a singular definition of Islam that resulted from patriarchal interpretation. Musawah continues to forge networks with women and men who are seeking justice from a variety of perspectives. Musawah methodology creates and sustains a complex engagement with religious knowledge while forging alliances across different perspectives. For example, those of us who choose to wear the hijab or find solace in its practice are not in competition with those who struggle to remove the hijab. All of us are equally subject to the mandate for human rights while establishing our Muslim identity. We come together across our differences to achieve greater dignity for all.

The Musawah secretariat moved to Morocco, and Fatema Mernissi came to greet them. I'd like to think of this meeting as a culmination of her decades of work, sometimes alone and sometimes in the trenches. I know she stayed longer than she had planned and that the Musawah members were thrilled to have her company. It was her last public event. When I arrived a few days later, she was no longer mobile.

It is difficult to express the heartbreak of losing her before our only opportunity to meet. No single name has accompanied the duration of my work more than "Fatema Mernissi." I appreciate how the formation of Islamic feminism owes some debt to secular feminists, whose difficult focus on women's issues had to move beyond the issues established with building the nation-states that were fought for at the end of empire. I understand the complexity of coming up against a religion that has been dominated by male authority for more than a thousand years. I still understand Muslim identity as forged through culture, experience, and interpretation. More importantly, though, I appreciate how the next generation will no longer be shaped by an unnecessary divide. In this millennium, we form critical and engaged intersectional alliances to achieve the collective goal of social justice and well-being for Muslim women. In this way, we are the beneficiaries of Fatema Mernissi, who stood up for this justice before it was popular to do so.

References

wadud, amina. [1992] 1999. *Qur'an and Woman: Rereading the Sacred Text from a Woman's Perspective.* Reprint. Oxford: Oxford Univ. Press.

Section Four

Mernissian Critiques of Coloniality, Orientalism, and Capitalism

13

Scheherazade and Sustainable Development

MOUNIRA HEJAIEJ

In her workshops for World Bank experts in Marrakesh in 1997, Fatema Mernissi demonstrated how development projects based on local social capital—networks of trust, caring, and shared responsibility—succeeded where World Bank and International Monetary Fund (IMF) structural-adjustment programs had failed miserably. Mernissi's groundbreaking fieldwork in rural Morocco had a tremendous influence in challenging the prevalent vision of development. In this chapter, I use Scheherazade as a code for women's voices to examine Mernissi's use of narrative and approach to development through the lens of water-related Women's Empowerment Projects in rural Tunisia conducted by the agency Deutsche Gesellschaft für Internationale Zusammenarbeit (GIZ, German Association for International Cooperation), Middle East and North Africa, in which women's social capital and women's voices are central to sustainable development. My analysis illuminates the power of communication "from below," which puts women's voices at the center of a web of competing narratives about sustainable development and brings women's local knowledge into dialogue with the larger global forces of development. Mernissi's genius was to insist that we attend to the power of those voices. I demonstrate how implementing Mernissi's recommendation to include local knowledge, social capital, and traditions maintained by Tunisia's female storytellers provided invaluable support in strengthening development efforts and allowing women's full participation in collective action.

Scheherazade is an emblematic figure in Mernissi's writing and understanding of narrative/voice and knowledge production. At the heart of this project is the recognition of the power of narrative and its importance for sustainable development. I explore here the ways women's traditional stories and practices were and have been translated into associative life in both premodern and postrevolutionary Tunisia and how current development projects are tapping into the power of women's narratives to teach practices around the conservation of water. Transnational feminism contributes to expand the scope of activism to important regional and international organizations and transnational networks. Central to my argument is the idea that we need to move away from relying solely on Western intellectual and imaginative frames because many are not relevant in non-Western contexts. With this movement away from solely Western ideas comes an increased focus on qualitative methodology, including narrative analysis, as opposed to purely quantitative methods that largely adopt Western intellectual frames.

In the past few years, a new humanist perspective on how to address the structural-development challenges prevalent in various postcolonial countries has moved away from conventional approaches dominated by science-based disciplines in favor of innovative methods that place a special emphasis on the role played by social capital and participatory processes in establishing economic development. The notion of "social capital" reflects the extent to which social trust and cooperative norms are present and assesses the density of interpersonal networks (Evans 1997).

The final report on an Organization for Economic Cooperation and Development (OECD) project identifies four main ways in which the concept of "social capital" can be conceptualized and measured:

- **Personal relationships,** referring to the structure of an individual's networks (i.e., the people they know) and the social behaviors that contribute to establishing and maintaining

these networks, such as spending time with others, exchanging news by telephone or email, and so on
- **Social network support,** which is formulated depending on the nature of an individual's personal relationships and refers to the emotional, material, practical, and financial resources available to each individual via their personal social networks
- **Civic engagement,** comprising the activities and networks through which people contribute to civic and community life via political participation, group membership, or various forms of community action—such as by volunteering
- **Trust and cooperative norms,** referring to the trust, social norms, and shared values that underpin societal functioning and enable mutually beneficial cooperation (Scrivens and Smith 2013)

To clarify a final set of terms present in my study, *trust* and *cooperative norms* refer to the trust, social norms, and shared values that underpin society's ability to function while also enabling the presence of mutually beneficial cooperation. When the World Commission on Environment and Development (Brundtland Commission) published its report *Our Common Future* in 1987, a new concept labeled "sustainable development" was introduced, referring to a kind of development that "meets the needs of the present without compromising the ability of future generations to meet their own needs" (Brundtland Commission 1987, para. 1). This concept has led to the emergence of one of the most successful approaches to be applied in many years. In fact, it has helped to shape the international agenda and the international community's attitude toward economic, social, and environmental development.

Centering Women's Voices, Giving Women Agency

In recent years, development studies have been subject to intense scrutiny, reflecting the influences of broader philosophical and theoretical debates that have marked Western and non-Western social and political sciences. An analysis of power that is rooted in postcolonial and feminist theories is central to contemporary studies on development (Radcliffe 1994). The possibility of producing decolonized knowledge in development studies became a subject of considerable debate during the 1990s.

Both postcolonialism and feminism attempt to recover the lost historical and contemporary voices of the marginalized through a radical reconstruction of history and knowledge production. In 1994, Naila Kabeer, a specialist in gender and development in Bangladesh, India, and Vietnam, summarized the complexity of the development concept at the time in her book *Reversed Realities: Gender Hierarchies in Development Thought*: "Highly ideologically loaded, [development] means different things to different people. Some see it in terms of a purposive planned project; others prefer to talk of processes of social transformation. Some define it as the enhancement of individual choice; others see it as the equalizing of opportunities. Some emphasize ends; others means; and still others focus on their interrelationships" (14).

A genealogy of the interplay between gender and development shows that significant changes in understandings of development can be linked to feminist critiques of the androcentric, colonial, and neocolonial approach. One way to historicize this large field and to focus it on North Africa more specifically is to look at key moments and iconic works that shaped the larger context of gender and development during Mernissi's time.

The Bretton Woods Agreement of 1944 among the forty-four Allied nations (which included France and its colonial domination of North African protectorates/departments—Tunisia, Morocco, Algeria) created the World Bank and the IMF, which would sketch out the development relationships between North and South as well as First World and Third World. The global revolutions of the 1950s and 1960s, the civil rights movement, and the feminist second wave challenged these development paradigms.

Margarita Aguinaga and her coauthors argue that in the early 1970s a "seminal contribution to feminist discourse" was made by the Danish economist Ester Boserup in her critique of development as being a system that excluded women in her book *Woman's Role in Economic Development* (1970). "Women had only been included in development policies as passive beneficiaries, or mothers and housewives," they write (2013, 42). Boserup had underscored that this Western model ignored the fact that in many cultures women worked in agriculture and food production (for example) and that there were different or much more flexible sexual divisions of labor. Aguinaga and colleagues (2013) highlight how women have always been an integral part of development and have sustained their societies.

Feminists began to challenge the exclusion of women from development on the global stage. A key landmark was the first World Conference on Women in Mexico in 1975, sponsored by the United Nations (UN). This event institutionalized women's voices as part of the development process. But we must ask which voices the second wave of feminism foregrounded. The neoliberal perspective expressed by Betty Friedan was center stage, while Domitila Barrios de Chungara, an impoverished Bolivian tin miner's wife, had to struggle to be heard, as she explained in her autobiography *Let Me Speak* (1978). The women-in-development movement of the 1970s added women's role in the home to development projects but did not challenge power dynamics or alter the neoliberal modernization paradigms. The late 1970s shifted to "women and development," which focused on equality and critiqued modernization but still framed change as women's entry into the economic status quo. An early challenge to the marginalization of non-Western women came with *Women in the Muslim World*, edited by Lois Beck and Nikki Keddie (1978). The gender-and-development movement of the third wave of feminism in the 1980s challenged both patriarchy and capitalism, putting women at the center of the inquiry. Women were seen as agents of change. Feminists began to examine the overlapping systems of oppression—race, class, gender—that shaped their lives. "At the second World Conference on Women in Nairobi in 1985, the network of women from the South, Development Alternatives with Women for a New Era (DAWN), challenged the assumption that the problem was simply that women did not participate enough in an otherwise 'benevolent' process of development and growth" (Aguinaga 2013, 46). There was nothing benevolent about "structural-adjustment" policies that favored debt repayment over human rights and quality of life.

The postcolonial feminists of the 1990s challenged the idea that countries were divided between developed and underdeveloped (rather than being maldeveloped in all cases), that so-called Third World women were objects, while First World women were agents. In the 1990s, the fourth World Conference on Women, "Action for Equality, Development, and Peace," was convened by the UN on September 4–15, 1995, in Beijing, China. In Tunis, Tunisia, the preparatory conference "Women and the Law in the Near East: Legal and Regulatory Constraints to Women's Participation in Development" was held on December 14–17, 1994. It brought together women legal experts from Tunisia, Egypt, Morocco, Yemen, Oman, Lebanon, Jordan, and Palestine. Like many earlier global forums, the Beijing conference illustrated the divide still evident between women with power (who represented governments) and women without power (who represented nongovernmental perspectives). As a corrective, progressive presses such as Zed Books, Verso Books, and Pluto Press moved marginalized voices to the center and provincialized Western development paradigms.

Fatema Mernissi's book *Les Aït-Débrouille: ONG rurales du Haut-Atlas* (1997) was part of this effort to reverse the top-down power dynamic of development. A possible translation of its title is the "DIY Tribe: NGOs of the High Atlas." She nicknamed the Aït community of Morocco the "Aït-Débrouille" to celebrate their ability to solve their problems without the help or aid of an expert or Western organization. When the World Bank asked Mernissi at the Marrakesh development conference in May 1997 to teach it about traditional forms of social capital, she took its representatives to the Amazigh village of Aït Iktel in the High Atlas to demonstrate the efficacy of grassroots development and "stories from below." In the late 1990s, both the World Bank and the IMF were well aware that their structural-adjustment programs had done harm in the worst development efforts and had led to endless talk without action in many of the rest (World Bank 2003). Using local networking, Aït Iktel had created roads, sunk sixteen wells, brought electricity to villages, reconstructed irrigation canals, and built and equipped a school. These projects leveraging local social capital were only the beginning (World Bank 2003, 75–76).[1]

At the beginning of the new century, a number of cross-sectoral works examined gender as it intersected with power, the state, and language. Starting in 2002, each annual *Arab Human Development Report*, written by experts from the regions examined, was a groundbreaking study (see UN Development Program [UNDP] 2002). While development studies have long had the environment as a focus, sustainable development, climate change, and the right of all to well-being are newer concerns. Activists such as Vandana Shiva and Arundati Roy have battled on behalf of humanity and the environmentally besieged.[2] Indigenous communities especially see well-being as the heart of sustainable development. Fatema Mernissi had a similar insight when she saw at the heart of sustainable development the Moroccan qualities of *hanan* (tenderness), *tiqa* (trust), and *ta'awun* (cooperation).[3]

---

1. The economic difficulties and social pressures of the 1990s had led to a burgeoning of civil society actions as Moroccan politics became more democratic. This civic energy was demonstrated by three efforts spearheaded by the faculty of Mohammed V University: Mernissi's work on local social capital—her Civic Synergy projects, Civic Caravans, and writings such as *Les Aït-Débrouille*, which told the story of how forty-five rural NGOs working in conditions of scarcity brought water and electricity to their village.

2. See *The Seeds of Vandana Shiva: A Documentary of Her Life* (Camilla Denton Becket and James Becket, 2021) and the interview of Roy in Simonson 2020.

3. "Ce livre raconte l'histoire de ces astucieux paysans du Haut Atlas qui arrivent à réaliser des projets dont rêvent à peine des citadin(e)s comme moi, super-diplômé(e)s et super-sophistiqué(e)s. Une des raisons du succès du mouvement associatif dans les zones rurales les plus défavorisées du Maroc, est l'esprit civique des intellectuels qui en sont issus . . . qui retournent vers leur pays d'origine, pour offrir leur précieuse expérience. . . . Nous avons une richesse; Le hanan (tendresse)

In the 1990s, global agencies such as the OECD began to center their search for alternative visions of development on community-based initiatives and to pay close attention to finding ways to measure the effects of social capital. The work of Fatima Mernissi and Gayatri Spivak became relevant for development academics, researchers, and practitioners. For the first time, to my knowledge, the World Bank sought out the help of feminist scholars on how to correct the "top-down" approaches to development that hadn't worked. Mernissi's *Aït-Débrouille* and some insights she learned from these rural problem solvers were presented to the World Bank Economic Development Forum organized in Marrakesh in 1997: "Prominent leaders and international agencies can play a catalytic role in raising awareness and promote promising initiatives. In 1998 a well-known Moroccan writer, Fatema Mernissi, published a book about the development dynamic in Ait Iktel. Her book was featured at the international gathering of the Mediterranean Development Forum in Marrakesh" (World Bank 2003, 75). The World Bank, in its efforts to elaborate theories to better understand the conditions under which development does or does not occur, also invited Gayatri Spivak to speak to them in 1999. She noted that "if the goal of development work is indeed people, then one of the hardest lessons to learn, is that some of virtues of human existence will be found at the very bottom

---

inconditionnelle, tiqa (confiance), ta'awn (cooperation), tadamun (solidarite). Un peuple qui ces qualités a un capital social énorme. Une population qui retrouve la confiance en soi, c'est retrouver le pouvoir de rever différemment, de s'inventer une nouvelle identité" (This book tells the story of those stubborn farmers of the High Atlas who managed to accomplish projects of which few city people like me, over-educated and oversophisticated, dream. One of the reasons for the success of these civil societies in the most marginalized rural zones in Morocco is the civic spirit of the intellectuals who come form there and who return to their native land to share invaluable experience.... We are blessed with unconditional wealth: *le hanan* (tenderness), *tiqa* (trust), *ta'awun* (cooperation), *tadamun* (solidarity). A people who have these qualities have an enormous social capital. A people who have regained confidence in themselves find once more the power to dream differently and invent a new identity for themselves) (Mernissi 1997, 3–4).

of society, which is the target area for change for development organizations." She recommended that "learning from the bottom has to take priority" (*World Bank* 1999).

The learning curve for Mernissi meant she needed to get out of the university confines and put herself in the role of student before assuming the role of expert before the World Bank forum. What was new in her activism was her focus on concepts such as *hanan* and the promotion of storytelling groups and forms of traditional-oral narrative as a means of enacting social change. Her work underscores the idea that social capital matters for women because they don't have much else sometimes. *Les Aït-Débrouille* (1997) related how women played a significant role in getting electric power and political power—in the form of Mernissi herself—to their village.

Mernissi had to put herself in the position of learner to write *Les Aït-Débrouille*. As she says in the dedication: "Ce reportage ne resemble a aucun des livres que j'ai deja écrit" (This report looks like no other report I wrote earlier) (1997, 5). To write it, she needed to get out of the ivory tower, buy espadrilles and a backpack from the flea market (as she says), and move out of her comfort zone to go up into the mountains. Mernissi explains early on that Tante (Aunt) Aicha called to say that forty local associations had brought electricity and clean water to many villages without the help of the government or experts. The development problem for Tante Aicha is simple: "Ici on dit que les gens de Rabat sont sourds!" (Here they say the people of Rabat are deaf) (Mernissi 1997, 8).

Mernissi was skeptical about the progress Tante Aicha reported, but she went to see. She learned how resilient these villagers are, and she had her own project of replacing the standard Orientalist narratives with this grassroots narrative of solidarity and self-sufficiency. Mernissi's contribution was as a translator. She had the status to present at the World Bank conference in Marrakesh. The villagers did not. But to learn something new about development, she needed to be humble enough to be willing to learn from below. She brought a series of photographs to the World Bank conference and described her experience of learning about this grassroots development effort that she saw as specific in some ways to Morocco's cultural traits. At the World Bank conference, she had to walk others through the steps she took to learn. As Tante Aicha said, "Rabat is deaf / doesn't listen." In many ways, Mernissi herself was "Rabat"; the World Bank and the IMF were "Rabat."

Water Management in Tunisia

The fact that water scarcity presents a global challenge in the twenty-first century is an issue that can no longer be avoided. A steady and sustainable supply of water is an essential ingredient to sustainable growth. Tunisia is no exception when it comes to facing the difficulties and challenges involved in providing its people with a reliable water supply and sanitation. In Tunisia, water-starved areas include the steppe city of Kairouan, the mountain city of Kef, and the island of Kerkennah—sites that have since become locations for GIZ developments. Safe drinking water forms the greatest challenge facing development cooperation in general and GIZ in particular. GIZ, the executing agency for German technical cooperation, actively participates with other partners, governments, administrations, businesses, the research sector, and civil society groups to develop local expertise and sustainable solutions for ensuring water supply in its partner countries. This effort has been initiated in multiple projects throughout 130 countries, including Tunisia (Gönner 2015, 1).

The story of water management in rural Tunisia is a multifaceted narrative illustrating the many forces at work shaping development policy. As such, it includes many actors on the local, state, and national levels. In North Africa, Tunisia, and Morocco, the major Western, transnational players in the region have been development agencies such as the UN Educational, Scientific, and Cultural Organization (UNESCO), the World Bank, the IMF, and other organizations focused on development cooperation, including Oxfam Québec, the Deutsche Gesellschaft für Technische Zusammenarbeit (GTZ, German Association for Technical Cooperation), the Agence française de dévelopement (AFD), and the US Agency for International Development (USAID). To describe their approach in broad terms, these agencies are focused primarily on so-called Western ways of life as reflected in development, democratization, good governance, sustainability, and environmental protection (Council of Europe 2003, 112). I would also describe them as competing forces, whether guided by interests in philanthropy or invested with an agenda of enacting influence upon the region.

The World Bank and the European Union have long partnered with Tunisia in support of this nation's efforts to preserve and more efficiently manage its water resources. Sadly, these efforts have not always succeeded. The European Union Water Project in Tunisia, for example, missed the genuine concerns of the women it targeted. This was especially true in the case of the most marginalized women living in Oueslatia.[4] By failing to identify these women's lack of social power and the challenges and social barriers they faced, the project's managers were not well enough positioned to structure water-management policies and economic allocations in a way that would have been more effective and ultimately far more successful. For example, today the only remaining sign of this attempt by the European Union is the empty building once used by the European experts and actors in charge of the project. To my mind, this building's ramshackle state perfectly illustrates the fact that good intentions are not enough. No matter how much financial backing a developmental project receives, taking the "top-down" approach, applying a "one-size-fits-all" set of solutions to complex problems such as water management, and ignoring local input, resources, and customs rarely lead to success.

Many cooperative development programs are currently involved in the sustainable management of groundwater resources. The primary executing agency for German technical cooperation was formerly GTZ, an association that preceded GIZ. GTZ was involved in thirteen rural development projects throughout Tunisia, nine of which were created to enable access to water in remote areas. This

---

4. Mohamed Kerrou, interviewed by Mounira Hejaiej, Tunis, Aug. 2016.

intervention by GTZ was, however, limited to providing technical support to village people, such as the installation of water posts and public lavatories and the drilling of individual wells. Technical assistance alone, however, is rarely effective in building long-term capacity. Without the ownership needed for implementation or a knowledge of the profile of the technology's users and their capacities, the plans and strategies created by consultants often fail, as in the European Union Water Project in Oueslatia referred to earlier. The problem may be a literary one: project participants are given a single storyline about what makes a good development strategy. This narrative is then discussed as if only one good plot possessing a happy outcome can possibly exist. In truth, myriad survival stories exist all around us, providing narratives that can give projects and their managers a variety of tools and techniques to enact change in a sustainable manner. It is my contention that instead of working from the top down, international development must work from below by engaging the local community.

Although the importance of promoting storytelling groups and forms of traditional, oral narrative as means of enacting social change is now perfectly clear to me, I was initially quite surprised when GIZ invited me—owing to my research on female storytellers in Tunis—to contribute to a development project focused on water management. I had never considered my book on storytellers in Tunisia, *Behind Closed Doors: Women's Oral Narratives in Tunis* (1996), as a source of information for such a project, but I knew that the tales it contained related stories of practical wisdom and the accumulated, lived experiences of women striving to imagine and create just and inclusive alternatives to their everyday issues. In many cultures around the world, women and girls function as homemakers and therefore remain in their households to cook, clean, and take on the primary responsibility of fetching drinking water (UNESCO Water Assessment Programme 2015). Women's knowledge of water resources and of how to make effective use of these resources is often transmitted through the stories women tell (Mernissi 1997). It can therefore be stated that the type of oral narrative conducted by traditional storytellers has never functioned merely as a form of entertainment; storytelling is one of the principal ways in which the surrounding community absorbs knowledge and brings social change. At the heart of my work on women storytellers in the city of Tunis, I found embedded in their tales notions that engaged and still engage people and their communities, such as equality, diversity, and justice. Their ability to voice these issues lifts female storytellers from the level of simple entertainers and empowers them instead with the tools for bringing about social activism and change.

The growing presence of storytelling projects (see, e.g., Lambert and Hessler 2018; Lejano, Ingram, and Ingram 2013; Morgan and Dennehy 1997; Ohler 2006; Solinger, Fox, and Irani 2008; Zipes 1995) clearly indicates the fact that now in the twenty-first century oral narratives represent a highly significant and crucial yet remarkably simple vehicle for stimulating engagement and active citizenship. Throughout this process, oral narratives simultaneously disseminate social equity. As the author Toni Morrison stated in her Nobel Prize lecture in 1993, "Narrative is radical, creating us at the very moment it is being created" (Morrison 1993), just as the issues of female power and progress are central to their narratives surrounding female survival, agency, and development.

To provide one instance of traditional, Tunisian culture that illustrates the power invested in women, I turn to the example of *el lemma* (social gathering). *El lemma* is a custom practiced in traditional and even modern Tunisian society involving a social gathering of relatives, neighbors, and friends for the purpose of preparing household food provisions vital throughout the year, such as a gathering to prepare couscous. These gatherings usually take place in the courtyards of traditional houses in the summer as the couscous dries in the sun: they also present the perfect opportunity for telling stories. These events demonstrate the tremendous solidarity, social tenderness, and sense of caring that characterize the social and emotional capital possessed by traditional Tunisian women. "Ishrat ma we milh" (Companionship of shared water and salt) is a common expression in Tunisian culture that captures the sense of sharing, generosity, and compassion. Although there are no specific stories addressing the issue of water management, storytellers often describe the special care given to preserving water in their daily routines and activities in order to have sufficient water for ablutions, the cooking of food, and sanitation.

For the past decade, the international management of research and development has opted to utilize more effective models of development that apply more culturally and socially oriented strategies to inform the development act. Development projects directed toward aiding women have often been small in scope and peripheral in comparison to the main aims of development. In rural communities, storytelling has proven to be a startlingly effective strategy, particularly when done by and among women as a means of building platforms to strengthen connections between scholars and partners in international developments that aim to address the challenges in water scarcity faced by postcolonial nations.

Development from Below: Valuing Local Indigenous Knowledge and Resources

To give development a human face, bottom-up development programs have moved toward complex models of innovation and become increasingly bottom-up and service oriented. Before providing a description of my own work, I must highlight the influence of Fatema Mernissi, who challenged the prevalent vision of development. Mernissi's articles "The Degrading Effects of Capitalism on Female Labour in a Third World Economy" (1979) and "Le prolétariat féminin au Maroc" ([1980] 2017) focus on the deleterious effects a capitalist economy has on women's status and on the need to give development a more humanist face. Her Civic Caravans (rural gatherings held to empower via communication) demonstrated the power of narrative to increase community awareness about the importance of social capital. In her workshops held for World Bank experts in Marrakesh in May 1997, Mernissi highlighted the success of development projects based on local social capital—networks of trust, caring, and shared responsibility—in cases where World

Bank and IMF structural-adjustment programs had failed miserably. Mernissi's genius was to insist that we pay attention to the power of the local people as the holders of the social capital central to achieving sustainable development.

Known for their strong opinions, female storytellers found their roles decreasing as women's stories were marginalized in Tunisia's postindependence, modernizing agenda beginning in the mid-1950s. As a legacy of colonialism, nonliterate women were considered symbolic of an ignorance that would hinder Tunisia's postcolonial, socioeconomic development. Since the 1980s, however, interest in reviving this heritage and the life histories of women expressed in their own words has grown. The increased availability of this wealth of traditional knowledge has enabled many contemporary development projects to view it as a previously untapped resource. The subsequent sections of my chapter describe how women's traditional stories and customs were put into action in both pre- and postrevolutionary Tunisia as current development projects channeled the power of women's narratives to teach water conservation. My work on storytellers in Tunis reveals that social capital as a resource is possessed by Tunisian women, who are closely united by bonds of trust, social care, networks, and mutual assistance in their community—symbolized by the commonly used expression "sharing (or shared) water and salt."

Al 'Ishra (Companionship): "Sharing Water and Salt"

Relations of trust and solidarity were present among the Tunisian women I grew up with and contributed toward mobilizing social capital on many occasions. The poet Amel Mousa demonstrates this proximity in poetic fashion:

> When I was little
> I called all men "Uncle"
> And all women "Auntie."
> (2015, 53)

The evidence of this can be seen in the successes achieved by small village nongovernment organizations (NGOs) throughout Tunisia.

Moncef Bouchrara's (1993) pioneering work describes how women from all walks of life and all parts of the country were—on their own initiative—challenging men's public role while showing great courage and enterprise. Bouchrara stresses the novelty of the enterprising spirit among women in the Maghreb, which he terms "civil feminism," and believes it is the basis of a new civil society in the region (Abd'ul Hamid and Binous 1996, 6). "Hanan," says Fatema Mernissi, "is the social caring that connects us to one another and makes us forget our individual interests and see more expansively" (1997, 37).

In Tunisian female communities, such as the ones in which I grew up, the social capital contained in social networks is highly prized. When proper education is added to this socially rich environment, efficiency is multiplied. With such an existing spirit, passage from the private to the public space, toward the path of organized cooperatives and civil society, has proven short and easy in present-day Tunisia. As women enter the public sphere, they develop a range of contacts and relationships outside of their immediate family and neighborhood. While traditional solidarity ties were already established within communities, new ties are established within the framework of these women's work and income activities.

Galvanizing Social Capital: From the Courtyard to the Public Square

In social science, the idea of social capital tends to be used to describe the resources of a community and the degree of shared values and trust within it (Bourdieu 1986; Coleman 1990; Putnam 2002). Pierre Bourdieu's (1986) concept of "capital" is connected to his theoretical ideas on class, and he narrows it down to three dimensions: economic capital (money, property, etc.), cultural capital (knowledge, skills, and educational qualifications), and social capital (connections and membership of groups). The OECD identifies four main ways in which social capital can be conceptualized and measured: personal relationships; social network support; civic engagement; and trust and cooperative norms (Scrivens and Smith 2013).

The concept of social capital is critically important to understanding the breadth and depth of civil society in present-day Tunisia, where associations of all kinds have become training grounds for community engagement and have fostered incredible civic activism in the transitional postrevolutionary period. In the two years following the Tunisian Revolution/Uprising and Zine El Abidine Ben Ali's departure from power in 2011, Tunisia witnessed a surge in the number of NGOs: from 9,600 in 1976 to 18,502 in 2015.[5] This is quite a big number in a country striving to build up a culture of democracy and pluralism, but it is an opportunity for Tunisians, especially women, to sustain new norms of civil engagement. Postrevolutionary Tunisia is a society in a state of flux. Economic crises, unemployment reaching 16.6 percent, and women's increased power and independence are already resulting in male backlash violence. Today, various associations exist to combat sexual harassment and domestic violence.[6] Women in the national capital are determined to play an important role in development—shaping the future and pushing for equality. From below, they are organizing, lobbying, and even reaching out to impoverished rural communities, providing clothes, water, food, and health services while engaging the members of such communities in their rights as citizens.

Even in the pre-revolutionary Tunisia of the 1990s, the proliferation of public-based micro-entrepreneurial activities, revolution, and civic feminism or female networking was undoubtedly creating a new reality in Tunisia that reflected the dynamism of female populations and the real extent of their contribution. Mernissi played an important role in moving women's voices from the courtyard to the public square. Her many books, which she wrote in English, French, and Arabic, show her belief in the centrality of women's voices to any sustainable-development project, and her activism in the field

---

5. For these statistics and others, see the Ifeda (Centre d'information, de formation, d'etudes, et de documentation sur les associations) website at http://www.ifeda.org.tn/fr/.

6. See the Ifeda website.

was felt not only in Morocco but also in the greater Maghreb and beyond. At an early age, she realized the importance of writing, and she saw it as an excellent way for women to free themselves from social constraints and to combat aging. Mernissi says: "That you write, for that reason alone means you have a voice! Power! When we talk about writing that is the essential idea. Writing is the best beauty treatment" (Mernissi 1992, 4). She was often invited by Tunisian women's associations to attend their formal and informal gatherings. She ran women's literacy and writing workshops in Tunis in 1991, the results of which were published as *Tunisiennes en devenir* (Tunisians in the Making) in two volumes, *Comment les femme vivent* (How Women Live) and *La moitié entière* (Full-fledged Citizens/Citizenship), by the Association des femmes tunisiennes pour la recherche et le dévelopement (AFTURD 1992a, 1992b).

Comment les femmes vivent is one of the healthiest, most inspiring nonfiction volumes of essays I have come across. The women speak out as Arab women, writers, mothers, academics, and feminists in fifteen pieces, ranging from the personal to the political. Among the contents are essays about other prominent feminists, human rights campaigners, and activists: an account of the protest movement against US intervention in Iraq in the 1990s, vivid accounts about traditional women networking not only as housewives holding the reins of the family's budget and contributing to it but also as poetesses, artists, chefs, healers, beauticians, midwives, creators, and procreators in their own right, celebrating nature, health, and well-being—human faces to which the writers have attributed all that is contemporary Tunisian civil society.

A Story from Below

The story of rehabilitating Tunisian women's voices in water management in rural Tunisia is also a heteroglossic narrative about the many forces at work shaping development policy. What happens when the water supply is disrupted, a situation currently happening in Tunisia today? In the areas of cooperation in which international bodies tend to represent their own interests, the emergence of free debate voiced by the Tunisian Assembly and the dissatisfaction expressed by Tunisia's civil society actors are forcing international organizations to enter into dialogue with the local population. The importance of participating in effective delivery has finally been recognized. Reviews of water projects conducted in Africa and Asia have found that "participation by beneficiaries and grass-roots institutions were [sic] a key factor in those long-term and community provisions of service" (World Bank 1994, 76).

To combat water scarcity, Tunisia is returning to traditional ways of water service and sanitation through the use of household cisterns (*majelles*) and giant basins (*fusqiyya*). Minister of Environment Samir Betayyib is advising Tunisians to resolve the water problem through traditional practices, such as collecting water in *majelles* and *fusqiyya*. In a radio broadcast, Betayyib declared, "Our problem is not in the lack of resources. Our problem instead resides in the management of these resources" (Betayyib 2016).

In many women's empowerment projects, activism is examining the possibility of using the power of words and the ancient intimacy of storytelling as channels (artist and audience) harnessed simply and effectively to build sustainable development. Through storytelling, audiences can become directly engaged in social justice issues regarding employment, health, water distribution, and the environment. This strategy is proving more useful than technical knowledge summarized in graphs and statistics. Storytelling, after all, involves a wide range of social, emotional, intuitive, and interpersonal skills that comprehensively provide a multitude of services to the community. Although narratives have been rooted in the social sciences since the 1980s, a more uniquely sociological approach has begun to examine stories in the interactional, institutional, and political contexts of where and how they are told. Scholars working from this perspective view narrative as a powerful tool and therefore focus on ways in which narrative competence is socially organized. When used in such a context, traditional narratives are an effective means of shedding light on enduring sociological questions, thereby rendering them an essential means of community development *from below* (Reinsborough and Canning 2010).

In this type of development, senior women living in the local community represent an important asset in terms of cultural continuity. The social capital they possess as the community's respected elders can be brought to bear on decisions about modernization (Rice and Hamdy 2008). "In rural water supply, probably more than in any other sector, sustainability is dramatically enhanced when women have key responsibilities" (Briscoe and de Ferranti 1989, 15). International policy statements now refer to the importance of women in water management, and the understanding of gendered roles in water-resource management is being incorporated into project planning.[7]

The power of communication initiated from below is taking place within the larger context of local and international NGO networks in rural Tunisia that support local actors in establishing empowerment programs for women. Tunisia's water, its liquid gold, is targeted by several of these projects, including Water Is a Human Right, sponsored by Les anciennes de Dar El Bacha association de femmes (Dar El Bacha Alumnae Women's Association). Commissioned by the Federal Ministry for Economic Cooperation and Development and implemented by GIZ, the water-management initiatives Les ambassadrices de l'eau (Water Ambassadors) and Les conteuses du Maghreb (Storytellers of the Maghrib) further illustrate how targeting local women can be used to spread water-preservation programs throughout Tunisia in a way that builds upon local tradition while also creating a sustainable network. The latter two projects (2014–16) were implemented in collaboration with the Center of Arab Women for Training and Research (CAWTAR), an international Arab women's

---

7. These practices encourage women to play influential roles in both water management and hygiene education. Capacity building is necessary to make community management effective and to enable women to play leading roles.

organization; the Société nationale d'exploitation et de distribution des faux (SONEDE), a national agency overseeing the exploitation and distribution of water; and the Urban Environment Development Organization (EMAR), a local NGO.

Rehabilitating Women's Voices: The Ambassadrices de l'eau and Conteuses du Maghreb

Undertaken by the sociologist Mohamed Kerrou, an earlier study of the European Union Water Project in the village Oueslatia showed women's invisibility in the development plans and the process of water management despite their decisive role in water management.[8] This invisibility additionally facilitated the exploitation of women while allowing the state and its development programs to elude the responsibility of not responding to women's needs and legitimate aspirations. Through an alternative focus on storytellers, in contrast, the invisible became visible: women were finally identified as the best actors in making a difference in other women's lives and communicating messages about good water practices. In Shebika, Les ambassadrices de l'eau (Water Ambassadors) represented a women's network created to ensure the sustainability of actions and provide a space for exchanging experiences and good methods. The purpose of this network was also to raise awareness among families, neighbors, and friends about the more responsible management of water. The two-year project (2014–16) illustrates how long-lasting change comes not from outside forces, such as the European Union, but rather from the existing and created collective social will that GIZ has tried to tap into.

Another important water collaborative project implemented by GIZ and commissioned by the Tunisian Federal Ministry for Economic Cooperation and Development is deeply connected to traditional forms of knowledge. Implemented in Morocco, Jordan,

---

8. Kerrou interview, Aug. 2016.

Egypt, and Tunisia, Les conteuses du Maghreb (Storytellers of the Maghrib) tapped into women's practical wisdom and central place in their communities. As part of this project, GIZ collected women's stories about water and water scarcity to serve as a narrative archive concerning water usage, practices, storage, and availability. To take the project a step further, storytelling events were organized, and women were also trained as storytellers. Activists insist on the power that stories possess to connect people and to generate understanding, engagement, and active citizenship. At the time that Mernissi first became involved with development projects, Stephen Heynemen (1989), a World Bank expert, insisted on the importance of cultural heritage in any development program and as an essential factor in the quality of education in the Middle East and North Africa.

Women are still the first victims of a lack of access to water in rural Tunisia. Mismanagement, global warming, and overexploitation are still making water one of the most vital social issues in Tunisia today. Long periods of drought have been increasing in recent years, and rainfall may drop by one-third by 2050. This crisis will overload an already tired infrastructure, and this general failure of the system will weigh heavily on the women, to whom fall the domestic servitudes in which water is the essential material. They are the ones who have to spend hours daily to get water supplies from standpipes or wadis (rivers in dry regions). Many in these conditions are unable to ensure the hygiene of their homes and their children, a crucial problem in this time of pandemic. But the stories of water in the landscape have been passed down, and local communities in rural Tunisia continue to use local knowledge to secure their own water supplies and build a resilient water future (see Brésillon 2021; EAUcole n.d.).

Conclusion

The most subaltern stories within a community project the hopes and dreams of those telling them or sitting nearby, hanging on the storytellers' every word. In addition, these stories are intrinsically connected to traditional forms of knowledge and communicate practical methods for dealing with issues such as water scarcity. Rejuvenating the work of storytellers literally taps into networks of traditional social capital that represent the foundation of Tunisian women's traditional culture. During the 1990s, leading international agencies practiced top-down methods intended to provide quick solutions to pressing issues; in the end, this approach instead led to failed results that closely resembled shock therapy.

"Stories or narratives provide the glue that binds people together in network, providing them with a sense of history, common grounds and future," say Raul Lejano, Mrill Ingram, and Helen Ingram (2013, 2), who suggest that by focusing on the stories people tell about their environments, agencies can do a better job of understanding what matters to people and why and how they take action. Although it would be unwise to deny the relevance of innovations in development strategies, Mernissi's influence on development protocols and the potential of narrative put to greater use in current development projects in Tunisia and Morocco demonstrate that home-grown development strategies have proven more effective.

In times of hardships, Tunisian women have always relied on the wisdom and aid found within their social capital. Tunisia's women have created survival strategies as a social means of adjusting to their circumstances. In other words, women have always contributed to solving problems or increasing their own economic activity by holding the key to the *bayt el muna* (storeroom), just as my own grandmother did. Illiterate and bound by tradition, my powerful grandmother reigned supreme over the bags of sugar, flour, semolina, spices, and jars of orange-blossom water, jasmine oil, and olive oil that represented our family's survival. Set aside for hard times like the supplies kept under lock and key in the *bayt el muna*, the fund of tales found in the intimacy of Tunisia's courtyards represents how women can turn their traditional power into a means of creating sustainable, long-lasting development—an essential means of community development "from below"—rather than continuing to rely on foreign expertise from international entities. Mernissi didn't invent the wheel on how to understand the importance of changing development models about gender and development, but she did open herself to learning a new field for herself and then followed up on her own to spread this wisdom.

References

Abd'ul Hamid, Yara, and Jamila Binous. 1996. *The Thousand and One Paths to Empowerment: Coping Strategies of Poor Women in Tunisia.* Tunis, Tunisia: Enda-Inter-Arabe, Ford Foundation, Cooperation francaise, Union europeenne.

AFTURD ouvrage collectif (Jamila Binous, Fathia Harzallah, Samira Hamzaoui, Habiba Ben Romdhane, Dorra Mahfoudh Draoui, and Léa-Véra Tahar Baklouti). 1992a. *Comment les femmes vivent.* Vol. 1 of *Tunisiennes en devenir.* Tunis, Tunisia: Cérès.

———. 1992b. *La moitié entière.* Vol. 2 of *Tunisiennes en devenir.* Tunis, Tunisia: Cérès.

Aguinaga, Margarita, Miriam Lang, Dunia Mokrani, and Alejandra Santillana. 2013. "Critiques and Alternatives to Development: A Feminist Perspective." In *Beyond Development: Alternative Visions from Latin America: Permanent Working Group on Alternatives to Development*, edited by Miriam Lang and Dunia Mokrani, translated by Sara Shields and Rosemary Underhay, 41–60. Quito, Ecuador: Transnational Institute and Rosa Luxemburg Foundation.

Barrios de Chungara, Domitila, with Moema Viezzer. 1978. *Let Me Speak: Testimony of Domitila, a Woman of the Bolivian Mines.* New York: Monthly Review Press.

Beck, Lois, and Nikki Keddie. 1978. *Women in the Muslim World.* Cambridge, MA: Harvard Univ. Press.

Betayyib, Samir. 2016. Interview. RadioExpressFM, Sept. 17. Formerly at https://radioexpressfm.com/fr/ but now no longer online.

Boserup, Ester. 1970. *Women's Role in Economic Development.* New York: St. Martin's Press.

Bouchrara, Moncef. 1993. "Esprit d'entreprise au feminin et politiques." Paper presented at the international conference "Les raisons d'entreprendre: Elles pensent la Sociète de Demain," Organization for Economic Cooperation and Development, Nov. 1993, Paris.

Bourdieu, Pierre. 1986. "The Forms of Capital." In *Handbook of Theory and Research for the Sociology of Education*, edited by J. G. Richardson, 241–58. Westport, CT: Greenwood.

Brésillon, Thierry. 2021 "Tunisie: Les femmes, premières victimes du manque d'accès à l'eau." Terre Solidaire, Feb. 3. At https://ccfd-terresolidaire.org/tunisie-les-femmes-premieres-victimes-du-manque-dacces-a-leau/.

Briscoe, John, and David de Ferranti. 1989. *Water for Rural Communities: Helping People Help Themselves*. Washington, DC: World Bank.

Brundtland Commission. 1987. *Our Common Future*. Geneva: World Commission on Environment and Development. At https://sustainabledevelopment.un.org/content/documents/5987our-common-future.pdf.

Coleman, James S. 1990. *Foundations of Social Theory*. Cambridge, MA: Belknap Press of Harvard Univ. Press.

Council of Europe, Committee on the Environment, Agriculture, and Local and Regional Affairs. 2003. *Globalisation and Sustainable Development*. Report. Strasbourg, France: Council of Europe. At https://assembly.coe.int/nw/xml/XRef/X2H-Xref-ViewHTML.asp?FileID=9961.

EAUcole. N.d. GIZ Tunisie. At https://www.facebook.com/EAUcole-785526988199891/.

Evans, Peter. 1997. *State–Society Synergy: Government and Social Capital in Development*. Berkeley, CA: Institute for International Studies.

Gönner, Tanja. 2015. "Speech by Tanja Gönner, Chair of the GIZ Management Board, at the 2015 Annual Press Conference: Global Results for Germany." Deutsche Gesellschaft für Internationale Zusammenarbeit, June 30. At https://www.giz.de/en/downloads/giz2015-speech-chair-of-the-giz-management-board.pdf.

Hejaiej, Monia. 1996. *Behind Closed Doors: Women's Oral Narratives in Tunis*. New Brunswick, NJ: Rutgers Univ. Press.

Heynemen, Stephen. 1989. *Textbooks in the Developing World: Economic and Educational Choices*. EDI Seminar Series. Washington, DC: Economic Development Institute, World Bank.

Kabeer, Naila. 1994. *Reversed Realities: Gender Hierarchies in Development Thought*. London: Verso.

Lambert, Joe, and Brooke Hessler. 2018. *Digital Storytelling: Capturing Lives, Creating Community*. 5th ed. New York: Routledge.

Lejano, Raul, Mrill Ingram, and Helen Ingram. 2013. *The Power of Narrative in Environmental Networks*. Cambridge, MA: MIT Press.

Mernissi, Fatema. 1979. "The Degrading Effects of Capitalism on Female Labour in a Third World Economy: The Particular Case of Crafts Women in Morocco." *Peuples méditerranéens: Revue trimestrielle* 6:41–57.

———. 1992. Preface to AFTURD ouvrage collectif (Jamila Binous, Fathia Harzallah, Samira Hamzaoui, Habiba Ben Romdhane, Dorra Mahfoudh Draoui, and Léa-Véra Tahar Baklouti), *Comment les femmes vivent*, vol. 1 of *Tunisiennes en devenir*, 4. Tunis, Tunisia: Cérès.

———. 1997. *Les Aït-Débrouille: ONG rurales du Haut-Atlas*. Casablanca, Morocco: Le Fennec.

———. [1980] 2017. "Le prolètariat feminin au Maroc." *Annuaire de l'Afrique du Nord*. Online reprint. At https://doi.org/10.4000/annee maghreb.7442.

Morgan, Sandra, and Robert F. Dennehy. 1997. "The Power of Organizational Storytelling: A Management Development Perspective." *Journal of Management Development* 16, no. 7 (Oct.): 494–501.

Morrison, Toni. 1993. "Nobel Lecture." The Nobel Prize (website), Dec. 7. At https://www.nobelprize.org/prizes/literature/1993/morrison/lecture/.

Mousa, Amel. 2015. "Little Girl Facing the Ruins." In "Revolutions in Tunisian Poetry," edited and translated by Laura Rice and Karim Hamdy. Special issue, *Pacifica: Poetry International*, no. 1: 53–55.

Ohler, Jason. 2005. "The World of Digital Storytelling." ASCD, Dec. 1. At https://ascd.org/el/articles/the-world-of-digital-storytelling.

Putnam, Robert D., ed. 2002. *Democracies in Flux: The Evolution of Social Capital in Contemporary Society*. Oxford: Oxford Univ. Press.

Radcliffe, Sarah A. 1994. "(Representing) Postcolonial Women: Authority, Difference and Feminisms." *Area* 26, no. 1 (Mar.): 25–32.

Reinsborough, Patrick, and Doyle Canning. 2010. *Re-imagining Change: How to Use Story-Based Strategy to Win Campaigns, Build Movements, and Change the World*. Oakland, CA: PM Press.

Rice, Laura, and Karim Hamdy. 2008. "Situating Senior Women in the Literacy Landscape of North Africa." *International Journal of the Sociology of Language* 190:27–47.

Scrivens, Katherine, and Conal Smith. 2013. *Four Interpretations of Social Capital: An Agenda for Measurement*. Organization for Economic Cooperation and Development (OECD) Statistics Working Papers No.

2013/06. Paris: OECD/OECD Publishing. At https://dx.doi.org/10.1787/5jzbcx010wmt-en.

Simonson, Rick. 2020. "*Azadi.*" Interview of Arundhati Roy. BookTV, C-SPAN2, Sept. 1. At https://www.c-span.org/video/?476710-1/azadi.

Solinger, Rickie, Madeline Fox, and Kayhan Irani, eds. 2008. *Telling Stories to Change the World: Global Voices on the Power of Narrative to Build Community and Make Social Justice Claims.* New York: Routledge.

UNESCO Water Assessment Programme. 2015. *Water for a Sustainable World.* United Nations World Water-Development Report. Paris: UNESCO Water Assessment Programme. At https://unesdoc.unesco.org/ark:/48223/pf0000231823.

United Nations Development Program (UNDP). 2002. *Arab Human Development Report.* New York: United Nations. At https://arab-hdr.org/.

World Bank. 1994. *World Development Report 1994: Infrastructure for Development.* Washington, DC: World Bank.

———. 2003. *World Development Report 2003: Sustainable Development in a Dynamic World: Transforming Institutions, Growth, and Quality of Life.* Washington, DC: World Bank; Oxford: Oxford Univ. Press. At https://documents1.worldbank.org/curated/ru/262521468337195361/pdf/247050REPLACEM00100PUBLIC00WDR02003.pdf.

World Bank. 1999. "Summary of Gayatri Spivak's Talk to the World Bank 1999." Apr. 20. Posted on dannybutt.net, Sept. 4, 2014. At https://dannybutt.net/summary-of-gayatri-spivaks-talk-to-the-world-bank/.

Zipes, Jack. 1995. *Creative Storytelling: Building Community/Changing Lives.* New York: Routledge.

14

Fatema Mernissi, Intersectionality, and the Decolonization of Knowledge

Rural Women's Work versus the Harem Myth

NASIMA MOUJOUD

Translated from French by Paola Bacchetta

In this chapter, I provide some reflections on what Fatema Mernissi brings to matters that are central to feminist theories and practices: the decolonization of knowledge and the interweaving of power relations or intersectionality as theorized in Black feminism (Crenshaw 1991, 2005). These topics, in fact, constitute a thread running through Mernissi's first writings in French from the late 1970s to the early 1980s (Mernissi 1978, 1979, 1980, 1981, 1983, 1986). They compose a doubled querying of both the materialized and ideological aspects of women's domination, which Mernissi offers us in her discussion of the Moroccan case. Her texts engage with the specific conditions of the most precarious, subaltern women. They address the gap between what women experience and articulate and what dominant discourses think because the latter obscure women's points of view, their subjectivities, their labor, and their exploitation. The major thematic of these first texts by Mernissi is the work that women of the popular, rural classes do. Mernissi puts these women at the center of her analysis before entering into discussion about the harem in later works (Mernissi 1994, 1996, 1998, 2001). However, I suggest that beginning with Mernissi's earliest publications there is a meeting point between her concerns with work and her concerns with the harem insofar as she was committed to deconstructing colonial categories, including the harem, by making work visible.

The doubled movement of Mernissi's oeuvre from the end of the 1970s to the beginning of the 1980s constituted by the thematics of work and the harem allows me to assert that her contribution is always contemporary and useful. We will see that the migratory and transnational contexts—which I evoke here from the spaces of France and Morocco—produce "new" discourses that echo the "old" ones (i.e., Orientalist discourses on the harem, religion, North Africa, etc.). Today these new discourses especially crystallize around religion even as they continue to deny the question of work and the effects of colonialism. Mernissi allows us to evoke religion but only as she reminds us that we must consider that which represents a central stake in current Muslim and other societies: work.

Why Work?

In France, where I am situated, work has been one of the main thematics in feminist research since the 1970s. Materialist feminist theories have demonstrated that the sexual division of labor constructs "women" and "men" and organizes all of society. This scholarship has revealed how an androcentric vision of work obscures the work that women do. The dominant definition of work, which this scholarship reproduces, has only the figure of the male worker as its referent. At the same time, although this construction seems relatively obvious in feminist critiques of industrial societies, the reductive categories prevent us from seeing it in societies deemed "underdeveloped" and consequently also in formerly colonized societies and among migrants from the latter. In fact, many feminist academics who specialize in questions of labor claim to study only industrialized societies, perhaps so as not to risk making comparisons that are difficult to support with evidence. For example, Héléna Hirata and Danièle Kergoat specify that their analysis of the sexual division of labor concerns only wage economies, as in the so-called global North (1998, 95). As with other points of view that represent "general" theories, these authors do not question the category of the societies they designate or the reasons for limiting the analysis to them. Their point of departure is an implicit epistemic bias: they presume the unity of an ensemble (the West) in opposition to another ensemble (the Rest). They thereby forget that colonization was a principal tool for the expansion of capitalism, as, in fact, Mernissi, among others, clearly demonstrates (e.g., in Mernissi 1981).

"General" theories in France ignore research coming out of the global South that likewise addresses the challenges and stakes of waged work. To make women's work visible, Moroccan scholars narrate its historical and sociological importance. Early studies by Aïcha Belarbi (1988, 1991) addressed the sexual division of labor in Morocco. Fatema Mernissi focused her first publications on the labor of formerly rural women who become workers on modernized farms that are affected by the introduction of wage labor and industrial technology or on the labor of domestic workers with families who change their status and the women thus experience access to "modern" privileges (schooling, wage earning, dominant languages, clothing, etc., introduced under colonialism in Morocco). Mernissi perpetually articulates work and (internal) migration. She analyzes new forms of exploitation of women's work as well as the effects of modernization on the daily lives of the most precarious among them. Mernissi said in an early phase of her writing that (formerly colonized, Moroccan) women have always worked, but the type of work they have done has changed since colonization. This shift in work enabled new hierarchies between women. Mernissi continually flags these hierarchies throughout her writing, using the words of the most subaltern women.

In this context, Fatema Mernissi was a pioneer of studies on women's work in Morocco and in the French-speaking world on both sides of the Mediterranean. She was an extremely thorough theoretician who did not forget the effects of colonization. But even though Mernissi was writing about a society that was formerly colonized by France, and notwithstanding the facts that work has been central to feminist studies in France and that literatures and discourse on Moroccan (and, more broadly, Maghrebian) women are abundant, she remains somewhat unknown in dominant (white) French feminist research on work. A notable exception is authors who study Morocco and are concerned about the effects of colonial history, such as Meriem Rodary (2007). It must be said that dominant (white) French feminist scholars have taken little account of colonial history, migration, and racism. The immense literature on women and work in France that they have developed since the 1970s is written from a homogenizing perception of French society as consistently white, and it ignores histories of both colonialism and slavery.

From 2000 on, however, questions of racism and hierarchies among women began to appear in dominant (white) feminist knowledge production in France. We are currently witnessing some success in translations of decolonial and intersectional studies, especially from the English-speaking world. Reflections on the decolonization of knowledge and themes such as women-of-color domestic workers appear—fortunately—by detour by way of translations of US Black feminists' texts. But this is occurring without much attention to the same thematics as developed in French-language works by francophone postcolonial authors from sites formerly colonized by France, such as Mernissi. Also, the reception of Black feminism in France has unfolded along with the ongoing invisibilization of knowledge produced by racialized academics from countries that are former or present colonies of France. French people of color are largely absent from lists of authors, references, citations, scientific committees, colloquiums, and international correspondence. This absence is flagrantly clear in academic journals, conference programs, and "new" French work that references Black feminism, postcolonial feminism, decolonial feminism, intersectionality, the idea of "imbrications" of multiple relations of power, and the coloniality of gender in France or in the (post)colonial context.[1] For example, Danièle Kergoat, the renowned specialist on gender and labor mentioned earlier, began

---

1. The only exceptions here are texts or events that include at least one academic from at least one of the sites colonized by France.

studying the racial division of labor at the beginning of the 2000s, but she does not cite any nonwhite researcher who works on labor or migration (see, e.g., Kergoat 2009). This lacuna is notable especially in light of the fact that the field of gender and migration is much older and was initiated by "women of foreign origin," as Catherine Quiminal (2000) points out in her essay on migration in the *Dictionnaire critique du feminisme* (Critical Dictionary of Feminism), edited by Héléna Hirata and others in 2000. Ignoring the prior work allows Kergoat to posit the racial division of labor as something totally new: it "is now appearing by way of the nanny, the maid, or caretakers of elderly family members—and *it's a new phenomena*—at the heart of families" (2009, 122, emphasis added). The other, the foreigner, is no longer situated in the peripheries, the outskirts of big cities, the suburban slums. Suddenly they live and work within families that just a short time ago were immune to this phenomenon. As Fatima Ait Ben Lmamdani and I argue in an earlier text, the invisibilization of contributions by French academics of color has allowed for forgetting the link between migration and colonial history in France (see Ait Ben Lmamdani and Moujoud 2012).

Thus, although dominant feminism in France currently recognizes the translated work of US feminists of color as valid feminist knowledge production, the same dominant feminists continue to neglect similar antiracism and decolonial feminist writing by French and francophone postcolonial feminists, especially those who are descendants of migrants from Africa. In addition, the period from 2000 on coincides with the dominant construction of the veil as a problem in France. Islam has become a major obsession in racist, Islamophobic, and antimigration discourses and practices (Hajjat and Marwan 2013). The term *immigrants* has become *Muslims*. Women's work disappears in speeches about "Muslims." But the question of work especially disappears in majoritarian debates about the veil. These discussions most often reduce the question of the veil to ideological dimensions, conveniently situating "difference" in "culture." They do so without any concern for the material dimensions of the lived experience of veiled and nonveiled women who have been subjected to racism regardless of their age, nationality, legal status, or "culture"—even well before the passage of France's infamous antiveil law in March 2004. Remarkably, in France there are no references to Mernissi in any publications or translations in journals or in collected books on intersectionality, Black feminism, or postcolonialism in France. Mernissi is cited as a main reference only on the harem, a topic that still attracts the kind of gaze that we can call "neo-Orientalist," instead of on the topics of work and racism.

The Traps of the Harem

Mernissi is not cited in dominant (white) feminists' analyses of issues that they consider to be central in France, such as women's work, intersectionality, and the decolonization of knowledge in the French context. Her contributions to these questions are completely neglected in dominant (white) feminism, even if the scholars who produce it cannot completely ignore Mernissi herself insofar as she is a world-renowned scholar and writer who published extensively in France. Thus, she is most often quoted only on questions of the harem—as fantasized in Orientalism. The main source for such quotes is Mernissi's first novel, which was translated by Claudine Richetin from the English original *Dreams of Trespass: Tales of a Harem Girlhood* (1994) as *Rêves de femmes: Une enfance au harem* (1996) and published in both France and Morocco. The novel immediately received acclaim in France, but in Morocco it created a certain distance compared to other writing by Mernissi. Moroccan feminists critiqued Mernissi's use of the word *harem*, which is not otherwise used (or even known) in the languages spoken in Morocco. The word *harem*, like many of its definitions in French, is totally unfamiliar to Moroccans, who are not saturated with Orientalist literature or painting and who speak neither classical Arabic nor French. Rita El Khayat remarks: "The word 'harem' is a Western invention of orientalist type: this word does not exist in spoken Arabic—at least not in the Arabic spoken in the western parts of Middle East as in

Morocco, and it is only after Orientalism that the word was used" (2002, 297).[2]

For example, the otherwise generally critical historian Christelle Taraud evokes "the harem of Fez where [Mernissi] was born in the 1940s" (2003, 429), thereby accepting the harem of fantasized Orientalism. Taraud takes literally the idea of Mernissi's birth in a harem. Yet Mernissi clearly states in a footnote in *Rêves de femmes* that the child narrator is a fictional character (1996, 234–35n2). *Rêves de femmes* is neither an autobiography nor necessarily factual. How are we supposed to believe that Mernissi was born in a harem? That a child of the harem—as such a child is invented and fantasized in Orientalism—can become a world-renowned researcher, as is Fatema Mernissi? Taraud falls into the same trap as journalists who have not been exposed to critiques of colonial history and Orientalism and who—unlike historians—believe that Mernissi was born in a harem. Taraud quotes Mernissi on the harem—and "North African sexuality" within it—but does not mention the questions at the center of Mernissi's studies, such as work, or even those at the center of Mernissi's novel, such as borders, dreams of transgressing them, and the role of colonization.

Yet, as Saadia Taouki remarks, "from the outset, Fatema Mernissi points out that this is the [imaginary] reality of a harem historicized by the culture and politics of the 1940s." Taouki continues: "The question of identity in the 1940s is defined in contrast to colonial otherness" (2017, 2). More generally, Mernissi uses the harem as a notion to articulate women's confinement by different male powers. In *Rêves de femmes*, states Taouki, "the imaginary is used to question the notion of *harem* as a space for women's identitary homogeneity.

2. I remember very well how my teachers in the Department of French Literature at the University of Agadir, Morocco, blamed Mernissi for reviving the harem as a category, for they tended to be vigilant about the reception of Moroccan novels promoted by the media in France. My life in France then made me discover the continued success of *Dreams of Trespass*/*Rêves de femmes*. But studies from the 2000s reduce the text to an autobiographical narrative and use it as the (sole) historical reference on the so-called North African harem, even though it is in fact a novel.

It allows us to move from the objectification of the *harem* norm to how women subjectively really experience it. It thus makes it possible to escape the ordinary and normative perception of reality" (2).

Mernissi refers to the harem to speak of confinement, dreams, and struggles. The stated goal of her first novel is to make visible the dreams of women who want to transgress the border. As Taouki argues, the harem is "an imaginary line," for "the frontier can only be mental; the *harem* is a discourse that tells itself only to perpetuate itself" (2017, 2). Mernissi (2001) later extends the meanings of the harem to realities in the West. In that sense, she uses imagination and humor but without ever forgetting to mention working-class women's work and the inequity between rich (urban, elitist) women and subaltern (rural, working-class, domestic-worker, etc.) women. The definition of the harem that dominant (white) authors in France reproduce from Mernissi do not take into consideration the complexities of how she deploys the idea of the harem to revisit it, to expand its meanings, and to invite "others" to deconstruct their colonial imagination.

The citations of Mernissi's writing on the harem thus indicate the paradox of how she is referenced as an author in France. One can say that her work is understood as limited to contributions concerning the harem and that these contributions are interpreted simplistically in Orientalist and colonialist ways. The treatment of Mernissi's work is an example of the double process of *concealment* and *misunderstanding* of writing produced by authors from societies that were formerly colonized by France and who critique French colonial history. It is also an example of how this postcolonial writing is instrumentalized to renew colonial knowledge instead of taking seriously the actual words of formerly colonized subjects and especially the words of the most subaltern subjects, such as those who are at the center of Mernissi's analyses.

Subaltern Women as a Point of Departure for Thinking Intersectionality

In her various publications from the late 1970s to the early 1980s, which are of major interest to us here, Mernissi studies subaltern women's work by highlighting the need to make their point of view central. Thus, in her book *Le Maroc raconté par ses femmes* (1986) Mernissi writes that these women "reveal that in low-income classes, the husband is often physically and economically absent; unemployment and emigration make him totally unavailable to his children." Historically, working-class women "were never able to be fed by their husbands without having to work very hard among the peasant masses who make up the majority of the population" (13–15). This observation is contrary to the dominant (elite-class and colonial-Orientalist) male discourse, which represents subaltern women as passive and as prevented from working by their men, their culture, or their religion. Mernissi instead demonstrates that subaltern women, like other subaltern workers, are exploited, discriminated against, and badly paid.

Without directly articulating this approach as such in a central way, in practice Mernissi recommends recognizing the knowledge of the subaltern women she engages by taking into account their oral literatures, proverbs, and jokes. She also makes it clear that the analyses and critiques that they convey to her as a person who is part of a more comfortable economic class and who is from an urban milieu are of utmost importance. Mernissi never forgets who is speaking and about whom. She very often focuses on what the subaltern women have taught her about the inequalities that separate her from them. An example is an interview with Aicha, a peasant woman whom Mernissi quotes in *Développement capitaliste et perceptions des femmes dans la société musulmane* (1981) and who reminds Mernissi of her own privileges:

> Women from wealthy families remain on their men's land, or they take exams and get degrees and hold permanent jobs just like men. They will not beg for poorly paid work outside, like me. When you go to beg for a job from a man on the wealthy farms, whether it's for the State or others for seven *durham*s (one dollar equals approximately four *durham*s) a day, and he hesitates, you feel like you are less than nothing, and you are ready to sell anything at that time. You understand? No, you do not understand, you cannot

understand, you with diplomas and a car. You are clean, have a nice haircut, you speak well. You need to understand what it's like to be an illiterate, poor woman who goes looking for work in dust and mud, dirty and tired, who asks for a pittance, seven *durham*s a day, from farm technicians of *Makhzen* (State). They are educated, well dressed, well cared for, with pens, folders, they write everything. No is no! Yes is yes! It's organized, everything is organized; there's only you who have no place in all that, and you come back the next day if you're told to come back tomorrow, and it starts again. Our mothers did not experience that. They fought with their fathers, brothers, husbands. We did not inherit land, but we were at home, our mothers did not beg from strangers. That's new, and it's worse. (12–13)

Listening to subaltern rural women allowed Mernissi to say that, contrary to popular belief, in Morocco colonization played only a marginal role in the positive improvement of women's status. The colonial introduction of the capitalist economy even aggravated the conditions of women from lower classes because colonization reinforced inequalities of class and between rural and urban populations. Mernissi highlighted the link among patriarchy, capitalism introduced by colonization, and the impoverishment of the familial economy and rural women who were quantitatively the majority before colonization. In city factories and on modernized farms, women have not had access to stable, recognized work. Few permanent jobs were created on modernized farms, and 97 percent of those jobs are occupied by men (Mernissi 1981). Popular-rural women have been impoverished even as other Moroccan women have benefited from new advantages linked to their belonging to the urban-elite milieu. The latter mainly reproduce the categories of colonial discourse that have been perpetuated since independence and that Mernissi deconstructs.

Continually Decolonizing Knowledge

Thus, Mernissi's work constitutes a historically primary and particularly solid basis for theorizing what she calls the *articulation* of social relations of sex, class, and colonization together. For Mernissi, in contrast to what dominant Orientalist or colonial discourse assumes, women are not a particular cultural category but rather a social group defined by (pre- and postcolonial) *social relations* of class and sex, which are historically constructed in a mode that is *articulated* together and organized around work during and since colonization. The link between patriarchy and capitalism is redirected in the postcolonial context under the effect of nationalist elites who propose the emancipation of women from their social milieu yet perpetuate the exploitation of subaltern women especially via what Mernissi calls "the dichotomization of women's world" (1981, a phrase repeated throughout the text). In her work, the latter process defines race.

Mernissi reflects upon the construction of colonized women in the colonizers' discourses and practices, highlighting their figuration as a different and impoverished group, as a rural group, as dominated, exploited, reduced to "tradition," the "veil," the "harem," and nonwork. By stigmatizing the colonized people's practices, colonial discourse aims to legitimize the exploitation of poor women and the marginalization of their group. But to deconstruct this stigmatization, Mernissi refers to the work of rural women—and often of rural men—pointing to their exploitation while describing their plurality of cultural practices, including the "veil" and "unveiling" and taking into account the circulation of colonial prejudices in nationalist discourse. I return to this point later.

Making the work of women from popular and rural backgrounds visible is one of the main tactics that Mernissi uses to escape from Orientalist, colonialist, capitalist, and sexist categories such as the harem and instead to demonstrate that these women's lives have been deeply, negatively affected by colonization both in transnational space and in the French migratory context, including in the postcolonial period. However, Mernissi's work on these topics is rarely engaged with in France, even though her first studies—in the early 1980s—were published at the same time as the emergence of an immensely stereotyped literature on "immigrant women," meaning

Maghrebian women. The latter are consistently imagined outside of work and via the kinds of Orientalist and colonialist categories that Mernissi had already long critiqued. Furthermore, according to these categories, "the Maghrebian people" cannot work, travel, or talk. I critically reviewed elsewhere the deployment of these categories across a variety of French publications (see Moujoud 2008). It was not until her book on the harem was released in French in 1996 that Mernissi was mentioned in France. Moreover, at that time attention to her was limited to a focus on the harem even as she was producing foundational work that would require a complete revision of dominant French thought about the formerly colonized and their descendants in France. Mernissi's writing on this topic could greatly contribute to decolonizing knowledge by redirecting its focus to connections among cultural prejudice, deprivation of resources, and exclusion from valued, paid labor.

Mernissi's writing on work from the point of view of popular and rural women constitutes an important base for continuing to decolonize dominant sexist, racist, (post)colonial, and classist discourses today. It is within the framework of such writing that Mernissi evokes a topical subject of our times: the veil. Yet Mernissi's approach is to understand the veil in the context of living conditions, work, and power relations among social groups in Morocco. She attacked Moroccan nationalist urban elites who reproduced dominant French discourses against the veil. For Mernissi, if these elites spoke of "isolated" women, of their necessary disclosure and "entry" into the workforce, it was because they were thinking only of urban bourgeois women and excluding popular and rural women who "were unveiled and worked in the fields from morning till night as they did for centuries before the nationalists" (Mernissi 1981, 27).

As a result, Mernissi's writing can contribute immensely to our current thinking against Islamophobia. On the veil, we can say that, for Mernissi, dress does not make the Muslim! Mernissi does not isolate clothing from the context of women's life and work. She allows us to broaden our focus on much that is generally taken for granted today, such as the idea of unveiling women during colonization, a notion based on forgetting that colonial domination has had contradictory effects, producing both unveiling and veiling. Some women (such as the middle-class women of whom Mernissi speaks) unveil to conform to European clothing standards or to avoid the intrusion of the colonial gaze, whereas other women (rural and from the popular classes) discover the veil in a colonial context when they migrate to cities and aspire to conform to locally dominant norms. Mernissi invites us to think about the veil as a category manipulated by politics to the detriment of disadvantaged women exploited by work. These women are never absent in her studies.

At the same time, Mernissi does not confuse the Islam of texts that appear in her later writing with the religion of everyday life that women develop in both subjective and collective ways and in different situations, and her studies in this area also center on work (e.g., Mernissi 1987). In rereading religious texts, she situates them in their context of production. Her study does not lead her to reject "religion," which allows her to avoid being instrumentalized by current Islamophobic discourse, and she makes strategic use of other authors from predominantly Muslim societies. She also does not confuse the texts and realities she observes in the daily life of women who—like their male counterparts in popular and rural milieu—often do not know the texts, often do not speak the language of religious texts, and sometimes began to make use of this language only during and since French colonization.

In sum, Mernissi's writings are to be read, reread, and recirculated, especially today. They are pathbreaking, numerous, multidisciplinary, and particularly dense. They constitute an example of decolonial criticism that does not separate social relations of power but considers their *coformation* (Bacchetta 2015) and insists on recognizing subaltern women's knowledge. The audacity of Fatema Mernissi's writings, their originality, and their theoretical and empirical contributions are capable of doing serious damage to the established order of ideas and systems of thought that are sexist as well as classist, racist, Islamophobic, and neo-Orientalist.

References

Ait Ben Lmamdani, Fatima, and Nasima Moujoud. 2012. "Peut-on faire de l'intersectionnalité sans les ex-colonisé-e-s?" *Mouvements* 72, no. 4: 11–21.

Bacchetta, Paola. 2015. "Décoloniser le féminisme: Intersectionnalité, assemblages, co-formations, co-productions." *Les cahiers du CEDREF* 20. At http://journals.openedition.org/cedref/833.

Belarbi, Aïcha. 1988. "Salariat féminin et division sexuelle du travail dans la famille: Cas de la femme fonctionnaire." In *Femmes partagées: Famille-travail*, edited by Fatema Mernissi, 79–98. Casablanca, Morocco: Le Fennec.

———. 1991. *Le salaire de madame.* Casablanca, Morocco: Le Fennec.

Crenshaw, Kimberlé Williams. 1991. "Mapping the Margins: Intersectionality, Identity Politics, and Violence against Women of Color." *Stanford Law Review* 43, no. 1241: 93–118.

———. 2005. "Cartographies des marges: Intersectionnalité, politique de l'identité et violences contre les femmes de couleur." *Cahiers du genre* 39, no. 2: 51–82.

Hajjat, Abdellali, and Mohammed Marwan. 2013. *Islamophobie: Comment les élites françaises fabriquent le "problème musulman."* Paris: La Découverte.

Hirata, Héléna, and Danièle Kergoat. 1998 "La division sexuelle du travail revisitée." In *Les nouvelles frontières de l'inégalité: Hommes et femmes sur le marché du travail*, edited by Marguaret Maruani, 93–104. Paris: La Découverte/Mage.

Kergoat, Danièle. 2009. "Dynamique et consubstantialité des rapports sociaux." In *Sexe, race, classe: Pour une épistémologie de la domination*, edited by Elsa Dorlin, 111–25. Paris: Presses universitaires de France.

El Khayat, Rita. 2002. "Foucault et le harem: Approche critique des notions de sérail et de despotisme." In *L'Orient des femmes*, edited by Marie-Elise Palmier-Chatelain and Pauline Lavagne d'Ortigue, 297–307. Lyon, France: ENS.

Mernissi, Fatema. 1978. "Des paysannes dans la ville." *Al Assas*, no. 9 (May): page numbers unavailable.

———. 1979. "The Degrading Effect of Capitalism on Female Labour in a Third World Economy: The Particular Case of Crafts Women in

Morocco." *Peuples méditerranéens / Mediterranean Peoples*, no. 6 (Jan.–Mar.): 41–56.

———. 1980. "Le prolétariat féminin au Maroc." *Annuaire de l'Afrique du Nord* 1980:345–56. At https://cinumed.mmsh.univ-aix.fr/idurl/1/67683.

———. 1981. *Développement capitaliste et perceptions des femmes dans la société musulmane: Les paysannes du Gharb*. Geneva: Bureau International du Travail.

———. 1983. "Women and the Impact of Capitalist Development in Morocco, Part II." *Feminist Issues* 3, no. 1: 61–112.

———. 1986. *Le Maroc raconté par ses femmes*. Rabat, Morocco: Société marocaine des éditeurs réunis.

———. 1987. *Le harem politique: Le Prophète et les femmes*. Paris: Albin Michel.

———. 1994. *Dreams of Trespass: Tales of a Harem Girlhood*. Cambridge, MA: Perseus.

———. 1996. *Rêves de femmes: Une enfance au harem*. Translated by Claudine Richetin. Paris: Albin Michel.

———. 1998. *Êtes-vous vacciné contre le harem? Texte-Test pour les messieurs qui adorent les dames*. Casablanca, Morocco: Le Fennec.

———. 2001. *Le harem et l'Occident*. Paris: Albin Michel.

Moujoud, Nasima. 2008. "Effets de la migration sur le femmes et sur les rapports sociaux de sexe: Au-delà des visions binaires." *Cahiers du CEDREF* 16:57–79.

Quiminal, Catherine. 2000. "Migrations." In *Dictionnaire critique du féminisme*, edited by Héléna Hirata, Françoise Laborie, Hélène Le Doaré, and Danièle Senotier, 111–16. Paris: PUF.

Rodary, Meriem. 2007. "Le travail des femmes dans le Maroc précolonial, entre oppression et résistance: Droit au travail ou accès aux bénéfices?" *Cahiers d'études africaines* 187–88, no. 3: 753–80.

Taouki, Saadia. 2017. "L'identité féminine dans le roman marocain: Déconstruction du réel à travers l'imaginaire dans *Rêves de femmes* de Fatema Mernissi." At https://hal.archives-ouvertes.fr/hal-01665796/document.

Taraud, Christelle. 2003. *La prostitution coloniale: Algérie, Maroc, Tunisie (1830–1962)*. Paris: Payot.

Editor and Contributor Biographies
Index

Editor and Contributor Biographies

Editors

Paola Bacchetta is professor and vice chair of research in the Department of Gender and Women's Studies at the University of California, Berkeley. She was the first chair of the Gender Consortium at Berkeley. She is currently cochair of the Decolonizing Sexualities Network. Her research and teaching interests are decolonial feminist and queer theory, lesbian and queer-of-color theory, epistemologies of the global South(s), subaltern archiving, analytics of power, right-wing movements, and space. Her geographical concentrations are France, India, the United States, and Brazil. Her sole-authored and coedited book-length works include *Co-motion: On Power, Subjects, and Feminist and Queer Alliances* (forthcoming); *Global Raciality: Empire, Postcoloniality, and Decoloniality* (coedited with Sunaina Maira and Howard Winant, 2019); *Femminismi queer postcoloniali* (coedited with Laura Fantone, 2015); *Gender in the Hindu Nation* (2004); *Right-Wing Women: From Conservatives to Extremists around the World* (coedited with Margaret Power, 2002). She has published more than seventy academic journal articles and book chapters in English, French, Italian, German, Spanish, and Portuguese.

Minoo Moallem is professor of gender and women's studies at the University of California, Berkeley. She was the chair of the Women and Gender Studies Program at UC Berkeley from 2010 to 2012 and the director of the Media Studies Program from 2017 to 2023. Trained as a sociologist, she writes on postcolonial feminist studies, transnational cultural studies, immigration and diaspora studies, Middle Eastern studies, and Iranian cultural politics and diasporas. She is the author of *Persian Carpets: The Nation as a Transnational Commodity* (2018) and *Between Warrior Brother and Veiled Sister: Islamic Fundamentalism and the Cultural Politics of Patriarchy in Iran*

(2005); the coeditor of *Between Woman and Nation: Nationalisms, Transnational Feminisms and the State* (with Caren Kaplan and Norma Alarcon, 1999); and the guest editor of the special issue "Iranian Immigrants, Exiles and Refugees" of *Comparative Studies of South Asia, Africa and the Middle East* 20, nos. 1–2 (2000). She is the author of numerous book chapters and articles in English, French, and Farsi. Her work has been translated into German, Portuguese, and Greek. Moallem has also ventured into digital media. Her digital project "Nation-on-the Move" (designed by Eric Loyer) was published in the special issue "Difference" of *Vectors: Journal of Culture and Technology in a Dynamic Vernacular* (Fall 2007).

Contributors

Fatima Ait ben Lmamdani is professor and researcher at the Institute of African Studies at the University Mohammed V in Rabat, Morocco. Professor Lmamdani's research focuses primarily on immigration and gender. A selection of her publications includes *Politique d'immigration au Maroc: Quelle intégration des femmes et des mineurs subsahariens au Maroc* (coedited with Hicham Hafid, 2024); *La vieillesse illégitime? Migrantes marocaines ou les chemins sinueux de la reconnaissance* (2018); "Senegalese Migrants in Morocco: From a Gender Perspective," in *Gender and Mobility in Africa: Borders, Bodies, and Boundaries*, edited by Kalpana Hiralal and Zaheera Jinnah (2018); "Femmes et émigration marocaine: Entre invisibilisation et survisibilisation, pour une approche postcoloniale," *Hommes et migrations*, no. 1300 (2012); "Peut-on faire de l'intersectionnalité sans les ex-colonisé-e-s?," *Revue mouvements*, no. 72 (2012); and "Dynamiques du mépris et tactiques des 'faibles': Les migrantes âgées marocaines face à l'action sociale en France," *Sociétés contemporaines*, no. 70 (2008).

Manal Hamzeh is full professor and cofounder of the Department of Borderlands and Ethnic Studies (BEST) at New Mexico State University (NMSU, 2022–) and director of the new BEST Research Center. Manal founded BEST's decolonial research and knowledge creation minor (2024). Manal is the sole author of *Women Resisting Sexual Violence and the Egyptian Revolution: Arab Feminist Testimonies* (2020) and *Pedagogies of Deveiling: Muslim Girls and the Hijab Discourse* (2012). She also led the artistic creation of *Three Women of Tahrir: Stories from the Egyptian Revolution* (2022), a graphic documentary, and *Shahadat* (2024), a theatrical production. Her teaching and research draw on antiracist educational theories and decolonial Arabyyah feminist research methodologies. Manal's research is distinguished by being transnational in scope, intimately collaborative, and based in qualitative methodologies. During her time at NMSU, Manal has been honored with three teaching awards (2012, 2015, and 2019), nominated by students in all instances. Manal earned a PhD in social justice education from NMSU in 2007.

Mounira Hejaiej is associate professor of literature at Sultan Qaboos University, Oman, and on the English faculty at the University of Tunis 1. She is the author of the groundbreaking work in women's studies *Behind Closed Doors: Women's Oral Narratives in Tunis* (1996). She has training in folklore and anthropology. Mounira Hejaiej's research interests have focused on comparative studies, cross-cultural relations, and academic exchange in an international context.

Suad Joseph is Distinguished Research Professor Emerita at the University of California (UC), Davis. She is the founder of the Middle East Section of the American Anthropological Association; the Association for Middle East Women's Studies (AMEWS); and the Arab Families Working Group. She founded and directed the Arab Region Consortium at UC Davis. She was president of the Middle East Studies Association of North America. She is cofounder of the Arab American Studies Association; the Association for Middle East Anthropology; and the *Journal of Middle East Women's Studies*. She is general editor of the prize-winning *Encyclopedia of Women and Islamic Cultures*. She has edited or coedited twelve books and published more than one hundred articles, most recently *Reporting Islam: Muslim Women in the* New York Times, *1979–2011* (2023); *Handbook of Middle East Women* (2023); *The Politics of Engaged Gender Research in the Arab Region: Feminist Fieldwork and the Production of Knowledge* (2021); and the award-winning *Arab American Women: Representation and Refusal* (2021). She is the founder of the Middle East/South Asia Studies Program and cofounder of the Feminist Research Institute at UC Davis. She was awarded the UC Davis Prize; the Middle East Studies Association Jere L. Bacharach Lifetime Service Award in 2019; the Association for Middle East Women's Studies and the Arab American Studies Association lifetime service awards; and the UC systemwide Constantine Panunzio Distinguished Emerita Award. Her research on her native Lebanon focuses on gender and citizenship, the state, family, children and youth, trauma, and the cultural politics of selfhood.

Hanane Karimi is assistant professor in the sociology of Islam at the University of Strasbourg in France. She is coholder of the Freedom of Expression, Religious Beliefs, and Identities axis of the Franco-Quebec Collective Research Chair on Freedom of Expression. Her research focuses on the collective mobilization of French Muslim women against Islamophobia and toward the extension of religious neutrality and a new *laïcité* (French secularism). Her most recent publications include *Les femmes musulmanes ne sont-elles pas des femmes?* (Are Muslim Women Not Women?, 2023). She is the author of multiple academic articles and book chapters, including "Overview: Islam and Feminism: Europe," in *Encyclopedia of Women and Islamic Cultures*, edited by Suad Joseph (2022); "Constructing the Otherness of Jews and Muslims in France," *Annual Review of the Sociology of Religion* 13 (2022); and "The Hijab and Work: Female Entrepreneurship in Response to Islamophobia," *International Journal of Politics, Culture and Society* 31, no. 3 (2018).

Azadeh Kian is Distinguished Professor of Sociology and Gender Studies, former director of the Social Science Department (2017–2021), and director of the Center for Gender and Feminist Studies and Research (and its journal *Les Cahiers du CEDREF*, https://journals.openedition.org/cedref) at Université Paris Cité. She earned her BA in Paris and obtained her MA and PhD in sociology at the University of California at Los Angeles. Her teachings include politics and society in the Middle East; gender, postcolonial, and intersectional perspectives; gender and feminist theories; and international relations. Her research focuses on gender and Islam, politics and society in Iran and Turkey, and gender and power in the Middle East. She has authored six books, edited twelve collected volumes and journals, and published more than 120 articles and book chapters. Her publications include: *Rethinking Gender, Ethnicity, and Religion in Iran: An Intersectional Approach to National Identity* (2023); *Femmes et pouvoir en islam* (2019); *Etat-nation et fabrique du genre, des corps et des sexualités: Iran, Turquie, Afghanistan* (coedited with Lucia Direnberger, 2019); "Individualization and the Emergence of Personalized Politics in Post-revolutionary Iran," *Iran Namag* 6, no. 4 (Winter 2021); and "Globalized Gender and Creative Strategies against Inequalities in Turkey: Capital City Women's

Platform (Başkent Kadın Platformu Derneği)," in *The Globalization of Gender: Knowledge, Mobilizations, Frameworks of Action* (2019).

Akila Kizzi is lecturer and researcher in gender studies at the University of Paris 8, Vincennes-Saint-Denis. She specializes in gender issues in North Africa. Her research deals with the rehabilitation of women figures forgotten by collective history, whether they be politicians, artists, or writers in North Africa. Her research aims to build an intellectual genealogy of women in the southern Mediterranean. She has published a monograph on the life and work of Taos Amrouche, *Passions et déchirements identitaires chez Marie-Louise Taos Amrouche* (2019). Another publication focuses on the Algerian artists Baya Mahieddine and Taos Amrouche, "Indigenous Algerian Women Artists in the French Landscape: Baya Mahieddine and Taos Amrouche," in *Under the Skin: Feminist Art from the Middle East and North Africa Today*, edited by Ceren Özpinar and Mary Kelly (2020).

Nasima Moujoud is professor of anthropology at the Université Grenoble Alpes in France and a member of the Rhône-Alpes Historical Research Laboratory. Her research focuses on Moroccan migration to France, Italy, and the Persian/Arabian Gulf countries (with a focus on Dubai). She recently compared the professional integration of Moroccan women in Dubai to their integration in Europe. She has published two books and many academic articles and book chapters. A recent article, cowritten with Chadia Arab, is "Decentering through Empirical Tests: An Intersectional Approach Based on Festive Spaces in Dubai," *Carnets de géographes* 16 (2022), at https://journals.openedition.org/cdg/8512.

Zakia Salime is associate professor of women's, gender, and sexuality studies and sociology at Rutgers University. She is a Fulbright Scholar and was the Presidential Visiting Associate Professor in the Department of Women's Gender and Sexuality Studies at Yale University in 2016–17 and a visiting professor at the University Paris 8, Vincennes-Saint-Denis in 2015. She is the author of *Between Feminism and Islam: Human Rights and Sharia Law in Morocco* (2011) and coeditor of *Freedom without Permission: Bodies and Space in the Arab Revolutions* (with Frances S. Hasso, 2016). She has published extensively on gender, women's movements, political Islamism, and youth cultural and political movements in the Middle East and North Africa region, and she is currently working on a book manuscript on gender and land rights in Morocco. Salime's work has been featured in the *New York Times* and the *Washington Post*.

Sima Shakhsari is associate professor in the Department of Gender, Women, and Sexuality Studies at the University of Minnesota, Twin Cities. Their book *Politics of Rightful Killing: Civil Society, Gender, and Sexuality in Weblogistan* (2020) received the Fatema Mernissi Honorable Mention Award from the Middle East Studies Association.

Dr. amina wadud is a world-renowned scholar and activist with a focus on Islam, justice, gender, and sexuality. After achieving the status of full professor, she retired from US academia, except as visiting researcher to Starr King School for the Ministry in Oakland, California. After fifteen years in retirement, she served as visiting professor in the Post Graduate Studies Program of the National Islamic University Sunan Kalijaga in Yogyakarta, Indonesia. She has residency in Indonesia, where she has been since 2018. She is the author of *Qur'an and Woman: Rereading the Sacred Text from a Woman's Perspective* ([1992] 1999), a classic in the development of epistemology and methodology of Islamic feminism, the most dynamic aspect of Islamic reform today. It has been translated more than ten times since its initial publication in 1992. Her second book, *Inside the Gender Jihad: Women's Reform in Islam* (2006), moved the discussion further to align with the mandate for ethics and activism in collaboration with scholarship and spirituality. Her fourth and most recent publication is a spiritual memoir: *Once in a Lifetime* (2022). After completing a three-year research grant investigating five hundred years of classical Islamic discourse on sexual diversity and human dignity, funded by the Arcus Foundation, she is founder of the International Center for Queer Islamic Studies and Theology, an online platform (QIST1.com) that is the first of its kind in the world. Mother of five and nana to six, she is best known as the Lady Imam.

Index

Italic page number denotes illustration.

Abbas I, Shah, 197, 199
Abbasids (people), 194
'Abd al-'Aziz, Caliph, 195
Abdo, Diya M., 62
Abou-Bakr, Omaima, 193–94, 204
Abu-Lughod, Lila, 187–88
academic knowledge production, 168–69
academic output, of Mernissi, 217
Académie française. *See* French Academy
"Action for Equality, Development, and Peace" (conference), 256
adab ("adding the brains of others to your own"), 63
Adichie, Chimamanda, 106
Agence française de dévelopement (AFD), 260
Aguinaga, Margarita, 254–55
Ahmad, Labiba, 202–3
Ahmed, Leila, 68nn9–10, 209
Aïcha Kandicha cult, 83
Aisha (specialist), 193
Ait Ben Lmamdani, Fatima, 17, 282
Aït-Débrouille, Les. See "DIY Tribe"
Aïth Mansour Amrouche, Fadhma, 55
Akbarzadeh, Shahram, 128n3

Alf Layla wa-Layla. See Arabian Nights, The
Algerian Civil War, 34
"L'Algérie se dévoile" (Fanon), 56
Ali, Zahra, 218, 223
alienation, *Dreams of Trespass* describing, 48–49
alienism, 86–97
Alloula, Malek, 69
Amazigh (language), 98n1, 112
ambassadrices de l'eau, Les. *See* Water Ambassadors
Amellouk, Fatiha, 177
Amin, Qasim, 158
L'amour dans les pays musulmans (Mernissi), 28
anciennes de Dar El Bacha association de femmes, Les. *See* Dar El Bacha Alumnae Women's Association
anglophoning, 102–6, 119–20
Anti-Racism Digital Library, 240
Anzaldúa, Gloria, 100–101, 110n7
Approches (Muqarabat) (research group), 34
Apter, Emily, 112, 114, 116
'aql. See reasoning
Arab culture, 64, 158, 245–46

Arab feminism, 24–25
Arab historians, women of power erased by, 196
Arab Human Development Report, 257
Arabian Nights, The (*Hezaar o Yek Shab*) (*Alf Layla wa-Layla*) (stories), 133n6
Arabo-Islamic patriarchies, Mernissi critiquing, 11
Arab women, 49
Ardistani, Ḥakim al-Malik, 199
area studies, queer studies bifurcated from, 130, 142n11, 143
Are You Vaccinated against the Harem? (*Êtes-vous vacciné contre le harem*) (Mernissi), 175
aristocratic women, 196–97
Arondekar, Anjali, 141, 143
articulation, of social relations, 288
art of dialogue and debate (*jadal*), 14, 27, 62, 64, 71, 73
Arwa (head of state), 194
Asad, Talal, 116
Asma (head of state), 194
Asmahan (singer), 49
assimilation, translation avoiding, 116
Association of Colonial Writers (Association des écrivains coloniaux), 103
Association of Muslim Women, 203
Association of Sea and Overseas Writers (Association des écrivains de la mer et de l'outre-mer), 103
Association of Writers in the French Language (Association des écrivains de la langue française), 103
Attar Nishapuri, Farid-ud-Din, 5n4, 140, 145–46

Attia, Kader, 99
autobiography, 46, 54; fictionalized, 174–75; North African autobiographical writing contrasted with, 52–53; North African women writers transforming, 43, 56; postcolonial, 52–54

Bacchetta, Paola, 79n4, 127n
Badran, Margot, 128n3
Barlow, Lorraine, 128n3
al-Banna, Hassan, 202
Banou, Princess Mahin ("princess sultan"), 196
Barrios de Chungara, Domitila, 255
Barthes, Roland, 60
bayt el muna. *See* storeroom
bazari. *See* merchant
beauty standards, in the West, 67
Beck, Lois, 255
Begum, Zeynab, 196–97
Behind Closed Doors (Hejaiej), 262
Beijing Conference, on women, 246
Belarbi, Aisha, 34, 280
Belqeys. *See* Queen of Sheba
Ben Ali, Zine al-Abidin, 34, 267
Bénani, Hamid, 98, 113
Benaouda, Lebdai, 50n4
Benjamin, Walter, 113–14
Bennani, Jalil, 79n4, 98n1, 99, 113
Ben Youssef Zayzafoon, Lamia, 128n3
Berber. *See* Amazigh (language)
Betayyib, Samir, 269
between two (*entre-deux*), 54
Bey, Maïssa, 50n4
Beygom, Maryam, 199
Beygom, Princess Shahr Banoo, 199
Beygom, Zeynab, 199

Beyond the Veil (*Sexe, idéologie, Islam*) (Mernissi), 2, 7, 24–25, 37, 44, 47, 187
Bhagavad Gita, Orientalists domesticating, 117
*bhut*s. *See* ghosts
Bhutto, Benazir, 9n6
Bilge, Sirma, 168
bin Abdelaziz, Umar, 193
bin Ibrahim, Ali ben Muhammad, 193
bint Ayyash, Fatima, 193
Bint Utba, Hind, 189–90
Black feminism: decolonization and, 281; French publications citing, 168n2; intersectionality theorized in, 278
Book of Kings (*Shahnameh*) (Ferdowsi), 146
Borderlands/La Frontera (Anzaldúa), 100–101, 110n7
borders (*hudud*), 171, 176–79, 217–18, 223–24, 226, 285
Boserup, Ester, 254–55
bottom-up development projects, 264–65
Bouchrara, Moncef, 266
Bouia Omar (village sanctuary), 82–84, 85n9, 86
boundaries: breaking, 159–60; Muslim women impacted by, 217; relationalities and connectivities and, 165–66; women damaged by, 226–27. *See also* self-boundaries
Bourdieu, Pierre, 139
boys, girls differentiated from, 153–54
Brandeis University, 24
Bretton Woods Agreement, 254
Bush, George, 227

"cage" system, Safavid dynasty changed by, 197
Cairo University, 204
Can We Women Head a Muslim State? (Mernissi), 9
Capital City Women's Platform (association), 204–5
capitalism, 128n3, 264; colonization spreading, 280; third-wave feminism challenging, 255; women objectified in, 67n8
capitalist patriarchy, 29
Caplan, Karen, 142n10
Casablanca Dream project, 128n3
Cassin, Barbara, 114
celebrity, cult of, 75n15
Center of Arab Women for Training and Research (CAWTAR), 270
Centre d'information, de formation, d'etudes, et de documentation sur les associations (Ifeda), 267n5
Chahrazad n'est pas marocaine (Mernissi), 73
chaines de transmetterus. *See* network of transmitters
Chajarat ad-dur (queen), 195
chaos (*fitna*), 68
chaos, digital, 72
Chaouni, Layla, 32, 37–38
Chardin, Jean, 198
Cheikh El Kamel (sanctuary), 78–79
childhood, of Mernissi, 43–44
Choua, Saddie, 3, 119
citation, 144
citizenship, oral narratives activating, 263
Civic Caravan (Caravan Civique) (gathering), 2, 177
civic energy, Mohammed V University spearheading, 257n1

civic engagement, 253
civil feminism, 266
civilizational imperialism, 65n5
civilizational thinking, 65n5
civil society, 34; fundamentalism opposed by, 35–36; intellectuals influencing, 257n3; in Morocco, 257n1; social capital influencing, 267
clairvoyant (*chouaffa*), 15, 83, 93
coformations, of social relations of power, 290
Collectif 95 Maghreb égalité (rights group), 33, 35
collectif du vivre ensemble, Le. *See* Living Together Collective
collective life, of women, 132–33
Collins, Patricia Hill, 57, 168
colonial amnesia, francophoning refusing, 104
colonial empire, end of, 155
colonial foreignization, 117
Colonial Harem, The (Alloula), 69
colonial history, French feminist scholars not accounting for, 281
colonialism, 116, 174–75; French spread through, 102; patriarchal system and Mernissi and, 169–73; translation influenced by, 117
colonial-Orientalist, 93, 111, 119
colonization, 41; capitalism spreading through, 280; inequality enforced by, 287; language and, 48–49. *See also* decolonization
colonized women, colonizers stigmatizing, 288
colonizers, 172, 288
Comment les femme vivent. *See* How Women Live
companionship (*'ishra, al*), 265

Conference of the Birds (*Mantiq ut-Tayr*) (Attar Nishapuri) (poem), 5, 140, 145–46
connectivities, boundaries and relationalities and, 165–66
contact zones, 110
contemporary legacy, 218–23
Contentious Traditions (Mani), 188
conteuses du Maghreb, Les. *See* Storytellers of the Maghrib
context, the text and, 70–72
cooke, miriam, 128n3, 131
cooperation (*ta'awun*), 18
cooperative norms, trust and, 253
cosmo-civics, 73
Critical Dictionary of Feminism (*Dictionnaire critique du feminisme*) (Quiminal), 282
critique, of Mernissi, 128n3
cult of celebrity, Mernissi resisting, 75n15
cultural and social inheritance, Mernissi examining, 61–62
cultural capital, 266
culturalism, 185, 230
cultural space, the harem as, 67–68

Dar El Bacha Alumnae Women's Association (anciennes de Dar El Bacha association de femmes, Les), 270
dargah. *See* Sufi shrine
Darija (language), 98n1, 107
debate, 27, 63–64
decolonial gestures, hybridity as, 106–7
decoloniality, in *The Lionesses*, 79n4
decolonial work, through *pretranslation*, 110
decolonization: Black feminism and, 281; of knowledge, 278, 287–90;

unlearning central to, 75–76. *See also* intersectionality
deep language learning, 66
deforeignizing, translation and, 112
"Degrading Effects of Capitalism on Female Labour in a Third World Economy, The" (Mernissi), 264. *See also* "prolétariat féminin au Maroc, Le"
Delacroix, Eugène, 14, 53
democratic writing, 17
Derrida, Jacques, 114
Détrez, Christine, 52
Deutsche Gesellschaft für Internationale Zusammenarbeit. *See* German Association for International Cooperation
Deutsche Gesellschaft für Technische Zusammenarbeit. *See* German Association for Technical Cooperation
Development Alternatives with Women for a New Era (DAWN), 255
development policy, 260–61, 268–69
development projects, 270; bottom-up, 264–65; Mernissi influencing, 273; social capital as base of, 264–65; "top-down" approach of, 256, 258, 261–62; in Tunisia, 251–52; women aided by, 264
development studies, scrutiny of, 253–54
Développement capitaliste et perceptions des femmes dans la société musulmane (Mernissi), 286
Dictionnaire critique du feminisme. *See Critical Dictionary of Feminism*
digital chaos, information technologies inducing, 72
digital Scheherazade, 72–73

al-Din, Qadi Kamal, 193–94
disciplinary lines, Mernissi blurring, 167
disease, social collective treating, 85
dismembering, emplacement of, 141
disorder (*fitna*), 226
displacements, epistemological, 140–46
"Displacing Queer Refugee Epistemologies" (Shakhsari), 127n
divine revelation through a voice that cannot be attached to any subject (*vahy*), 65
division of labor, 279–80, 282
"DIY Tribe" (*Aït-Débrouille, Les*) (Mernissi), 256–59
Djebar, Assia, 41–44, 51, 115
Doing Daily Battle (*Maroc raconté par ses femmes, Le*) (Mernissi), 29–30, 171n4, 177, 286
domestic status, North African women refusing, 94
Doran, Nouria, 205
Dreams of Trespass (*Rêves de femmes*) (Mernissi), 14–16, 43, 44n1, 57, 127–31; alienation described in, 48–49; cover of, 52; frontiers centered in, 153–54; El Khayat critiquing, 283; kinship unsettled in, 137–40; Orientalist stereotypes and, 188–89; patriarchal connectivity expressed in, 165–66; power of women discussed in, 171; queer kinship in, 128–29; queer theory and, 143–44; Richetin translating, 45; as semiautobiographical, 128n2; symbolic territoriality in, 223–24; Taouki on, 284–85; US academia ignoring, 140–41
dynastic system, Islam as, 191

East, the, power structures impacting women in, 230
Ebn-Eddin, Forouq, 207
École normale supérieure, 43
economic capital, 266
"Effects of Modernization on the Male–Female Dynamics in a Muslim Society" (Mernissi), 2
electricity, women and, 259
embedded counterpublic, 36
emplacement, of dismembering, 141
English (language), 105–6, 109–11, 116
Ennaifer, Rachida, 51n6
epistemological displacements, temporal areas and, 140–46
equality, Islam and, 225–26
Erasmus Prize, 3, 44
essentialism, 185–87
Êtes-vous vacciné contre le harem. See *Are You Vaccinated against the Harem?*
Ethical Hijab, 236n3, 239
Euro-American (term), 127n2
Euro-American epistemologies, transnational queer scholarship recentering, 142
Eurocentric hegemonic feminism, 11–12
Eurocentrism: Mernissi decentering, 138; of queer and feminist studies, 141; queer theory and, 141n9, 144–45
European Union Water Project, 261–62, 271
everyday life, Islamic texts contrasted with, 290
exegesis (*tafsir*), 7
Ezzat, Heba Raouf, 203

Fadl, Abul, 220
fakhr al nisa'. See women's pride
Falk, Nancy Auer, 87n11
family relationships, in Lebanon, 165
Fanon, Frantz, 118
Farhoud, Samira, 55, 173–74
farmers, in High Atlas, 257n3
Farouk (king), 159
Fatema (mother of Imam Hussein), 191
Fatema Is Fatema (*Fatemeh Fatemeh ast*) (Shari'ati), 191
Fatema Mernissi Book Award, Middle East Studies Association establishing, 3
Fatema Mernissi Chair, at Free University of Brussels, 180
Fatema Mernissi la pensée féministe au Maghreb (Talahit and Ennaifer), 51n6
Fathi, Hassan, 74
Fatima (specialist), 193
Fatimid dynasty, women empowered during, 194–96
Federal Ministry for Economic Cooperation and Development (Tunisia), 270–72
female storytellers, 262–63, 265
feminine ideal, 78–79
femininity, 218, 227, 229
feminism, 33–34, 51, 245, 282; Arab, 24–25; civil, 266; Eurocentric hegemonic, 11–12; Islam and, 128n3; materialist, 279; Mernissi neglected by, 283; third-wave, 255. See also Black feminism; Islamic feminism
Féminismes islamiques (anthology), 218

feminist critiques, of industrialized societies, 279
feminist debates, 179–80
feminist knowledge, 33, 41, 281–82
feminist press, 37–38
feminist reading, of Islamic texts, 26–27
feminist scholars, World Bank seeking out, 258
feminist theory, 30
femme dans l'inconscient musulman, La (Aït Sabbah), 24, 60, 176
Femmes d'Alger dans leur appartement (painting). *See* Women of Algiers in Their Apartment
femmes dans la mosquée, Le. *See* Women in the Mosque
Femmes en trance (Mehssani), 79
Fennec, Le (press), 37, 174
Ferry, Jules, 103
fiction, memoir mixed with, 128n2
fictionalized autobiography, 174–75
50 noms de l'amour, Les (Mernissi), 28
first name, spelling of Mernissi's, 1n1
First World women, Third World women contrasted with, 256
fitna. *See* chaos; disorder
Fondation Hassan II. *See* Hassan II Foundation
foreignization, colonial, 117
Forgotten Queens of Islam, The (Mernissi), 8–10, 217
Forum of Women's Creativity (Multaqa al Ibda'e al-Nisa'i), 31–32
Four Hijabs, The (short film), 3, 18, 234, 235, 239, 240–41
France: feminist knowledge production in, 281–82; Mernissi ignored in, 288–89; the veil problematized in, 282–83
France, Algérie et colonies (Reclus), 103
francophone (francophonie) (term), 104
francophoning, 102–6, 119–20
Frederick Ebert Stiftung (foundation), 35
freedom, of North African and Arab women, 49
Freeman, Elizabeth, 16, 136n7
Free University of Brussels, Fatema Mernissi Chair at, 180
free woman (*al-hurra*), 10
French (language), 46, 101, 103–6, 109, 116; colonialism spreading, 102; North African women writing in, 42–43, 48–50; pretranslation challenging, 118; reclamation of, 50; translation in English contrasted with, 110–11
French Academy (Académie française), 102
French colonizers, Mernissi critiquing, 172
French culture, Arab culture contrasted with, 158
French feminist scholars, colonial history not accounted for by, 281
French-language versions, of works, 170n3
French publications, Black feminism cited by, 168n2
French public spaces, the veil in, 220
French readership, Orientalist imagination influencing, 55–56
French schools, the veil banned in, 227

French-speaking academy, intersectionality in, 168–69
French state, Islamophobia of, 17
Freud, Sigmund, al-Ghazali contrasted with, 7
Friedan, Betty, 255
frontiers (*hudud*), 45n2, 57, 132, 153–54, 157–58, 285
Full-fledged Citizens/Citizenship (moitié entière, La) (Mernissi), 268
fundamentalism: civil society opposing, 35–36; imperialism converging with, 69; Muslims and, 10–11; petro-, 69
Fundamentalist Obsession with Women, The (Mernissi), 10
funding, 35, 37
fusqiyya. See giant basins

Galland, Antoine, 133n6
Galland Manuscript, 133n6
Garaoun, Massinissa, 118
Garden of Lovers, The (Raoudatul muhibbin wa nuzhatul-nushtaaqeen) (al-Jawziyya), 28
gender asymmetry, Mernissi challenging, 245
gender equality, in Qur'an, 204, 206–7
gender-justice movement, 244
gender order, Islamic law enforcing, 210–11
gender phase, 34
gender power relations, 212
gender relations, 226
gender spaces, Mernissi unsettling, 32
gender studies, 26, 30

geopolitical power relations, private feminine space devalued by, 47
German Association for International Cooperation (Deutsche Gesellschaft für Internationale Zusammenarbeit) (GIZ), 251, 260, 270–72
German Association for Technical Cooperation (Deutsche Gesellschaft für Technische Zusammenarbeit) (GTZ), 260–62
gharib. See stranger
al-Ghazali, Zainab, 7, 203
ghosts (*bhuts*), 100
giant basins (*fusqiyya*), 269
girls, boys differentiated from, 153–54
global agencies, social capital measured by, 258
globalization: *Islam and Democracy* discussing, 12; Mernissi resisting, 174–75; Muslim women activists and, 208
global North, 12, 279
global South, 12, 175, 280
goddesses, pre-Islamic, 68
Gomri, Sid El, 89–90
Graham-Brown, Sarah, 66
Grewal, Inderpal, 67n7, 142n10
Gross, Rita M., 87n11
Guardian, The (newspaper), 3
Guessous, Nouzha, 178–79
Gulf War, 26, 70n14

hadith. See words and acts of the Prophet
Haeri, Abdolkarim, 206
al-Hakim, Fatimid Caliph, 6, 195
Half of a Yellow Sun (Adichie), 106
Hall, Stuart, 66n6
Hallidy, Fred, 186n1

Hamzeh, Manal, 3, 234
harassment (*ta'arrud*), 220–21
harem, the, 69, 119, 130, 131n4, 197, 284n2; borders evoking hijab and, 218; colonial construction of, 19; as cultural space, 67–68; of the East contrasted with of the West, 170; hierarchies and, 158, 198; kinship complicated by, 136, 138; Mernissi challenging concept of, 66, 170–71, 285; Moroccans as unfamiliar with, 283; rural women and, 278; traps of, 283–85; the West projecting onto, 175
harem et l'Occident, Le (Mernissi), 170
harem politique, Le. *See Veil and the Male Elite, The*
Haritaworn, Jin, 112
Hassan II Foundation (Fondation Hassan II), 177
Hatem, Mervat, 128n3
Hayden-Roy, Anna, 239
hegemonic femininity, "Muslim" femininity contrasted with, 227
Hejaiej, Mounira, 262
Heynemen, Stephen, 272
Hezaar o Yek Shab. *See Arabian Nights, The*
Hezar afsaneh. *See Thousand Stories, The*
hierarchical social order, 210–11
hierarchies: the harem and, 158, 198; Mernissi flagging, 280; among women, 281. *See also* patriarchy
High Atlas (mountains), farmers in, 257n3
hijab: borders evoking the harem and, 218; Ethical, Spatial, Visual, and Spiritual, 236n3, 239; Mernissi critiquing, 224–25, 231; Muslim women wearing, 220; Qur'an on, 236n3, 240; radical alterity constructed through, 229; sexual aggression responded to with, 220–21; social order represented by, 226; symbolic territoriality or, 223–26; Western intellectuals rejecting, 227–28. *See also Four Hijabs, The*
Hirata, Héléna, 279, 282
Histoire de ma vie. *See Story of My Life, The*
history, use of, 6–7, 9
horizon d'attente. *See* impending horizon
Hossein, Imam, 199
household cisterns (*majelles*), 269
How Women Live (*Comment les femme vivent*) (Mernissi), 268
hudud. *See* borders; frontiers
humanist perspective, on structural-development challenges, 252
Hungry Translations (Nagar), 144n12
hurma. *See* modesty
al-hurra. *See* free woman
hybrid "I," 54–57
hybridity, as decolonial gestures, 106–7
hygiene education, women influencing, 270n7

"I": fictionalized use of, 173–76; hybrid, 54–57
I Believe You Are Confused (*Je crois qu'il y a une confusion chez vous*) (film), 3, 119

Ibn 'Arabi, 7, 211
Ibn Hazm, Abu Mohammad, 28
Ibn Khalliqan, 193
Ibn Mohammad, Ali, 194
Ibn Taymiyya, 193
identity, Muslim, 248
Ifeda. *See* Centre d'information, de formation, d'etudes, et de documentation sur les associations
ijtihad. *See* interpretation
imitation (*mujtahideh*), 206
immigrant women, literature stereotyping, 288–89
impending horizon (*horizon d'attente*), 55
imperialism, 65n5, 69
imprisonment, the veil associated with, 69
inadvertent silence, pretranslation influencing, 115
industrialized societies, feminist critiques of, 279
inequality, colonization enforcing, 287
information technologies, digital chaos induced by, 72
Ingram, Helen, 273
Ingram, Mrill, 273
"In Search for Pro-faith Feminism in Islam" (grant), 245
Institute of Scientific Research (Institut de recherche scientifique), 24
intellectual legacy, 23
International Islamic University in Malaysia (IIU), 244–45
International Monetary Fund (IMF), 251, 254, 256
International Organization of Francophonie (Organisation internationale de la francophonie) (OIF), 103
interpretation (*tafsir*) (*ijtihad*), 73, 206
intersectionality, 179; Black feminism theorizing, 278; in French-speaking academy, 168–69; positionality contrasted with, 168–69, 172–73; subaltern women and, 285–87
invisible rule (*qa'ida*), 162
Iran: under Safavid dynasty, 196; Soukeina not mentioned in, 191; the veil mandated in, 69
Iranian Revolution (1979), 69
Iraq, 26, 227
Isfahani-Amin, Alavi, 205–6
'ishra, al. *See* companionship
Islam, 10, 64, 68n9, 204–5, 217; Arab culture collapsing with, 245–46; conversion to, 245–46; as dynastic system, 191; equality and, 225–26; feminism and, 128n3; historical context of, 68; Mernissi rethinking, 3–4; as method of control and governance, 216; modernity and, 228; property rights of women in, 200–202; psychoanalysis compared with, 226; queer interpretations of, 9n6; racist ideas about, 65; sexist interpretations of, 8–9; women seeking power through, 192–96. *See also* Muslims
Islam and Democracy (*Islam et démocratie*) (Mernissi), 5–6, 12, 26, 179, 217, 226
Islamic discourses, Mernissi challenging, 75
Islamic feminism, 179, 246–47; Islamic texts interpreted in, 7; Mernissi contributing to, 128n3, 180; Western feminists contesting with, 209
Islamic jurisprudence, women barred from, 209

Islamic law, gender order enforced under, 210–11
Islamic Republic Civil Code, 206, 207n6
Islamic State of Iraq and Syria (ISIS), 64n4
Islamic texts: everyday life contrasted with, 290; feminist reading of, 26–27; Islamic feminism interpreting, 7. *See also* Qur'an
Islamists, social order reinforced by, 18
Islamophobia, 289–90; of French state, 17; Muslimophobia distinguished from, 187n1; after September 11, 2001, 236
Ismail, Shah, 197
Issawa sect, 78

jadal. See art of dialogue and debate
Jadeh Bozorg School, 199
Jadeh Koochak School, 199
Jain, Devaki, 177
Jam'iyyat Tarqiyat al Mar'a. *See* Society for Women's Progress
Jauss, Hans Robert, 56
al-Jawziyya, Ibn Qayyim, 28–29
Je crois qu'il y a une confusion chez vous. See I Believe You Are Confused
jihad. See struggle
jinns. See troublesome spirits

Kabeer, Naila, 254
Kairouan (Tunisia), 260
kalam. See speech act
kalameh. See words
Kaplan, Caren, 67n7
Karimi, Hanane, 13

Keddie, Nikki, 255
Kef (Tunisia), 260
Kergoat, Danièle, 279, 281
Kerkennah (Tunisia), 260
Kerrou, Mohamed, 271
khai'n. See traitors
Khanom, Delaram, 199
Khanom, Hoori Nam, 199
Khanum II, Pari khan, 196
Khatibi, Abdelkbir, 30
El Khayat, Rita, 283
Khoury, Jamil, 234, 237–39
kinship, 136n7; *Dreams of Trespass* unsettling, 137–40; the harem complicating, 136, 138; practical, 139; queer, 128–29
kinship theory, 143–44
knowledge: decolonization of, 278, 287–90; feminist, 33, 41, 281–82; situated, 169; storytelling and, 263; traditional, 271–72
knowledge production, 168–69, 254, 281–82
Konrad Adenaur (foundation), 35
Kuntsman, Adi, 112

labor: racial division of, 282; sexual division of, 279–80; of women, 19. *See also* waged work
laïcité. See secularism
Lalla Aziza Tagurrami (saint), 95–99
Lamrabet, Asma, 223, 243
language, 65, 67–70, 108–9; Amazigh, 98n1, 112; colonization and, 48–49; Darija, 98n1, 107; inequity and violence within and among, 116–17; as site of resistance, 66; subalternized, 106; *verlan*, 118; written, 71. *See also* English; French

Lebanon, family relationships in, 165
Leccese, Francesco Alfonso, 63
legacy, 23–26, 218–23, 231
Lejano, Raul, 273
Lejeune, Philippe, 52–53
lemma, el. See social gathering
Let Me Speak (Barrios de Chungara), 255
Lewis, Bernard, 196
Liberation of Women (Amin), 158
#lifeofamuslimfeminist, 230
Lionesses, The (*Lionnes, Les*) (Mernissi), 1, 8, 14–15, 96–97, 110, 120; *Borderlands/La Frontera* compared with, 100–101; Darija in, 107; decoloniality in, 79n4; pretranslation of, 111–12; silence formations in, 115; subalternized languages concealed in, 106; as text-as-subject, 118; translation-pauses in, 113–16
Living Together Collective (collectif du vivre ensemble, Le), 180
local officials (*mokkadem*), 90n20
local social capital projects, structural-adjustment programs contrasted with, 251, 264–65
Louis IX (French ruler), 195
love, Mernissi focusing on, 28–29

Mabanckou, Alain, 104
Macron, Emmanuel, 103–4
Madueke, Sylvia Ijeoma, 106–7
Maghreb 2000 (women's rights group), 33
Maghreb Feminist Days (workshops), 51n6
Maghrebian people, 289

Mahabharat (epic), 117
maintenance of wife (*nafaqeh*), 207n6
majelles. See household cisterns
Majid, Anouar, 128n3
male witch (*sorcier*), 79n4, 111
Mamluks (dynasty), 195
Mani, Lata, 188
Manoubia, Aïcha (Lella or Saïda Manoubia), 193
Mantiq ut-Tayr. See Conference of the Birds
marabout. *See* religious figure; sacred space
marbut. *See* person who is garrisoned
March 8 (*Thamania Mars*) (magazine), 33
marital control, rebellion against, 190
Maroc raconté par ses femmes, Le. See Doing Daily Battle
marriage, 92–93, 135–36
materialist feminism, 279
Mbembe, Achille, 104
McGill University, 60
media, importance of, 73–74
medicine, Western, 82–83
Mehssani, Jamal, 79
MEM. *See* Muslim Women in Movement
memoir, fiction mixed with, 128n2
Menon, Ritu, 177
menopause, 93
merchant (*bazari*), 206
Mernissi, Fatema ("Fatna Aït Sabbah"). *See specific topics*
"Mernissi for Our Times" (conference), 127n
Michel, Albin, 170
Middle East, women participating in revolutions in, 186

Middle East Studies Association, Fatema Mernissi Book Award established by, 3
al-Mihiyya, Sarah, 202
Mikdashi, Maya, 143
mission civilizatrice, 68
Moallem, Minoo, 127n, 141
modernity, Islam and, 228
modern state institutions, women defining, 29
modesty (*hurma*), 14, 56
Mohammed V University, 1–2, 257n1
Mohanty, Chandra, 227
moitié entière, La. See Full-fledged Citizens/Citizenship
mokkadem. See local officials
monumental buildings, women funding, 199–200
Moroccan culture, feminine ideal of, 78
Moroccan nationalists, women subordinated by, 171–72
Moroccan nationalist urban elites, against the veil, 289
Moroccans, the harem as unfamiliar to, 283
Moroccan universities, without gender studies, 26
Moroccan women, liberation desired by, 178
Morocco, 83n6, 87n11, 89–90; civil society in, 257n1; independence of, 155; psychiatry in, 83–84, 87; sexual division of labor in, 280
Mossadeq, Mohammad, 74
Moujoud, Nasima, 17, 168, 227
Mousa, Amel, 265
moussem. See saint

Muʻawiya (ruler), 191
muhaddithat. See women specialists: in words and acts of the Prophet
Muhammad (prophet), 26, 225
mujawarah. See sacred places
mujtahideh. See imitation
al Mulk, Sitt, 195
Multaqa al Ibdaʻe al-Nisaʼi. *See* Forum of Women's Creativity
Muqarabat. *See* Approches
murabit. See person who is garrisoned
murderous inclusion, 112
Musawah (global movement), 246–47
Muslim and Arab worlds, the West in relation to, 70
Muslim Brotherhood, 202
"Muslim" femininity, hegemonic femininity contrasted with, 227
Muslim identity, 248
Muslim law, Mernissi subverting interpretation of, 180
Muslimophobia, Islamophobia distinguished with, 187n1
Muslim queer activist groups, 9n6
Muslims: culture of love reconnected with by, 28; fundamentalism and, 10–11; racist ideas about, 65
Muslim societies, women respected in, 194
Muslim values, Western values differentiated from, 185–86
"Muslim woman," 228–29
Muslim women, 203; boundaries impacting, 217; double oppression of, 185; hijab worn by, 220; power and, 196–200; Western women contrasted with, 7–8

Muslim women activists, globalization and, 208
Muslim Women in Movement (Musulmanes en mouvement) (MEM) (group), 218–22
Muslim women's movements, fragility of, 243

nafaqeh. *See* maintenance of wife
Nagar, Richa, 144n12
Najafi, Mar'ashi, 206
naked (*'awra*), 221
National Endowment for Democracy, 35
national movement, Mernissi critiquing, 172
ol Nesa Begum, Kheyr, 196
network of transmitters (*chaines de transmetterus*), 61
Neyestani, Mohammadreza, 198
Nimaward School, 199
nongovernment organizations (NGOs), 265, 267
North Africa, women saints in, 95
North African autobiographical writing, autobiography contrasted with, 52–53
North African women: domestic status refused by, 94; freedom of, 49; French written in by, 42–43, 48–50; self-writing by, 42
North African women writers, 54; autobiography transformed by, 43, 56; literary space broken into by, 51; Mernissi encouraging, 52
novel (*roman*), 174
novels, 31

nushuz. *See* rebellion against marital control

obedience (*ta'a*), 164, 190
objectivation, 168
occult spirits (*esprits occults*), 112
OIF. *See* International Organization of Francophonie
"One Million Signature Campaign against the *Mudawana*" (petition), 31
oral narratives, citizenship activated by, 263
Organisation internationale de la francophonie. *See* International Organization of Francophonie
Organization and Charities of Isfahan, 198
Organization for Economic Cooperation and Development (OECD), 252, 266
Organization of Muslim Sisters, 203
Orientalism, 283–84
Orientalist discourses, writing decentering, 65–66
Orientalist fantasies, 133n6
Orientalist imagination, French readership influenced by, 55–56
Orientalists, Bhagavad Gita domesticating, 117
Orientalist stereotypes, *Dreams of Trespass* and, 188–89
Orientalist traditions, Mernissi challenging, 75
Ottoman empire, 199–200
El Ouardi, Houcine, 85n9
Oueslatia (Tunisia), 261

Our Common Future (World Commission on Environment and Development), 253

Pandolfo, Stephania, 86n10, 99n2
paradoxical femininity, 227
Patel, Geeta, 141, 143
"Pathways to Maghrebian Feminism" ("Des voies vers un féminisme maghrébin") (symposium), 51
patriarchal connectivity, *Dreams of Trespass* expressing, 165–66
patriarchal social practices, 65
patriarchy, 169–75; Arabo-Islamic, 11; capitalist, 29; third-wave feminism challenging, 255; Western democracies investing in, 6
Payam-i hâjar (journal), 207
Pedagogies of Deveiling (Hamzeh), 234, 237
personal relationships, 252–53
person who is garrisoned (*marbut*) (*murabit*), 79n4, 111–12
petro-fundamentalism, Saudi Arabia exemplifying, 69
pious bequest (*waqf*), 198, 200
political practice, situated perspective influencing, 176
polygamy, 207
popular culture, importance of, 73–74
Portraits de femmes (Mernissi), 49
positionality, 168–69, 172–73
Posocco, Silvia, 112
postcolonial autobiography, 53–54
post-translation, 116–20
power (*sulta*), 164; Muslim women and, 196–200; social relations of, 290; translation and, 101; women and Islam and, 192–96. *See also* hierarchies
power of women, *Dreams of Trespass* discussing, 171
power relations, 278; gender, 212; geopolitical, 47; women and, 188–89
de Praconta, Mona, 106
practical kinship, 139
Pratt, Mary Louise, 110
pre-Islamic goddesses, 68
pretranslation, 109, 113; decolonial work by, 110; inadvertent silence influenced by, 115; of *The Lionesses*, 111–12; *pretranslation* languages, 106–8, 111; *pretranslation*-scape, 106; translation impacted by, 112
Prince of Asturias Prize, 3, 44
private feminine space, geopolitical power relations devaluing, 47
"prolétariat féminin au Maroc, Le" (Mernissi), 264. *See also* "Degrading Effects of Capitalism on Female Labour in a Third World Economy, The"
property rights, of women in Islam, 200–202
pseudonym, used by Mernissi, 5
psychiatry, in Morocco, 83–84, 87
psychoanalysis, Islam compared with, 226
Puar, Jasbir, 143
publication, of Mernissi, 4–5
public sphere (*umma*), 187

qaʿida. *See* invisible rule
qiwama, meaning of, 219

Qizilbash (guardians of princes), 197–98
Qom religious seminary, 206
Queen of Sheba (*Belqeys*), in Qur'an, 210
queer and feminist studies, Eurocentrism of, 141
"Queer Geopolitics" (seminar), 143
queer interpretations, of Islam, 9n6
queer kinship, in *Dreams of Trespass*, 128–29
Queer Maroc (Zaganiaris), 8n5
queer scholarship, transnational, 142
queer studies, area studies bifurcated from, 130, 142n11, 143
queer theory, 141–42; *Dreams of Trespass* and, 143–44; Eurocentrism and, 141n9, 144–45; Mernissi contributing to, 7
Quiminal, Catherine, 282
Qur'an: gender equality in, 204, 206–7; on hijab, 236n3, 240; Queen of Sheba in, 210; women addressed in, 27
Qur'an and Woman (wadud), 244

Rabat (Morocco), 83n6
racial division of labor, 282
racialized academics, invisibilization of, 281, 283
racialized women, double alienation of, 47–48
racism, 237–38, 281
Radia, Sultana, 195
radical alterity, hijab constructing, 229
Rafael, Vicente, 118
Rangarajan, Padma, 117

Raoudatul muhibbin wa nuzhatulnushtaaqeen. See *Garden of Lovers, The*
Rashid, Fatima, 202
readings, as reframings, 119–20
reasoning (*'aql*), 68, 190
rebellion against marital control (*nushuz*), 190
Reclus, Onésime, 103
Réflexions sur la violence des jeunes (Mernissi), 29
reframings, readings as, 119–20
refugee world making, 130
relationalities, connectivities and boundaries and, 165–66
relationality, translation and, 110
religion, Mernissi embracing, 24
religious authority, women exercising, 208–9
religious femininity, 218
religious figure (*marabout*), 79n4
religious sciences, women specialists in, 192–93
representational practices, Mernissi deconstructing, 64–65
reproductive silence, 115
resident, situating oneself as, 173–76
Reversed Realities (Kabeer), 254
Rêves de femmes. See *Dreams of Trespass*
Reza, Imam, 199
Rhouni, Raja, 128n3, 217
Richetin, Claudine, 45
rites, description of, 84–85
Rodary, Meriem, 281
roman. See novel
Roque, Maria-Àngels, 177
Roussillon, Alain, 208
Roy, Arundati, 257

royal court, 196–97
rural women, the harem and, 278

sacred places (*mujawarah*), 194
sacred space (*marabout*), 79–80, 111
Safavid dynasty, 196, 199–200; "cage" system changing, 197
Safavid Persia, as main learning center of religious sciences of Shi'ism, 199
Safi, Shah, 198
Said, Edward, 117
Saidzadeh, Hojjat-ol Eslam Mohsen ("Mina Yadegar-Azadi"), 208n7
saint (*moussem*) (*wali*), 80, 82, 99
Sakhawi (scholar), 194
Salama, Umm, 189
Salé (Morocco), 83n6, 89–90
Salma, Umma, 9
Sami, Mustapha, 173, 176
Samini, Naghmeh, 74
sanctuaries of saints for healing (*zaouias*), 79n4, 80, 88–91, 96–97, 99, 112–13; flexibility of, 92; visits to, 84–85; women in relation to, 81–83
sanctuary (*sanctuaire*), 87n11
Sarah (specialist), 193
Saudi Arabia, 69, 70n14
Scheherazade Goes West (Mernissi), 67, 68n9, 128n3, 188
Schneider, David M., 137n8, 138
secular femininity, 218
secularism (*laïcité*), 217, 228
self-boundaries, 162–63; obedience violating, 164; social boundaries combated with, 160–61; women making, 155–56

self-writing, by North African women, 42
September 11, 2001 (attacks), Islamophobia after, 236
Sexe, idéologie, Islam. See *Beyond the Veil*
sexual aggression, hijab responding to, 220–21
sexual desire (*shahwa*), 68
sexual division of labor, 279–80
sexual dynamics, social order and, 68n11
sexuality, 7–8, 47, 226
Shahnameh. See *Book of Kings*
Shahrzad (TV show), 74
Shakhsari, Sima, 127n
Sha'rawi, Huda, 203
Shari'ati, Ali, 191
Shi'ism, 196, 199
Shiva, Vandana, 257
Shohat, Ella, 140–41, 144
shrine (*tombeau*), 87n11
Shuhda, Shaykha, 193
Sidi Ali Ben Hamdouch (sanctuary), 94
Sidi Ben Achir (sanctuary), 83, 90
silence formations, in *The Lionesses*, 115; *inadvertent silence*, 115; *inevitable silence*, 115; *reproductive silence*, 115; *strategic silence*, 115–16
Silk Road Rising (organization), 234n1, 237
Sisters in Islam (SIS), 245–46
situated knowledge, 169
situated perspective: fictionalized autobiographical "I" expressing, 174–75; political practice influenced by, 176; systems of power intersecting with, 167–68

situated planetarity, 101
Slimani, Leïla, 103
social boundaries, self-boundaries combating, 160–61
social capital, 252–53, 257n1, 257n3, 266, 268; civil society influenced by, 267; development projects based on, 264–65; global agencies measuring, 258; local, 251, 254–56; women relying on, 273–74
social collective, disease treated by, 85
Social Forum in Tunis, 221
social gathering (*lemma, el*), 263–64
social network support, 253
social order: hierarchical, 210–11; hijab representing, 226; Islamists reinforcing, 18; sexual dynamics and, 68n11. *See also* hierarchies
social relations, articulation of, 288
social relations of power, coformations of, 290
Société nationale d'exploitation et de distribution des faux (SONEDE), 271
Society for Women's Progress (Jam'iyyat Tarqiyat al Mar'a), 202
Society of Egyptian Women's Awakening (association), 202
Soleiman, Shah, 199
solidarity, among women, 135
Sonmez, Berrin, 204
sorcier. *See* male witch
Soukeina (great-granddaughter of the Prophet), 190–91
space, 223–26
Spatial Hijab, 236n3, *239*
speech act (*kalam*), 62
spelling, of Mernissi's first name, 1n1

Spiritual Hijab, 236n3, *239*
Spivak, Gayatri Chakravorty, 51, 66, 258
status, the veil symbolizing, 198
Stoler, Ann Laura, 117
storeroom (*bayt el muna*), 273
Story of My Life, The (*Histoire de ma vie*) (Aïth Mansour Amrouche), 55
storytellers, female, 262–63, 265
Storytellers of the Maghrib (conteuses du Maghreb, Les), 270, 272
storytelling, 272–73; art of, 72–73; knowledge and, 263; sustainable development built through, 269–70. *See also* writing
stranger (*gharib*), 6
strategic silence, 115–16
structural-adjustment programs, 251–52, 264–65
structural-development challenges, humanist perspective on, 252
struggle (*jihad*), 243
subalternized languages, *The Lionesses* concealing, 106
subaltern women, intersectionality and, 285–87
subordination (*ta'ha*), 226
Sufi shrine (*dargah*), 100
Sufyan, Abu, 189–90
Sulayhids (people), 194
Suleiman (sultan), 200
Sultan, Hurrem, 200
Surat al-Nisa'. *See* Women, The
sustainable development, 253, 269–70
symbolic territoriality, 223–26
synergies, 23
systems of power, situated perspective intersecting with, 167–68

taʿa. See obedience
taʿarrud. See harassment
taʿawun. See cooperation
tafsir. See exegesis; interpretation
taʾha. See subordination
Tahmasb, Shah, 196
Talahit, Fatiha, 51n6
Taliqani, Azam, 207
Taliqani, Mahmoud, 207
Taouki, Saadia, 284–85
Taraud, Christelle, 284
"Tarrying with the Irreparable" (workshop), 99n2
Ṭawq al-hamāmah (Ibn Hazm), 28
temporal areas, epistemological displacements and, 140–46
temporality, importance of, 226–31
tenderness (*hanan*), 18
territoriality, symbolic, 223–26
text, the, context and, 70–72
text-as-subject, 117–18
text interpretation, art of dialogue and debate and, 71
Thamania Mars. See March 8
third-wave feminism, 255
Third World women, First World women contrasted with, 256
Thousand and One Nights, The (stories), 133–34, 163, 177
Thousand Stories, The (*Hezar afsaneh*) (book), 133n6
Tiffelent, Imma, 94–95
time, 226–31
tombeau. See shrine
"top-down" approach, of development projects, 256, 258, 261–62
traditional knowledge, water collaborative projects connected to, 271–72

traitors (*khaʾin*), 158
translation, 109, 144; assimilation avoided by, 116; of *Borderlands/La Frontera*, 110n7; colonialism influencing, 117; deforeignizing and, 112; in French contrasted with English, 110–11; post-, 116–20; power and, 101; *pretranslation* impacting, 112; relationality and, 110. *See also pretranslation*
translation-pauses, in *The Lionesses*, 113–16
transnational audience, 3
transnational queer scholarship, Euro-American epistemologies recentered by, 142
troublesome spirits (*jinns*), 83n8, 86n10, 92–93, 112
trust (*tiqa*), 18
trust, cooperative norms and, 253
Tuksal, Hidayet Şefkatli, 204
Tunisia, 270–72; development projects in, 251–52; NGOs in, 267; water management in, 260–64; World Bank partnering with, 261
Tunisian Assembly, 269
Tunisian culture, women invested in by, 263–64
Tunisian Revolution/Uprising, 267
Tunisians in the Making (*Tunisiennes en devenir*) (Mernissi), 268
Twelver Shiʿism, 199

umma. See public sphere
Ummayad dynasty, 191
UN Educational, Scientific, and Cultural Organization (UNESCO), 260

Union of Egyptian Women (organization), 203
Union of the Maghreb Arab (Union du Maghreb Arabe), 34
United Nations (UN), 255
United Nations University for Women, 35
United States (US), 26, 237–38
University Mohamed V, 24
University of Agadir, 284n2
University of Montreal, 60
University of Rabat, 2
unlearning, decolonization centralizing, 75–76
Unspoken Words (Falk and Gross), 87n11
untranslatables, 113–15
unveiling, writing as, 176
Urban Environment Development Organization (NGO), 271
US academia, *Dreams of Trespass* ignored by, 140–41
US Agency for International Development (USAID), 260
al-Uzza (pre-Islamic female divinity), 224–25

vahy. See divine revelation through a voice that cannot be attached to any subject
Valparaiso University Center for the Arts, 238
veil, the, 205, 288; France problematizing, 282–83; in French public spaces, 220; French schools banning, 227; imprisonment associated with, 69; Iran mandating, 69; Moroccan nationalist urban elites against, 289; status symbolized by, 198; veiled and nonveiled, 282–83. *See also Beyond the Veil*; hijab
Veil and the Male Elite, The (harem politique, Le) (Mernissi), 25–26, 30, 44, 221–22, 236, 238
Venuti, Lawrence, 114, 116
verlan (language), 118
Visual Hijab, 236n3, *239*

wadud, amina, 244
waged work, challenges and stakes of, 280
wali. See saint
waqf. See pious bequest
Watani Party, 202
Water Ambassadors (ambassadrices de l'eau, Les), 270–71
water collaborative projects, traditional knowledge connected to, 271–72
Water Is a Human Right (project), 270
water management, 260–64, 268–72
West, the, 170; beauty standards in, 67; the harem projected onto by, 175; Muslim and Arab worlds in relation to, 70; power structures impacting women in, 230. *See also* France
Western democracies, 6, 11
Western femininity, 229
Western feminists, Islamic feminism contested by, 209
Western intellectuals, hijab rejected by, 227–28
Western medicine, 82–83
Western values, Muslim values differentiated from, 185–86

Western women, Muslim women contrasted with, 7–8
wife, maintenance of, 207n6
woman, free, 10
Woman's Role in Economic Development (Boserup), 255
women, 10, 35, 203; Arab, 49; aristocratic, 196–97; Beijing Conference on, 246; bodies of, 67n8; boundaries damaging, 226–27; capitalism objectifying, 67n8; centering voices of, 253–60; collective life of, 132–33; colonizers stigmatizing colonized, 288; development projects aiding, 264; *Dreams of Trespass* discussing power of, 171; electricity and, 259; exploitation of labor of, 19; during Fatimid dynasty empowering, 194–96; First World contrasted with Third World, 256; freedom fought for by, 231; hierarchies among, 281; high status of aristocratic, 196–97; hygiene education influenced by, 270n7; immigrant, 288–89; Islamic jurisprudence barred from, 209; modern state institutions defined by, 29; monumental buildings funded by, 199–200; Moroccan nationalists subordinating, 171–72; Muslim societies respecting, 194; pious bequest legitimizing, 198; *in possession*, 99–100; power in Islam sought by, 192–96; power relations and, 188–89; power structures in the East and West impacting, 230; property rights in Islam of, 200–202; Qur'an addressing, 27; religious authority exercised by, 208–9; revolutions in Middle East participated in by, 186; sanctuaries of saints for healing in relation to, 81–83; self-boundaries made by, 155–56; social capital relied on by, 273–74; solidarity among, 135; Tunisian culture investing in, 263–64; voices of, 271–72; water management by, 268–69, 270n7, 272; work of, 280–81; writing freeing, 268. *See also* Muslim women; North African women; North African women writers
Women (*Zanan*) (magazine), 208
Women, Families, Children (group), 177
Women, The (Surat al-Nisa') (Qur'an), 207
"Women, Saints and Sanctuaries in Morocco" (Mernissi), 87n11
Women and Memory Forum, 204
"Women and the Advent of Islam" (Ahmed), 68n9
"Women and the Law in the Near East" (conference), 256
Women in the Mosque (femmes dans la mosquée, Le) (group), 219n1, 221
Women in the Muslim Unconscious (Mernissi), 5n3
Women in the Muslim World (Beck and Keddie), 255
Women of Algiers in Their Apartment (*Femmes d'Alger dans leur appartement*) (painting), 14
women of power, Arab historians erasing, 196
women saints, in North Africa, 95
Women's Awakening (journal), 203
Women's Empowerment Projects, 251

women specialists: in religious sciences and jurisprudence, 192–93; in words and acts of the Prophet (*muhaddithat*), 192
women's pride (*fakhr al nisa'*), 193
words (*kalameh*), 62
words and acts of the Prophet (*hadith*), 62n3, 192–93
World Bank, 251, 256; Bretton Woods Agreement creating, 254; feminist scholars sought out by, 258; Tunisia partnering with, 261
World Bank Economic Development Forum (1997), 258
World Commission on Environment and Development, 253
World Conference on Women, 255–56
world making, refugee, 130
World War II, 155
writers, North African women. *See* North African women writers
writing, 42–43, 48–51, 177, 290; democratic, 17; North African autobiographical, 52–53; Orientalist discourses decentered in, 65–66; power of, 50; as rejuvenation cure, 51; self-, 42; as unveiling, 176; women freed through, 268. *See also* North African women writers
written language, impact of, 71

Yadegar-Azadi, Mina. *See* Saidzadeh, Hojjat-ol Eslam Mohsen
Years of Lead, 51
Yegenoglu, Meyda, 117
YouTube, 13

Zaganiaris, Jean, 8n5
Zahra El Kouch, Sida, 95
Zanan. See Women
zaouias. See sanctuaries of saints for healing
Zayzafoon, Lamia Ben Youssef, 228
Zeynab (sister of Imam Hussein), 191
Zidane, Moulay, 95

www.ingramcontent.com/pod-product-compliance
Lightning Source LLC
Chambersburg PA
CBHW030256050225
21322CB00005B/13